THE SHARED PARISH

The Shared Parish

Latinos, Anglos, and the Future of U.S. Catholicism

Brett C. Hoover

NEW YORK UNIVERSITY PRESS
New York and London

NEW YORK UNIVERSITY PRESS
New York and London
www.nyupress.org

References to Internet websites (URLs) were accurate at the time of writing.
Neither the author nor New York University Press is responsible for URLs that
may have expired or changed since the manuscript was prepared.

Library of Congress Cataloging-in-Publication Data
Hoover, Brett C., 1967–
The shared parish : Latinos, Anglos, and the future of U.S. Catholicism /
Brett C. Hoover.
pages cm   Includes bibliographical references and index.
ISBN 978-1-4798-5439-4 (cl : alk. paper)
1. Church work with Hispanic Americans—Catholic Church.
2. Catholic Church—United States—History—21st century. I. Title.
BX1407.H55H66   2014
259.089'68073—dc23   2014009795

New York University Press books are printed on acid-free paper,
and their binding materials are chosen for strength and durability.
We strive to use environmentally responsible suppliers and materials
to the greatest extent possible in publishing our books.

Manufactured in the United States of America

10 9 8 7 6 5 4 3 2 1

Also available as an ebook

With gratitude to the people of "All Saints" parish, for all their hospitality, kindness, and willingness to share.

A la comunidad hispana de la parroquia de "All Saints / Todos Los Santos" con todo mi agradecimiento. Gracias por toda su confianza y por recibirme con tanto cariño.

Thanks to "Fr. Adama" for his generosity and feedback.

Agradeciendo también al "Padre Nacho" por todo su apoyo en este proyecto.

And most of all, this work is dedicated to the members of the parish research team.

Sobre todo, esta obra está dedicada al equipo de investigación de la parroquia.

I thank / Les agradezco a:
J.D., N.G., S.G., E.M., M.N., C.E.N., T.P., D.R., V.L.R., K.T.

CONTENTS

ACKNOWLEDGMENTS

I wish to thank those scholars whose comments or general advice helped to shape this work along in different ways: Eduardo Fernández, Faustino Cruz, Timothy Matovina, Stanley Brandes, Kathleen Garces-Foley, R. Stephen Warner, Gerardo Martí, and Kenneth McGuire. I am grateful to Jennifer Hammer, my editor, and the anonymous scholars who offered comments through the publisher.

AUTHOR'S NOTE ABOUT TERMINOLOGY AND
THE IDENTITY OF PERSONS AND PLACES

This study employs certain terms for cultural groups as if they were a settled matter, but I must acknowledge that this is not the case. There is no generally agreed upon terminology for the cultural groups described in this study, and there are complications in the terms the people themselves used. The Spanish-speaking people of Havenville generally used *mexicano* or *hispano* to refer to themselves and *americano* (occasionally *anglo*) to refer to the white midwesterners they encountered there. The English-speaking people did not know quite how to refer to themselves as they transitioned from being the overwhelmingly dominant group to a group existing side by side with another group. Sometimes people would say "Anglo" of themselves. They usually referred to people of Latin American descent or origin as "Hispanics," a term that emphasizes their language and Iberian heritage and comes to us mostly from government use (especially the Census Bureau).

In these pages, I have generally chosen the term "Latino" to refer to people living in the United States of Latin American or Caribbean heritage. I admit that this term—which highlights the Latin American origins of the people it describes—has more currency in academic circles and on the West Coast where I teach and live. When I am referring to the specific Mexican national or cultural background of the immigrants at All Saints, I say "Mexican." For the English-speaking whites in Havenville, I have generally used the term "Euro-American," an academic term that emphasizes the broad European cultural origins of midwestern whites rather than their nationality (as with "American" or *americano*), their language (as with "Anglo," which some people of Irish descent object to because of its association with England), or their race (as with "white"). All these terms are somewhat imprecise social constructions, though they have also become significant descriptors of identity for some individuals and groups.[1]

Given the sensitive nature of many of the topics explored in this study—immigration status, racism, cultural conflict—I have taken significant measures to protect the identities of those who agreed to participate. The chief geographical names—Havenville, Brookton County, Port Jefferson Diocese—are pseudonyms as are the parish names All Saints and Our Lady of San Juan de los Lagos. All the names of parishioners, priests, and local leaders are pseudonyms. The endnotes and bibliographic information indicate the tiny number of locally oriented primary and secondary sources that have been given pseudonyms as well. The publication information for those sources also contains pseudonyms and omits the state of publication. The latter precautions especially may seem excessive to some, but the use of true source names would have immediately led an inquisitive reader to the real people who participated, especially in the age of the Internet. I have occluded this information for the protection of the good people who consented to share their stories, some at considerable risk. Necessary questions about such matters should be directed to the author through the publisher.

Introduction

The Shared Parish

All Saints Catholic Church sits across Main Street from a national chain drugstore a few blocks south of downtown Havenville. All kinds of drivers pass by, from local shoppers and parents en route to schools to truckers making deliveries along the long state highway. Probably few recognize the red brick building with a steeple as a Roman Catholic church. You would have to slow down to read the marquee sign, or even park and get out in order to see the two statues of the Virgin Mary on the lawn. On my first visit in the spring of 2007, despite a map downloaded from the Internet, I drove right by. Much later I discovered that this church was dedicated in 1970, replacing an older, smaller structure built farther back on the same lot. The previous church had a recognizably Roman Catholic configuration for a small town in a historically Protestant section of the Midwest—it was compact, traditional, and discreet. A handful of German and Irish Catholic families built it in Gothic Revival style in 1860–1861. Even when renovated in the 1940s, the church remained artfully hidden from the main road behind a grove of trees.[1]

Until the second half of the twentieth century, that little Gothic church served the small parish community admirably. Just before World War II, however, a handful of new employers had arrived in town. By the end of the war, the population—including the Catholic population—began to grow more rapidly. That growth necessitated the construction of a much larger church. In the late 1960s, parish leaders opted to build right on the main road in a Colonial Revival style then popular among Protestants.[2] In those heady days of ecumenical cooperation after the Second Vatican Council, the pastor wanted an architectural statement that showed that Catholics belonged in this town dominated by the Reformation churches. Yet even as the winds of social and ecclesial change blew through Havenville in those years, no one realized that even greater changes were yet to come. By the late 1980s, local factory labor shortages drew a steady stream of immigrants from Mexico. A priest and some parishioners organized a fledgling Hispanic ministry outreach. That ministry grew rapidly when a priest arrived from Mexico in 2000 to assist the pastor. The parish ensconced in the red brick church on Main Street no longer catered exclusively to an English-speaking people of mid-nineteenth-century German vintage. Indeed, within a few years, hundreds of people gathered each weekend for two different masses in Spanish in addition to the three in English. Parallel ministries and programs developed in English and Spanish. All Saints had become what I call a "shared parish."

Roman Catholics, Orthodox Christians, Episcopalians (Anglicans), and Lutherans refer to their local faith communities as parishes; these communities generally function as the only church of that particular tradition in a defined geographical area.[3] I define shared parishes like All Saints as Catholic parishes with two or more cultural groups, each with distinct masses and ministries, but who share the same parish facilities. This setup makes the shared parish a decidedly hybrid structure. On the one hand, immigrants and their families find a safe space in which to congregate and worship in their own language and in a culturally familiar idiom. They do so without disrupting the worship and ministry of groups already in residence. Yet this structure also forces parishioners at a shared parish to periodically interact with one another, sometimes for joint worship but most frequently to negotiate the way they share the space. You might say that, in this way, the shared parish institutionalizes both avoidance and connection. Most parishioners remain in their own cultural world and never have much contact with people from other groups. But a few do take up opportunities to interact across cultural lines, sometimes out of curiosity, more frequently because they simply have to do so in order to get things done in a parish that includes multiple groups.

This shared parish structure has proliferated in recent decades. Cultural diversity within U.S. Catholicism has increased dramatically in response to postwar waves of immigration from Latin America and Asia. Rather than form new churches (as nineteenth-century European immigrants did across a Protestant land), immigrants have moved into parishes already in existence, gradually creating shared parishes in an ad hoc manner. Especially since immigration moved out of traditional gateway cities and states after 1990, these parishes have spread across the country into the Midwest, the South, and the Pacific Northwest. Despite this growth, the shared parish remains understudied, often examined episodically amidst broader studies of how local faith communities (usually termed congregations) deal with cultural diversity. This book offers the first specific and thorough look at the shared parish structure, seen through the lens of one parish. An in-depth examination of the historical development and contemporary parish life of All Saints in Havenville will help us to see in greater relief what the shared parish structure is, how it works, what its specific challenges might be, and how it addresses cultural diversity in the wake of demographic transformation.

*   *   *

In the late summer of 2007, I moved to Havenville to study All Saints as a shared parish. Having served in such parishes as a Catholic priest in New York City and Northern California (and visited others in various parts of the country), I recognized the shared parish as a unique and increasingly common organizational structure. Now I was immersed in a doctoral program in the interdisciplinary study of religion at the Graduate Theological Union, an ecumenical consortium of seminaries in Berkeley, California. The program had afforded me the opportunity to study the sociology of culture and ethnographic methods at the University of California, Berkeley, at the same time. After completing my comprehensive examinations, I looked around for a shared parish where I could spend several months in residence. I visited All Saints in the spring of 2007 and received permission from the pastor and pastoral staff there to spend the next year trying to understand the shared parish they had become. Although I came to that midwestern city as a middle-class Euro-American man originally from the suburbs of Southern California, I had learned to speak Spanish with some fluency during my years of ministry. Living in the northeast part of Washington, DC, in midtown Manhattan in New York City, and then in Berkeley in the San Francisco Bay area, I had been turned into an urbanite. After driving across the West and the Plains states in a small Saturn sedan, I arrived in the small city of Havenville feeling like something of an alien. On that Saturday afternoon in August, I passed by the vintage downtown district, the county fairgrounds, the old courthouse with the clock tower, and the old wooden houses near the local college. This was not like any place in which I had lived of late.

The pastor at All Saints, Fr. David Adama, asked me to introduce myself the next day at Sunday masses. At the English masses, I experienced what felt to me like a warm welcome from a significant number of the parishioners, even though some initially had trouble understanding my purpose in being there. Repeated explanations and consistent presence over the following weeks and months helped with the latter. On that very first Sunday, I disclosed that I was there to understand the experience of two cultural communities sharing the same parish. I also told them that I was a Catholic priest (I have since left the active priesthood), which no doubt put me in a recognizable role apart from researcher. Also, early in my time in Havenville, both the pastor and the associate pastor asked me to help with masses and other sacramental duties. Though initially reluctant to do so, I acquiesced, feeling that I was in some way paying my debt to these communities in a relatively priest-poor area of the country. During my time in Havenville, being a priest made my entry into the community easier and sometimes established trust that facilitated research, but it also complicated my role and made me and many All Saints parishioners cautious about the potential for misuse of power. I address these concerns more fully in the methodological appendix.

That same Sunday I also explained myself at the Spanish masses, where I received a more muted welcome. In the weeks that followed, some Spanish-speaking parishioners remained suspicious of my motives for being there. Some of that was likely a problem of language. The formal word for research, *investigación,* has the same ambiguity as its cognate. Some people wondered aloud if I were there on behalf of the diocese to subject the community to some ecclesial scrutiny. I cleared up that misunderstanding over time, but a deeper caution remained, the reasons for which will become clearer as this book progresses. Weeks later, when I asked for some help from a handful of parishioners, some of them still gave me wrong telephone numbers. In the Spanish-speaking community, however, the strong support of the associate pastor, Father Ignacio (Padre Nacho), served to soften that suspicion over time. My persistent presence at community events also helped, as did my linguistic skills. Many Latino parishioners were recent immigrants. Especially in this part of the rural Midwest, they had never met a Euro-American priest who could competently pronounce their language. Eventually, people in both communities got used to my presence. Over time, most people seemed to appreciate that someone had come simply to hear their stories and learn what it was like to be them.

*   *   *

What was it like to be them? In truth, the shared parish structure created not a little cross-cultural confusion. I elaborate by sharing a couple of brief anecdotes courtesy of two very different parishioners at All Saints.

At the parish school at All Saints, I met Helen Duffy, a blond, Euro-American mother who had grown up in Havenville. Her aging father remained an influential parish leader during my time there. He and his wife had first come to Havenville in the late 1940s from another part of the state; they had served the parish for many years in many capacities. Helen grew up in the parish, and she and her husband met at a church event for young people. They appeared each Sunday at one or another of the English masses, and Helen was especially involved in the life of the parish school. She watched the changes in the parish initiated by the arrival of so many Catholic immigrants. When she was young, hardly a Latino family lived in town. Now, as she approached middle age, 36 percent of the students who attended All Saints School with her son were Latinos, mostly of Mexican descent. Helen saw this as a positive development. It increased the enrollment and energy at the school. But she knew that other people did not feel as comfortable with what had happened.

She told the story of how her son went to a classmate's birthday party one afternoon. When she came to pick him up, the party was still going, so she stood in the kitchen with the other mothers to wait. Looking at the children enjoying themselves, she realized that her son's was the only head of red hair in the raucous room. At first she thought little of this, but then she saw that all the other children were Latino. Then she took a look around her in the kitchen. All the other mothers were speaking Spanish around her. "I had stood there for thirty minutes and then all of a sudden I was like, oh, my gosh, I'm the only white person." Then it dawned on her what this meant. Of all the classmates, her son was either the only white child invited or, more likely, the only one who had come to the party. It was a poignant object lesson in the intercultural avoidance that goes with sharing a parish (and a school), a strategy people in both communities at All Saints adopted as often as they could.

Early on in my time in Havenville, I ran into Francisco Martinez. We shared a ride through town in another parishioner's car. Though not a longtime Havenviller like Helen Duffy, Francisco had been at the parish for close to a decade when I arrived. A compact, middle-aged man, he had migrated to Havenville from a small town in the mountains of central Mexico in search of work to support his wife and children. They remained there in central Mexico. In an interview, he described himself upon arrival in Havenville as weary and overwhelmed. A lifelong Catholic at home, he had sought solace by going to mass. Noting a tall beautiful building with a clock tower sitting astride a plaza in the center of town, he assumed this had to be the Catholic church. Many churches in Mexico loom over the central square of a town in that way. When he approached one Sunday morning, however, he saw no one and no activity. This puzzled him. Then he noticed a police officer standing just inside the door. He became nervous. Having come so far, he could not afford to tangle with the law in any way. He left, disappointed.

Later Francisco found out this was not the Catholic church but the county courthouse. With the help of a friend from his hometown, he found his way to All Saints. The way he describes it: "I came with a thirst to find a church in order to feel tranquility, to unburden myself. When one comes as an immigrant, one arrives with that weariness and one desires to pray, to rest with God." When he met Fr. Ignacio Barba, the Mexican priest who worked at All Saints, Francisco asked almost immediately if he could help in some way. Padre Nacho, as everyone called Father Ignacio, invited him to serve as an usher (*ujier*), helping to distribute missalettes (worship books) and bulletins, direct congregational traffic, and collect the money for the church in long-handled baskets. By the time I came to All Saints, Francisco was the head usher, always crisply dressed, cheerful and friendly, apparently a mentor to the mostly young men and women who served as *ujieres*. His experience of confusion about intercultural life in Havenville was typical, as was its denouement in leadership and participation for a small but devoted number of involved Hispanic parishioners.

Immigrants and Parishes

The kinds of cultural collisions and dilemmas that Helen Duffy and Francisco Martinez experienced in Havenville only begin to demonstrate the complex dynamics and tensions created when immigrant newcomers and longtime residents come together to share the same Catholic parish. But such dynamics are not really new in American Catholicism. Shared parishes count as the latest development in a historical endeavor as old as the United States itself. From the beginning, Roman Catholic parish life in the United States has attuned itself to ministry in a culturally diverse context, and especially among immigrants. In 1785, the newly appointed pastor of the first parish in New York City, Charles Whelan, wrote a letter to the papal nuncio in France, describing the situation of his new parish. He had discovered a community of mostly poor Irish immigrants, many Irish-speaking. He also found a smattering of Anglo-American Catholics as well as immigrants from several other places. He wrote to the nuncio that a good priest in his situation would possess skills for ministering not only in English and Irish but also in French, Dutch, Spanish, and Portuguese.[4]

From roots like these, the tiny U.S. Catholic Church grew exponentially when Catholic immigrants from Germany and Ireland began to arrive in the middle of the nineteenth century. As they did, the structure of the U.S. Catholic parish developed in a new direction. A fledgling network of national or ethnic parishes—eventually called personal parishes in church law—was crafted to accommodate the various cultural-linguistic groups of newcomers. Such parishes preserved but also reshaped European Catholic customs as communities gradually adjusted to life in this country.[5] National parishes continued to domi-nate the landscape as Germans and Irish gave way to immigrants from southern and eastern Europe—among Catholics, especially Italians, Poles, Hungarians, Czechs, Slovaks, Croats, and Ukrainians.[6] National parishes did not prevent infighting among the different Catholic cul-tures, but some were established as a result of such internecine battles. Nor was every neighborhood or town able to sustain a national parish; especially in rural areas, interethnic parishes contributed to accultura-tion to Anglo-American culture, although often with an Irish or Ger-man accent.[7] Mid-nineteenth century Catholicism dealt with cultural diversity through a parish system with two arms. National parishes favored cultural pluralism—an approach where diverse cultural groups worship in their own space—while other parishes favored assimilation to Anglo-American culture, often with other cultural accents integrated in. This latter approach to assimilation is sometimes called melting pot assimilation.

National parishes dominated the Catholic scene until, in the early twentieth century, the Church began to reverse course. World War I made assertion of German identity suspect, at least outside of cer-tain midwestern communities culturally and politically dominated by Germans.[8] Bishops started to oppose the formation of new national parishes and encourage the development of pan-ethnic organizations like the Catholic Youth Organization, the Holy Name Society, and the Altar and Rosary Society.[9] The focus turned to Catholic uniformity of thought and action across groups.[10] At the same time, a wave of racially tinged nativism—accompanied by a heightened consciousness of the now reduced birthrate among Anglo-Saxon Protestants—turned Anglo-American public opinion against immigration. Government policies shifted from preventing the entry of "undesirable" people—the indigent, criminals, and anarchists—to preventing the entry of spe-cific ethnic and racial groups—that is, Asians, Eastern Europeans, and Southern Europeans.[11] The restrictions joined with the Great Depres-sion to bring immigration to a virtual halt, at least in comparison with the century before.

The decades between the world wars saw the beginnings of a trans-formation among the immigrant families that made up a large percent-age of the Catholic population:

The hiatus starting in the 1920s virtually guaranteed that ethnic communities and cultures would be steadily weakened over time. The social
mobility of individuals and families would drain population from these
communities and undermine the cultures they sheltered, since there
were few newcomers to replace those who were departing. General shifts
would have a similar impact because there was little replenishment of
the immigrant generation . . . The hiatus undoubtedly contributed to
the extent of assimilation among Americans of European and Asian
ancestry.[12]

In the nineteenth and early twentieth centuries, parishioners at national
parishes looked on language and culture as the major guarantors of
Catholic faith, even if that language and culture already demonstrated
adaptations necessary for life in the United States. But the interwar
period accelerated these adaptations; it saw parish life shift from trying to preserve Old World cultures to celebrating an ethnic heritage
reshaped in the United States. English became more and more the language of Catholic sermons and devotions, encouraged by a generation
of bishops determined to demonstrate to Protestants the rising status
and patriotism of Catholic Americans.[13] At the time, church leaders
referred to this approach to cultural diversity as Americanization, but it
also is a form of what immigration scholars call assimilation.

Thus, by the middle of the twentieth century, many Catholics recognized their parishes not as ethnic way-stations[14] but as bastions of an
omnipresent "Catholic culture" (really, an American Catholic culture)
in contradistinction to the mainstream Protestant culture. This Catholic culture had many identity markers, from eating fish on Fridays to
positioning crucifixes in homes and institutions. Many of these cultural
markers pointed toward Rome. Unlike Protestants, for example, Catholics of that era advocated for the political independence of the pope
against the Italian secular state.[15] Bishops fundraised for the "embattled"
pope and pushed a theological agenda initiated by Rome. At the same
time, they denied that such attentions made them anything but equals
on the American stage.[16] The Catholic counterculture had its unique
vocabulary—novena, "Father," fast and abstinence, transubstantiation,
mortal sin.[17] It had a familiar cast of characters—mostly priests and sisters—as well as its unique institutions—parishes and parochial schools,

hospitals and universities. Catholicism in the United States began to function as a semi-encapsulated cultural world presided over by a distinct philosophy (scholasticism), distinct politics (the urban Democratic machine, anticommunism), and an intellectual and literary scene set apart (from Catholic professional societies to Catholic newspapers, from J. F. Powers to Dorothy Day).[18]

After World War II, however, suburbanization and the G.I. Bill gave birth to a more "mainstream" perspective among Euro-American Catholics.[19] A different narrative of U.S. Catholic life began to take root in the parishes. Catholics had left their immigrant past and their counterculture behind and had joined the modern, middle-class world.[20] This collective rags-to-riches assimilationist narrative sat well with the greater American narratives of progress and success, of leaving the Old World behind and embracing the new. This narrative, however, mostly articulated the suburban experience of the descendants of European immigrants. It left out a great number of people, including rural German Catholics who retained a strong sense of ethnicity and African American Catholics in Louisiana and the industrial cities.[21] The fastest-growing group that existed outside this narrative, however, was a group of postwar immigrants, most from Latin America and East Asia. Through the 1970s and 1980s, that group grew exponentially. The Euro-American assimilationist narrative was rapidly overwhelmed by new demographic realities. Parish life once again began to attune itself to Catholic immigrants and their families. For a great number of parishes—but still not the majority—this translated to a wider concern for Latino or Hispanic parishioners.

Latino people had lived in the southwestern part of the United States for centuries, long before the United States annexed the area after its war with Mexico (1846–1848). Workers from Mexico migrated to the U.S. Southwest in the 1880s to serve in agricultural and railroad work, and the violence of the Mexican Revolution (1910–1917) spurred a wave of emigration to the United States. In 1942, Mexican immigration began to accelerate. The U.S. government negotiated a guest worker program with Mexico to assist with agricultural and industrial worker shortages during World War II. In its first decade, the *bracero* program—along with economic and political pressure to limit enforcement—actually facilitated an increase in unauthorized immigration, that is, immigration of people without legal permission to live and work in the United States. A 1954 crackdown, however, coincided with a dramatic increase in the number of braceros recruited for farm work. Unauthorized immigration declined precipitously, but it picked up just as precipitously when the guest worker program came to a close in the early 1960s. Agricultural work in the Southwest now depended on Mexican workers. As the guest worker program ended, the Immigration and Naturalization Service also increased the number of workers legally permitted to cross back and forth as "commuters."[22]

As these factors impacted Mexican immigration in the Southwest and California, economic and political chaos in Puerto Rico and Cuba spurred migration to Florida and the Eastern Seaboard. Central Americans dramatically increased their share of immigration by the 1980s, their arrival connected to the political and military involvement of the United States in civil wars in their homelands. Throughout the postwar period, dioceses and parishes in destination states responded slowly to an influx of largely Roman Catholic immigrants. Ad hoc solutions like itinerant Spanish preaching teams gave way to de facto national parishes in Latino neighborhoods.[23] In some places, such as New York City, migrants found themselves forced into existing parishes, often under inhospitable circumstances.[24]

In 1965, immigration law formally changed to favor family reunification and special skills rather than the discriminatory quotas of the 1920s. By the early 1980s, Catholic immigrants from Latin America, the Philippines, and Vietnam were among the largest groups of newcomers. The Church response had begun to change as well. After ethnic pride movements emerged in the 1970s, Roman Catholic leaders abandoned their insistence that immigrants assimilate or "Americanize."[25] Nevertheless, most leaders did not return to supporting national or ethnic parishes, the historical means of incorporating immigrants.[26] Though some such parishes did emerge, in most cases older parishes were restructured to allow migrant communities a modicum of their own space. This form of parish life avoided the difficult financial and personnel questions involved in building new worship spaces or appropriating older ones. In the new arrangement, different cultural groups share parish space but retain distinct masses and ministries. These are the shared parishes I described above, and this book tackles their story.

The Anatomy of a Shared Parish

There exist different terminologies to describe this phenomenon of parishes with parallel "tracks" for different cultural groups. Sociologists tend to use the term "parallel congregations,"[27] while Catholic pastoral leaders have generally spoken of "multicultural parishes," a term that only succeeds in offering basic demographic information. A few resort to "mixed parish" or "integrated parish," terminology that tends to imply far more integration among groups than is generally the case. I prefer the term "shared parish," my own creation, for two reasons. For one thing, "parish" is emic terminology. The word is familiar to Roman Catholics. "Congregation" is a less familiar moniker for local faith communities and is, in fact, frequently used to refer to Catholic religious orders. Furthermore, the other terms do not draw attention to the art of the ongoing negotiated arrangement created by the presence of multiple cultural groups in the same parish space. In short, these terms do not acknowledge the *sharing* of the parish.

Each shared parish situation functions differently. Nevertheless, most structure themselves as a kind of federation of distinct cultural groups operating mostly independently under one roof. Each group accesses its unique cultural expression of Catholicism. Some have shared leadership, some do not. Many have occasional bilingual (or trilingual or more) liturgies on important feast days. Some have shared parish committees or service programs. Whatever the case, all cultural groups make use of the same parish facilities. The bishop names one pastor as head of the entire operation, though other priests may function as quasi-independent leaders of particular communities. The parish has only one set of administrative procedures and records through which it relates to the diocese.

This juxtaposition of distinctness within a common physical space creates an unusual dynamic. Two (or more) cultures find themselves compelled to interact—or collide—across the landscape of the one facility. Sooner or later, they must negotiate with one another, even as they frequently try to avoid it. This dynamic of sharing has sociological (and some theological) consequences. Who will hold on to power and resources? How will the communities influence one another? What kind of understanding of church unity works in a divided setting? This book spends a great deal of time addressing these questions and their practical consequences. The complexity of the findings suggests that recent Catholic models for understanding cultural diversity—especially assimilation and multiculturalism—have proven inadequate. The Church requires new models. The models must learn how to keep cultural distinction *and* some form of interlinked experience in creative tension. As we will see, some of that creative tension can be found in theological models of the Church described as communion.

But it serves little purpose to address such questions only as theory. We need a case study to understand them in any depth. Historian Jay Dolan once said about the Catholic parish, "It is a window in the wall, through which Catholic life can be observed."[28] In this book we will peer through that window at one particular parish. We will take a detailed, interdisciplinary look at All Saints Parish. All Saints is the only parish in a midwestern city of about 30,000. Its parish life has developed in response to a particular cultural, historical, and ecclesial context. Most recently, immigration from Mexico has transformed its makeup and created a shared parish over the course of a decade. Using different forms of social scientific analysis, we will explore the historical, cultural, and ecclesial context, particularly in the midst of that demographic transformation. We will then look at the response of the people to that transformation, capturing a snapshot of how migration transformed U.S. Catholicism, at least in this small corner of the world.

Demographic Transformation and the Shared Parish

The experiences of parishioners like Francisco Martinez and Helen Duffy in and around All Saints Parish allow us—just for a moment—to peer through that "window in the wall" into the everyday dynamics of Catholic life where different cultures meet. As already noted, Catholic life in the United States has always involved intercultural dynamics (and intercultural conflict), but national parishes once offered "cushioning space" while each cultural group struggled with its immigrant identity and attempted to coexist with others. The demise of the national parish and the rise of the shared parish have eliminated some but not all of that cushioning space. At shared parishes like All Saints, Catholics from distinctive cultures find themselves face to face with one another in parking lots and church facilities, at bilingual worship services and committee meetings, and within the parochial school (and at its ancillary events such as birthday parties). This was bound to happen. The number of foreign-born citizens and residents has reached levels our nation has not seen since the earliest part of the twentieth century.[29] And just as in that era, a disproportionate number of those immigrants remain Roman Catholic.[30] Meanwhile, the longtime residential population of American Catholics—dominated by Euro-Americans but possessing a considerable amount of racial and cultural diversity—ages, in part because of the disaffiliation (or indifference) of young white Catholics.[31]

Shared parishes manifest the massive demographic transformation currently underway in the United States. A hundred years ago, the 1910 census calculated the population of the United States to be 88.9 percent white and 10.7 percent black, percentages that more or less held steady until the 1960s.[32] Since then, the nation's ethnic and racial makeup has grown more broadly diverse, principally due to immigration from Latin America and the Pacific Rim.[33] Some have called this the "browning of America."[34] Latinos, for example, now constitute 16.3 percent of the national population, the largest "minority" group. Asians and Pacific Islanders are 5.0 percent of U.S. residents, and blacks constitute 12.6 percent. Non-Hispanic whites are now 63.7 percent of the U.S. population.[35] In four states (California, Texas, Hawaii, and New Mexico) and the District of Columbia, whites are not the majority group. Given continued immigration and higher birth rates among people of color, we can expect many of these trends to continue.[36]

This diversity has engendered an even more profound transformation within the Roman Catholic Church. Roman Catholicism remains the largest religious group among immigrants, a chief player in "the de-Europeanizing of American Christianity."[37] Only Muslims, Buddhists, and Jehovah's Witnesses offer a more diverse profile in the United States, and each of these groups is much smaller than Roman Catholicism.[38] Nevertheless, analysts disagree about the precise demographic makeup of contemporary U.S. Catholicism. For example, different surveys estimate Latinos to make up between 29 percent and 39 percent of Roman Catholics in the United States and African American Catholics between 2 percent and 3.4 percent.[39] Whatever the precise numbers, trends are clear. The proportion of Catholics of Latin American ancestry is likely to increase as the proportion of Euro-American Catholics decreases. This is both because of higher birth rates among Latinos and because a large proportion of migrants come from the disproportionately Roman Catholic nation of Mexico.[40]

Statisticians calculate diversity broadly, but human beings experience it locally. The diversity of experience within shared parishes demonstrates this. Before the onset of Latin American migration to Havenville (and All Saints) in the 1990s, only a handful of Mexican families had settled there permanently. Large cities with their multiple immigrant neighborhoods were hours away. Few Euro-American parishioners knew any words of Spanish or had ever eaten a taco or tasted mole sauce. The influx of immigrants in the 1990s arrived as a shock. It did not happen in the same way in other parts of the country. In Southern California, where I grew up, Spanish city and street names abound. Native-born and immigrant Latinos have always been part of the cultural landscape, though persistent racial discrimination, white flight, and class divisions historically put cultural groups at a distance from one another. Everyone in Southern California eats Mexican food, and Euro-Americans typically know at least a few phrases in Spanish: *Hola, ¿cómo está? ¿Dónde está el baño? Otra cerveza, por favor.*[41] Enormous, affluent parishes in the suburbs there have long had mass in multiple languages—English, Spanish, and Vietnamese were typical in the suburban Orange County of my youth, even as far back at the 1970s, and still are. English masses today are often dominated not by Euro-Americans but by English-speaking Hispanics, Vietnamese, Koreans, and Filipinos. After decades of experience, diversity provokes little sense of shock, even if such parishes continue to struggle with cultural misunderstanding and changing power dynamics.

Urban shared parishes in parts of Los Angeles, Chicago, or New York City demonstrate a third dynamic. Most European-descended Catholics disappeared from these neighborhoods long ago. Other cultural groups negotiate with one another—immigrant and native-born Hispanics, Filipinos and Mexicans, Salvadorans and Mexicans. A particularly poignant dynamic surrounds Black Catholic parishes that more recently have had to accommodate immigrant Catholics from Latin American or Caribbean countries. In Los Angeles, the demographic decline of

African American Catholics has created some tensions between new-comers from Central America or Mexico and the longtime resident population. In Harlem in New York City, I served a parish where the African American and Dominican communities—racially similar—shared the parish more or less harmoniously, but gentrification and worries about younger African Americans' Catholic identity also gave urgency to the project of an African American–identified parish.

Every shared parish's experience of cultural diversity is unique. On the one hand, this emphasizes the importance of larger statistical data about diversity across representative samples of Catholics and their parishes. Local manifestations of demographic transformation do not offer us the big picture. Surveys, census data, and large-scale structured interviews bring demographic trends into focus. On the other hand, these forms of data have limitations. Cultural diversity is not just a demographic fact. It involves people facing social, cultural, and religious changes. Uncovering how they participate and react to those changes requires more detailed information culled from particular cases. It is not enough to know that a certain percentage of Roman Catholics of different races and ethnicities worship side by side in shared parishes. We need to know what that experience looks and sounds like in order to develop frameworks to understand it in detail. It makes sense to investigate how this complex intercultural encounter unfolds in a single parish.

To accomplish this, I spent ten months, from August 2007 to July 2008, engaged in ethnographic fieldwork at All Saints Parish. I observed and carefully noted the details of parish life, received tours of the par-ish and local area from people in both cultural communities, and asked endless questions both at church and around town. I also conducted twenty-two interviews and oral histories, and I collected considerable historical archival information from both the parish and the diocese. Following trends in postmodern ethnography and action research, I did not attempt to develop an "objective" account of parish life at All Saints, and I participated in parish life as I normally would as a Catho-lic priest.[42] Following traditions of community interpretation in action research, halfway through the year I recruited a team of parishioners to work with me on the project. These ten men and women (four Span-ish-speaking, five English-speaking, and one fully bilingual) conducted twenty interviews with their fellow parishioners and also helped me interpret results. Multiple critical perspectives emerged instead of just one. I also discussed the results with other parishioner informants, with parish leadership, and with various experts—social scientists, theologians, and pastoral workers. In the end, major findings were reported to the parish at large as well.[43]

Such attention to one parish brought to light a host of dynamics unique to the local scene—a common experience of working-class labor, a May–December situation where Latinos tended to be younger and Euro-Americans older, a lack of bilingual people and resources. In reality no parish, shared or not, is totally unique. Parishes model themselves on other parishes, and they do what they have heard that others do. Dioceses issue rules and make demands. Parish communities find that there are limited options to select in a cultural and religious environment when they establish and maintain their structures and practices, a point frequently made by sociologists of institutions. All Saints had become a shared parish because, in most areas, the shared parish had become the most practical among limited options for addressing increasing cultural diversity within the Roman Catholic Church in the United States. Other parish forms—the national parish, the ethnic mission, the assimilating or "Americanizing" parish—still exist, but various factors have made shared parishes the more practical option in places like Havenville. National parishes and ethnic missions require an investment of personnel and money in an era of declining resources and numbers of priests. They can lead to charges of "separatism" by Euro-Americans or of favoritism by cultural groups not receiving such treatment.[44] Americanizing parishes only appeal to a slice of the immigrant population, usually a more educated and upwardly mobile slice. Most would rather not surrender their traditions and customs if they can avoid it. One might say that shared parishes exist as an imperfect answer to the tension between immigrant groups' desires to maintain their distinct Catholic culture and practices and Euro-American preoccupations over stability and unity in a changing landscape, a dynamic to be explored later on in this volume.

Certain social and economic factors promote shared parishes. In the past, housing discrimination and "white flight" segregated neighborhoods (and churches). While neither has vanished from the scene, now multiple dynamics are at work. We see a shift from a manufacturing to a service economy, from urban to suburban workplaces, and the rise (and perhaps fall due to fuel prices) of exurban communities. Upward economic mobility has occurred for select immigrants and African Americans while diverse groups of young professionals have moved to city centers in New York, Chicago, Philadelphia, Denver, San Francisco, and other cities. Meanwhile, older Euro-Americans remain in working-class urban neighborhoods as new immigrants arrive there. All these factors create residential mixing or, at least, neighborhoods of different cultural groups existing in proximity. Mobility combined with a more robust focus on personal choice also favors shared parishes. When people feel free to choose their parishes, church authorities cannot easily shuffle cultural groups around from parish to parish. Newcomers demand their mass where they want it, and declining populations—often Euro-American or African American—refuse to leave. These factors tend to keep parishes shared.

It is difficult to surmise if any one parish—let alone All Saints— strictly represents (that is, provides generalizable data about) the wider experience of U.S. Roman Catholics contending with demographic transformation in shared parishes. But All Saints does fall into this larger trend toward shared parishes and draws upon the cultural and ecclesial resources and structures available because of the trend. All Saints also mirrors the larger demographic transformation of U.S. Roman Catholicism. It contains the two largest cultural groups in the U.S. Roman Catholic Church—the Americanized descendants of European Catholic immigrants and Catholics of Mexican heritage. Like the larger Church in the United States, it struggles with questions of identity in the wake of immigration from Latin America. That includes questions of acculturation and adaptation for Latino immigrants and questions of new cultural consciousness for Euro-Americans in a more heterogeneous society.

An Ad Hoc Model for Ministry

To my knowledge, no meeting of bishops or any other body of Roman Catholic leaders sat down and designed the shared parish as it exists today. Instead, demographic change created the conditions in which shared parishes arose. At All Saints, the need to provide pastoral services to a new cultural group emerged quickly in the 1990s. The shared parish form was adopted gradually for pragmatic reasons. A similar process has come about in various locations across the country where a rapidly developing need is followed by the pragmatic development of a new ministry within an existing parish. The formation of shared parishes as a result has created a discernible ad hoc pattern. Almost no one adopted the shared parish form purposefully according to a plan. Rather, the process has moved functionally, step by step.

An established parish with a relatively stable population, often skewing slightly older than the surrounding community, experiences a demographic transformation in its locality. The old neighborhood or town begins to look different. Perhaps, as in the case of All Saints, a local need for labor starts a round of migration from Latin America. Perhaps people simply shift to the area from another part of the metropolitan region, as has happened in many parts of Los Angeles. Eventually, some proportion of Catholic newcomers venture to church. Others go elsewhere in order to find a service in their language or according to their cultural expectations. Eventually something initiates a special ministry or a mass on-site in the newcomers' language. At All Saints, parish and diocesan leadership noticed what was happening within the parish boundaries and initiated a ministry and a mass.[45] In other cases, delegations of immigrants come to the pastor or bishop and ask for services. Maybe a third party such as a business, nonprofit organization, or civic leader requests more attention to a particular group. However it occurs, this first stage of attention begins with what might be termed a "special ministry." At this stage, the residential community has little traffic with the newcomers and does not have to share much of the parish with them. Those who do know may feel generous that they have extended hospitality.

The movement from special ministry to shared parish may require a lengthy transition. Or it may happen quickly if the newcomers come in droves and the residents are few. In some cases, it may never occur. It depends on (1) the growth of the newcomer cultural group (or groups) involved, (2) the size and demographic profile of the residential group, (3) local church politics, and (4) the willingness of the newcomers to find a home in the parish. In today's environment of increasing

immigration, newcomer growth is seldom an obstacle. A mass in Spanish, for example, frequently draws large numbers of people. This happened at All Saints after the arrival of the priest from Mexico in 2000.
This may take church leaders and resident parishioners by surprise.
Especially in areas with a number of undocumented immigrants working to remain as anonymous as possible, no one may have an accurate
idea of the actual number of Latino Catholics. Ministries for other
cultural or linguistic groups such as Vietnamese, Koreans, or Francophone Africans may also increase exponentially, especially if few such
communities exist across a wide geographical area. As people fill the
church, they may even begin to match or outnumber the residential
community. At that point, it becomes particularly difficult to think of
newcomers as recipients of a "special ministry."

The demographic profile of the residential community matters as
well. At All Saints, the Latino community had grown until the two communities had roughly equal numbers of mass goers. Thus, the shared
parish presented itself as a kind of fait accompli over time. The large
number of people over sixty in the residential community at All Saints
compared to the childbearing age of most adults in the immigrant community created a complicated tension. The Euro-American community was relatively fixed and stable in comparison to the Latino community. They had fewer children, raising questions about the parish
and the city's future. At another, more rural parish in the same state,
a small Euro-American community had found themselves completely
outpaced by Latino growth. Over time, many local residents left for a
parish in a nearby town. But a small number of elderly Euro-Americans
held out, some happy about the infusion of energy, some resentful. For
both, this had been their parish for decades and perhaps generations;
they would not leave.

Yet demographics alone do not accelerate the transition. Politics
enters in. In Roman Catholicism, church law gives jurisdiction solely
to the pastor locally and to the bishop regionally. In reality, of course,
pastor and bishop do not have unlimited power and must contend with
various groups and factions. But the expansion of a newcomer community's role within a parish generally requires the support of both.
All Saints grew because the bishop recruited a priest from Mexico and
sent him to the parish. That priest, Father Ignacio (also known as Padre

Nacho), required the permission of the pastor to put many of his pro-grams and reforms into action. The distinct masses and ministries that formed demonstrated to Euro-American parishioners—often to their surprise in a previously culturally homogenous area—that assimila-tion or "Americanization" was no longer the Church's chief approach to immigration. But immigrant communities also need pastor and bishop support to help them negotiate through the almost inevitable resis-tance that builds up among residential communities. Change is difficult for the latter. Overtly and covertly, they fight surrendering control of resources, committee seats, and leadership. People feel strong owner-ship for their parishes, and they do not like the idea of turning over facilities to newcomers who have not yet contributed what they and their families have. The language barrier, constant cultural misunder-standing, and bouts of racism make communication and mutual under-standing difficult.

Meanwhile, perceptions about unequal status can grate on new-comers, especially if they confront such challenges in the workplace as well. At All Saints, Gabi Moreno, a volunteer ministry head at All Saints, observed that Latinos generally received lesser salaries for fac-tory work in Havenville (something I was unable to confirm). She also repeatedly questioned me about where Euro-American parish staff members got money for their seemingly abundant parish resource materials, since she had to buy such things with her own money. In some cases, perceptions of unequal status push newcomers to keep to themselves entirely. One Latino leader at All Saints told me how, after all the unreasonable demands from Euro-Americans, he hoped a new Hispanic ministry office would mean no entanglements with "Anglos" at all. At other times, the movement toward separation seems to come as much from a determination to preserve culture and retain a sense of internal solidarity. For example, several Korean Catholic communities in the United States celebrate liturgy and conduct religious education at churches mostly inhabited by other cultural communities. Generally, however, they have minimal to no contact with them or even with the local church in general. Some rotate in priests from dioceses in South Korea.[46]

Despite such obstacles, however, shared parishes do come about. No doubt U.S. Catholic bishops' consistent acceptance of cultural diversity and defense of immigrants plays a role in ensuring that they do. So does the work of pastors who recognize a responsibility for all the cultural groups charged to their care. Even the residential community, albeit grudgingly, generally sees the inevitability of the changes producing the new arrangement. As one woman at All Saints told me,

> I don't like to see things changing to the point, I don't like to see—it just is the wrong mix to go down Main Street and see so many stores that have Spanish on the front of them. I don't want to sound like I'm prejudiced; it's not that, it's just that it's not Midwest America to me because I'm older. . . . But I may as well get over it. As well as should the rest of my friends.

Over time, an imperfect process of pragmatic negotiation between cultures sets in. Masses and ministries form in parallel. Religious education, youth ministry, prayer meetings, and socials emerge for each community. Some programs, such as St. Vincent de Paul, may be administered across communities. Depending on the situation of the parish, there may be joint or separate leadership committees. Some parish councils and finance committees are more or less balanced according to the demographics of the parish. Often, however, a Euro-American–dominated parish council oversees the whole parish while a separate leadership committee works for the immigrant-rooted community. Some shared parishes with three or more cultural groups have leadership committees that integrate some of the groups, while others (often Korean or Vietnamese) remain more on their own. Whatever the situation, a shared parish necessarily functions as a living but imperfect union of distinct communities always negotiating their sharing of one parish.

How Common Are Shared Parishes?

How common is the shared parish phenomenon? No precise statistics exist, yet indications suggest a widespread presence. The 1999 PARAL study of Latino religion in the United States found that 75 percent of Latino Catholic faith communities shared facilities with a different faith community.[47] In 2008, Ken Johnson-Mondragón, a researcher with the

Instituto Fe y Vida in Stockton, California, prepared a comprehensive study on multicultural ministry in U.S. Catholicism. Unable to find or create precise national statistics regarding cultural diversity in the Church, he culled a number of interesting findings in different ways. Using language as an indicator of culture, Johnson-Mondragón studied linguistic diversity in parishes in five dioceses geographically distributed across the country—Brooklyn, New York; Charlotte, North Carolina; El Paso, Texas; Oakland, California; and Wichita, Kansas. He found that 45 percent of parishes in all five dioceses were "bilingual"— had masses in two languages. Another 15 percent in two immigration state dioceses, Brooklyn and Oakland, had mass in three or more languages.[48]

Following Ken Johnson-Mondragón's approach, I looked at linguistic diversity in my own search to find data on the prevalence of shared parishes. In mid-2009, I found that 16 percent of the parishes in the midwestern Port Jefferson Diocese (where All Saints is located) had mass in more than one language. Though some parishes there had historical roots as national or ethnic parishes, only one could be considered as such today. Seeking a contrast, I checked the parishes of the immigrant-rich Archdiocese of Miami in Florida. Seventy-one percent of its parishes, missions, and shrines had mass in more than one language. Given the concentration of Latinos there, however, it perhaps surprises that only 7 percent strictly follow the national or ethnic parish model (mostly mission parishes ministering to Haitians). In the Oakland Diocese (which Johnson-Mondragón also included in his study), 52 percent of parishes had mass in more than one language. At least two parishes (Korean and African American), perhaps a few more, could be considered ethnic or national parishes. On the other end of the spectrum, the Diocese of Helena (Montana) had only two parishes with scheduled weekend masses in both English and Spanish out of ninety-two parishes and missions.[49] The Diocese of Baker (Oregon) registered in between. A mostly rural diocese comprising the eastern two-thirds of the state, it too underwent transformation through post-1990 immigration.[50] Twenty-three percent of its parishes and missions had mass in both English and Spanish.[51]

There are, however, disadvantages to making language a measure of the presence of multiple cultural groups. Depending solely on language ignores African American and other English-dominant cultural groups (such as Filipinos and Indians). Some parishes that effectively function as national or ethnic parishes retain masses in English to accommodate those who prefer the English language but retain strong cultural ties (for example, second- or third-generation Latinos).[52] Since the 1990s, the Pew Charitable Trusts has funded several studies of religion and immigrants, but most—like the present study—provided ethnographic data rather than comparative statistics about migrants' local faith communities. Among its most recent Gateway Cities Initiative studies, however, one included a survey of local faith communities serving select immigrant groups in the Washington, DC, area. That 2002 survey found that 73 percent of Catholic immigrant worshipping communities were part of a larger parish, while 27 percent were stand-alone national parishes.[53] To move in a completely different direction, we can look at figures collected in 2007 by the Archdiocese of Chicago on the "ethnic or racial identity" of its parishes. Sixty-six of the 170 parishes that professed a specific cultural identity identified themselves as "various mixed." The archdiocese had 364 parishes that year.[54]

All this confirms anecdotal evidence. To be certain, the national or ethnic parish retains a place in the Church's response to cultural diversity in the United States. Nevertheless, the shared parish has the greater presence. It has become, whether in incipient, intentional, or ad hoc form, the primary local way in which Roman Catholics address cultural diversity within the Church.

Structuring This Study

In this introduction I have introduced the idea of the shared parish and have established its place within the history of Catholic immigration and the contemporary demographic transformation of American Christianity in general and U.S. Catholicism in particular. I have also offered a snapshot of the parish that will serve as extended case study of the phenomenon. Most of the rest of this book is devoted to an in-depth analysis of field research at All Saints. The next chapter lays out the history of All Saints within the larger context of American Catholic parishes, including how it became a shared parish. The second chapter presents ethnographic data on current issues—such as social order and the connection between worship and identity—engendered by the demographic transformation of All Saints as a shared parish. It probes the concerns raised by people in the parish, applying theoretical analysis from sociological and cultural anthropological sources. It builds on that theory in a few situations. The following chapter explores the specific issue of intercultural relations at All Saints, including a sociological analysis of different constructions of parish unity.

Other more general theoretical questions follow from this ethnographic reporting. What *is* the parish in Roman Catholicism? How is that role unique for the historical, cultural, and ecclesial context of the United States? Does the shared parish represent a unique manifestation of the parish or does it fit into previous models? This penultimate chapter of the book attempts to make a contribution to the so-called "new paradigm" in the sociology of religion. A part of the new paradigm trajectory includes R. Stephen Warner's finding in the 1990s that the de facto congregational form dominates American religious life across religious boundaries.[55] In the United States, this tendency has to contend with Roman Catholic theological traditions emphasizing the Universal Church as well as authority structures that focus on the bishop and pastor. A more in-depth discussion of this dynamic forms the bulk of the fourth chapter.

The final chapter assembles the concluding argument of the book. It builds up an extended theoretical reflection on cultural diversity in the Catholic Church in the United States. It also asks how the Church might contend with the mutual isolation of cultural groups—perpetuating misunderstanding and a lack of empathy—even within shared parishes. How should the Roman Catholic leadership respond in order to incorporate immigrants and welcome internal cultural diversity? Roman Catholic bishops in the United States underwent a significant shift in principles for the incorporation of immigrants from the 1970s to the present. They went from embracing assimilation (Americanization) to promoting an ecclesial version of multiculturalism.[56] The question arises as to whether such a shift has really proved adequate to the environment of diversity as manifested in shared parishes like All Saints. I argue, based on the data from earlier chapters, that the Christian theological vision of church as communion may provide us with a better blueprint for understanding cultural diversity as an experience of both distinction and difference and unity and interconnectedness.

For those interested in questions of methodology, an appendix describes how I approached ethnographic study at All Saints. The Episcopal priest and organizational consultant Eric Law protests that U.S. churches typically respond in a shallow manner to the deep challenges of a culturally diverse society.[57] Catholic parishes like All Saints have complex roots. They exist as the result of multiple, intersecting responses that arose within different historical contexts. That was the case even before the demographic changes effected with the arrival of Latin American immigrants. These changes raised new practical dilemmas and required new responses in the lived religion of the people on both sides. What sort of approach to research adequately addresses this milieu? I have proposed a collaborative approach to ethnographic listening, one that provides community members with tools for assisting in the inquiry. Combined with my own investigations over the ten months of a "parish year," this approach delivered multiple perspectives to help fill out the picture. It also demanded that I share conclusions with parish leaders and other community members. The appendix describes this approach in more detail.[58]

All Saints has secured some stability as a shared parish for the present. After my year there, the bishop transferred Father Nacho, who became pastor in a "national parish" for Latinos in another town. But there was no question of not assigning him a replacement, and a recently ordained Latin American man who had attended seminary in the United States came to serve at All Saints. Both communities continued with their ministries and masses, even as variations in their collaboration and negotiations also continued. On a follow-up visit, volunteer religious education teachers from both communities described their cooperation in a joint demonstration table at a parish ministries' fair. But others suggested a gradual attrition in attention to intercultural relations that my research had accented and brought to the surface. Yet I attended a wedding where a handful of white American men married to Mexicans occupied a table together and described their consistent presence at such events. Both communities continued to allow space for the other and to interact in different ways, as circumstances suggested or demanded. Still, the future remained and remains uncertain. Will the local diocese continue to be able to provide adequate clergy support to both communities in both languages? How will the unstable local economy impact the vulnerable lives of migrants as well as certain contemporary cultural narratives that bill them as a threat?

Once again, the parish experience mirrors that of the larger demographic transformation of U.S. Roman Catholicism. A certain ambiguity envelops the future there as well. Given the long-term trends, the Catholic Church will continue to have to attend to the influx of immigrants and their families, especially those of Latin American provenance. At the same time, negative views of immigration exist as surely among Euro-American Catholics as they do among the general population.[59] This ambiguity was well captured when the bishop of Sacramento, California, told a diverse audience of Catholic leaders that bishops receive more hate mail for their support of immigration reform than on any other issue. The future indeed remains uncertain.

1

All Saints from Village Church to Shared Parish

In early 2008, I facilitated the creation of a bilingual display on the history of All Saints Parish. In preparation, a group of older parishioners sorted through their memories, I sorted through parish archives, and a handful of us looked through the photographs, newspaper articles, and other materials provided by the same group of elderly parishioners. A teacher with an artistic bent designed the display space and helped me set out the materials. We set out old photographs, first-person accounts of the past, anniversary booklets, newspaper articles, and artifacts. Over the next few weeks, parishioners filed by the exhibit after mass or during the Lenten fish fries sponsored by the Knights of Columbus. They examined photographs of the old Gothic Revival church—inside and out—and the old parish school building (also formerly a house for priests and then nuns), both now long gone. Some of the Euro-American parishioners pointed out their own ancestors in first communion photographs from 1906 and baptism photos from 1914. There were reproduced accounts of turmoil in the town of Havenville from the early years of the parish. People looked at Altar Rosary Society medals from the 1940s and 1950s, an anniversary booklet from the 1990s, and a grayed photograph of the twin angels that once flanked the old Gothic Revival church's entrance. It was pointed out how photographs of Catholic Youth Organization activities during World War II contained only young women, most of the young men being away at war. People remembered with pride the women's choir from the early 1960s, a group of housewives who had made popular records of sacred music and toured internationally.

Although almost all of the materials came from elderly members of the Euro-American community, the exhibit gathered interest in the Mexican community as well. Several people remarked on how different the parish's past was from what they had expected. They looked at photographs of the previous parish church and saw strong similarities between its Gothic Revival style and the churches they had known back in Mexico. Reading a story about the first parish school's makeshift desks (planks nailed over pews in the church), one man spoke of his own family's struggles to piece together a makeshift parish church in their poor neighborhood in central Mexico. The parish's history of struggle and traditional Catholicism resonated with its newest parishioners. Meanwhile, on the Euro-American side, parishioners reveled in a public display of their heritage. The exhibit provoked new anecdotes. A married couple told me how they had met at a church social decades before. A retired schoolteacher described how she was hired to teach in the parish school after the public school district refused to hire her because she was a Catholic. One elderly man, noting the record of the name of a former pastor, spoke of temporarily moving to another parish when he and his wife could no longer bear the man. Exhibit photos of the parish during World War II brought out war stories from several of the older men.

Parishioners in both communities found themselves drawn in by the exhibit's evocation of times past. Some found themselves surprised about the difference between the economic struggles of the parish's past and the relative success of today. Most saw similarities and differences across time. The exhibit had, in a sense, opened up a path between then and now, displacing the nostalgia and amnesia that often rule our conceptions of the past. In a different way it raised the question, "How did we get to where we are now? Who has made up this worshipping community and how has that changed over time?" Of course, modern historiography accepts that history never simply equates to an assembly of facts about the past but is instead an interpretation of the fragmented information we have. The pages that follow here mold the record of memory—written, oral, archival, material, and photographic—into an narrative interpretation of what happened at All Saints over the years. This testimony, like all, remains incomplete and partial, but we cannot move forward in understanding All Saints as a shared parish today without understanding whence it came. We cannot understand, for example, contemporary resistance to demographic changes without a feel for the fraught intercultural encounters of the mid-twentieth century, when Havenville was a homogenous Euro-American cultural environment and differences were not well tolerated. On the other hand, history can offer hope. Reconstructing intercultural encounters of a more distant past—for example, the relatively uneventful nineteenth century rapport between Germans and Irish, between Catholics and Protestants—might provide surprising resources for wading through the intercultural tensions of today.

*   *   *

The history of All Saints Parish can be roughly divided into four distinct periods. All Saints began in its early years as a tiny Roman Catholic parish in a small Protestant town. During those "village church" years, it was one of the few English-speaking parishes in an area dominated by German Catholics and other ethnic Catholics in national parishes. After many decades as a small-town parish of this kind, population growth after the Great Depression made it into a "social parish," a comprehensive social environment for Catholics. This period lasted well into the 1970s (in part through the long tenure of one pastor), but it eventually surrendered to multiple social forces that made its community less tight and cohesive. By the 1980s, a more "decentralized parish" came to birth, which by the late 1990s had slipped into the "shared parish" era when parishioners began to share their church with an immigrant community from Latin America.

There is a temptation to think of intercultural relations, one of the major themes of this study, as a product of the shared parish era at All Saints. But long before that epoch began, encounters, perspectives, and clashes between cultural groups shaped the parish community at All Saints. In the description of the history of the parish that follows, intercultural perspectives offer a frequent lens through which to view the unfolding story. Though certainly not the only lens, this one raises consistent questions about the negotiation of religious and cultural identity in Havenville, even from its earliest days. But these issues take the fore in the era of All Saints as a shared parish.

Village Church in the Protestant Midwest, 1860–1940
The Context: Roman Catholic Parishes in the Midwest

The United States is, even today, a nation of regions, and All Saints Parish and Havenville belong squarely in the history and traditions of the midwestern states. Originally known simply as "the West," the area first opened to Anglo-American settlement when parts of it were included in the Northwest Territory in 1787 and in the Louisiana Purchase from France in 1803.[1] The first Catholics in the area were French missionaries, and up to the nineteenth century, all of the mission parishes were French. Maryland Catholics moved across Kentucky into Ohio and established a parish there in 1818.[2] Several midwestern indigenous peoples, including Potawatomis and Miamis, became Catholics in large numbers. All were removed from the region by the federal government, often brutally and sometimes accompanied by their priests, between the 1830s and the 1850s.[3]

From the middle of the nineteenth century onward, Catholicism grew rapidly across the Midwest, due mostly to immigration. Nevertheless, both dioceses and parishes often covered great swaths of territory. A constant shortage of priests meant perennial challenges with the clergy—itinerant priests, clergy suddenly defecting to other dioceses and locales, and priests in their frontier isolation struggling with alcoholism and gambling. The clergy situation in dioceses and parishes remained as unstable in these early years as church finances did. On the brighter side, despite a national peak of anti-Catholicism in the 1840s, the Midwest did not suffer as much as in the northeastern cities. Suspicion of Catholics was not absent, but in the Ohio Valley, for example, the multitude of different Protestant religious groups established a moderate acceptance of religious pluralism advantageous even to Catholics and Jews.[4]

Although some Anglo-American Catholics did settle in the Midwest (and in Havenville), Irish and German immigrants dominated midwestern Catholicism in the mid-nineteenth century. Both settled in what became the larger cities—Cincinnati, Chicago, and St. Louis. In general, the Irish were disproportionately urban in their patterns of settlement, the men employed as low-wage workers on the railroads, canals, and in the factories, and the women working as domestics.[5] About a quarter of the Germans who came settled in agricultural areas.[6] So many Germans settled in the Ohio and Mississippi River Valleys that the area between Milwaukee, St. Louis, and Cincinnati became known to historians as the "German triangle." A pattern developed among Catholic parishes for these Irish and German immigrants. Ethnic or national parishes—parishes for single ethnic or language groups, established either de jure (by church law) or de facto (by circumstance)—dominated the cities, while the rural areas, with fewer concentrated immigrant communities, sported a mix of territorial and ethnic parishes.[7]

Irish migrants frequently formed national parishes, but these parishes often morphed to accommodate other cultural groups. Irish Catholics spoke English and disproportionately supported Americanization, that is, faster accommodation to the Anglo-American culture. At the same time, Irish-American Catholicism decisively shaped Catholicism in the United States. Irish and Irish-American prelates dominated the episcopacy for decades, and Irish-American Catholic culture became the foundation of the twentieth-century American Catholic counterculture.[8] In the rural Midwest, however, German Catholicism remained in ascendency. Indeed, the most enduring and salient form of nineteenth-century parish life in the Midwest was the German parish.

German national parishes became significant sites to reconstruct and enact a unique German Catholic identity for the United States. This identity-producing effort worked in part though social boundaries. Social boundaries can be defined as "a categorical distinction that members of a society recognize in their quotidian activities and that affects their mental orientations and actions toward one another."[9] German parishes established social boundaries over and against Anglo-American Protestant institutions, especially the public school system. Large numbers of German parishes had German-language (or bilingual) parochial schools, and German Catholics initially resisted reconciling arrangements with the public school system. Midwestern German bishops argued for requiring Catholic schools in every parish.[10] German Catholic identity was further cemented by the marking of boundaries with German secular liberal thought (such as that associated with the revolutions of 1848). German priests encouraged parish missions and local societies to combat liberalism. Finally, German Catholic parishes resisted the Americanization efforts of Irish Catholic prelates. For many

German Catholics, there was an explicit connection between the preservation of language and culture and the endurance of Catholic faith.
"Language saves faith" was the catchphrase.[11] German cultural practices
and language also permeated the network of societies and organizations in the parishes: devotional confraternities, mutual-aid societies,
trade organizations, and music and theatre groups.[12]

The twentieth century brought historic challenges to this state of
affairs. World War I made German cultural identity suspect in the
larger society, and many though not all parishes ceased their German-
language activities. Yet even without that dramatic event, changes were
afoot. By the beginning of the twentieth century, Germans no longer
constituted one of the major groups migrating to the United States.
The industrial economy of the German state had grown, especially in
comparison to the still agriculturally dominant economies and politically developing states in eastern and southern Europe. These nations
now provided the major migration flows to the United States.[13] As the
generations raised in the United States grew in influence, it became
more and more common to hear one sermon in English and one in
German, though this provoked no little consternation on the part of
previous generations of German Catholics.[14] Nevertheless, the German
parish did not disappear. Social boundaries remained, but they were
recalibrated; in effect they became "blurred."[15] The focus on protecting
cultural and linguistic identity gave way to the management of cultural
memory—for example, with anniversaries, parades, and other demonstrations of heritage and pride. Herbert Gans famously called this "symbolic ethnicity."[16]

By the beginning of the twentieth century, southern and eastern
European Catholics had begun developing ethnic parishes in midwestern cities, but these Poles, Italians, and many other groups still had less
influence in the rural Midwest. The national experience of southern
Italians in that era, however, still merits attention. Perhaps more than
any other group of European migrants, they were characterized negatively by the larger society in ways parallel to the Mexican community of
the late twentieth century. Classified in scholarly publications as geneti-
cally inferior to northern Europeans, Italians suffered from urban over-
crowding, gang violence, discrimination, and economic exploitation.
Roman Catholic religious leaders spoke of the "Italian problem." They

found themselves sometimes consigned to the basement of a church they themselves had built.[17] Priests complained about scant church attendance. The saint festivals, or *feste*, however, drew great numbers to church and to the streets. Initially, many dioceses experimented with "duplex parishes" for Italians—a predecessor to the shared parish of today. Eventually, ethnic parishes run by Italian religious orders like the Pallottines and Scalabrinis worked more successfully.[18]

In any case, ethnic parishes—mostly German—remained the dominant approach to parish life in the Catholic Midwest through most of the nineteenth and early twentieth centuries. In 1900, for example, a Kentucky bishop sent the Propaganda Fide, the Vatican congregation that supervised U.S. Church appointments, a profile of the Port Jefferson Diocese where All Saints Parish is located. He counted 141 parishes, 39 without resident priests, and only 17 of the parishes English-speaking.[19] Nevertheless, by the end of World War II, the ethnic or national parish was on the wane for multiple reasons. There were first of all ecclesial reasons: bishops shied away from permitting them. Yet the bishops themselves were influenced by larger societal changes.

American society itself underwent a process of "boundary blurring" through the mid-twentieth century. Multiple factors weakened the social boundary between the mainstream Anglo-American culture and various immigrant cultures. Economic transformation meant some jobs previously filled by Catholic immigrants disappeared. Their children sought other, higher-status work as new migrants—African Americans from the South, Puerto Ricans, Mexicans—filled many low-paying jobs. Higher education received substantial government help and became available to the children of Catholic immigrants. Suburbanization, promoted by federal law, brought home ownership to working-class whites—a good many of whom were Catholic—though less to African Americans or Hispanics.

Cultural factors also contributed to the boundary blurring. Nativism and xenophobia, the latter provoked by World War I, jump-started a strong society-wide drive for the Americanization of immigrants. At the same time, the war made the assertion of German cultural identity unsavory, inspiring many German parishes to downplay their Germanness. Military service and patriotic unity during World War II intermingled Catholics and Anglo-American Protestants. At the same time,

Hitler's anti-Semitism made discrimination less acceptable to Americans, though even anti-Catholic forms of discrimination did not disappear entirely.[20] Finally, the National Origins Act of 1924 and other 1920s restriction laws had a dramatic stifling effect on Catholic immigration. As the second and third generations became more influenced by the mainstream culture, few new immigrants arrived to provide counterinfluence or to reinforce firmer boundaries against the mainstream culture.[21] The national parish met a gradual demise.

A Small Parish among Protestants, 1860–1940

Histories of the Roman Catholic parish in the Midwest rightly emphasize the ethnic or national parish, but All Saints Parish in Havenville was not established as an ethnic parish. In 1860, thirty families of mixed heritage were organized as part of a diocesan drive to establish parishes in county seats and major towns just before the Civil War. An 1863 parish census confirms the mixed makeup; it describes All Saints as consisting of 78 families—40 German, 20 Irish, 2 mixed German-Irish, 1 German-American, and 1 [Anglo-]American. Fourteen families do not have any cultural description. The parish had three single people, one designated as Irish and two without cultural description.[22] What parish records cannot tell us is how these families from different cultural groups got along. Germans clearly dominated. A school was established in 1868, initially meeting in the church. The pastor hired his brother—both of them German immigrants—as the single teacher. The parish's first priest, who had the church built in 1860–1861, did not live in Havenville but presided over this and several communities from a solidly German parish nearly 50 miles away.[23] All Saints had its first resident pastor, also a German, in 1861.[24] Nevertheless, Irish and Anglo-American names continued to show up in parish records, suggesting that the different cultural groups did not splinter apart.

To understand the development of All Saints, it is best to trace the rise of Havenville itself. Like many midwestern towns, it was born from the ashes of forests cleared and—more tragically—native peoples removed.[25] Settlers moved to the area from other parts of the Midwest in the late 1820s and early 1830s, and newly appointed county commissioners were quickly empowered by the state legislature to select and organize a county seat—it had only 200 inhabitants. The town grew as a merchant center for local farmers. The first courthouse went up in 1831, and by 1852 there was a railroad spur to nearby Brookton. In 1867, local engineers diverted the Brookton River and built a canal to attract mills and other forms of basic industry.[26] By 1860, the population of the town was already 2,053, and it gradually but steadily increased through the nineteenth century. By 1900 there were 7,810 residents in town.[27]

Unlike in other parts of the Midwest, Catholics never constituted a major force there. When the first thirty families from across Brookton County organized the Catholic parish at Havenville in 1860, Presbyterians, Methodists, and Baptists already had churches in town, the Methodists being the first. In the same years, Lutherans and Episcopalians were on the verge of building their houses of worship in Havenville, and within a few decades, Reformed and Congregationalist congregations would come to town as well. Havenville had more religious diversity than many midwestern towns. After the Great Awakening, Methodists and Baptists had become the dominant religious groups through most of the nation. But Havenville reserved a place for more marginalized groups. Already by 1860, Anabaptists—Brethren, Mennonites, and Amish—had moved into the area and organized churches or meetinghouses. In 1878, a congregation of Jews bought the Baptists' former meeting house and converted it into a synagogue.[28]

Religious diversity does not appear to have disturbed the waters in nineteenth-century Havenville. Since 1840, long before the Catholics built their church, priests had come to town from nearby Port Jefferson to give talks at the courthouse and celebrate mass in private homes.[29] By the time the Catholic church was built and the parish firmly established in 1863, fifteen of its seventy-eight families were denominationally mixed, ten of them Catholics married to Lutherans (all Germans). In the sociological literature, research shows that intermarriage depends on three factors: the number of eligible spouses, the social distance between groups, and the internal attitudes regarding exogamy within groups.[30] While Catholic attitudes toward exogamy in this era were generally negative, between Germans of different faiths there would have been less social distance. Across the Midwest, Germans had the reputation for moderately friendly relations across religious lines.[31] Furthermore, with Catholics making up such a small percentage of the population in Havenville, the limited availability of coreligionists as spouses may have overcome any resistance to exogamy. In any case, the proportion of exogamy in the rolls of the Catholic parish reinforces the idea that Havenville was not an interreligiously hostile environment in the mid-nineteenth century. A similar study of one midwestern state during settlement backs up this assertion.[32]

Despite this apparent openness to religious diversity and Havenville's increasing population, All Saints did not grow into a large parish in this period. It did not even draw enough families to consistently keep a resident pastor until 1878. Even by 1907, the parish still had only 90 families and 362 members, not many more than in 1863. The parochial school remained a two-room schoolhouse into the 1920s. First communion was held only once every few years until the 1930s.[33] All Saints did not expand into a larger parish in part because of the establishment of other parishes in the neighboring towns and cities. Catholics no longer had to travel from across the county to Havenville for mass. But perhaps more significantly, the town was hardly touched by the waves of Catholic immigrants from southern and eastern Europe at the end of the century. Its own population surge in that time of local industrial growth was native-born and midwestern, that is, largely Protestant.[34]

Into the twentieth century, All Saints continued to keep a low profile in its immediate environment—Catholic in a Protestant town, English-speaking in a mostly German Catholic diocese. Physically, the church sat on a side street astride an alley with an orchard between it and Main Street. Its only mention in the sesquicentennial history of Havenville concerns the "curiosity" of a murdered Roma (gypsy) woman whose funeral rites were performed by the priest from All Saints.[35] Nevertheless, internally it developed a robust life of devotions and devotional societies that carefully asserted Catholic identity in contrast with Protestant congregational life. In an era of highly formalized Sunday worship, these societies also ensured, through the effective use of ritual space and practice, that church teaching and discipline impacted everyday life.[36] By 1906, the parish had distinct devotional societies for married men, married women, young unmarried women, boys, girls, and small children.[37]

By the 1920s, a new wave of anti-Catholic nativism spread across the Midwest. Part of a nationwide anti-immigrant, anti-Semitic, and

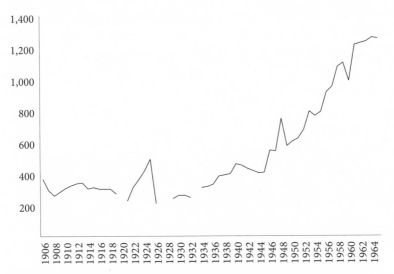

Figure 1.1. Number of parishioners at All Saints, 1906–1965 (as indicated in annual reports by the pastor to the diocese)

anti-Catholic movement, it included the refounding of the Ku Klux Klan in 1915. The KKK grew active in the Midwest in the 1920s, seizing control of the Republican Party in one midwestern state, though actual violence was rare. Havenvillers lived far from the center of such activity, and the immigrant population in town remained relatively low. Nevertheless, a cross burning took place in Havenville on Christmas in 1922. Some months before, out-of-town Klan leaders, one from a neighboring state, had attempted to build a local chapter, but the city police chief absolutely forbade it, even going to the trouble of breaking up an organizational meeting at the downtown theater. On Christmas Eve, a hooded Klansman paid a visit to a local minister seeking support. By the end of the evening, signs were posted around town, and several townspeople received telephone calls about the cross burning. As a result, several hundred people walked over west of downtown to observe what the newspaper claimed citizens described as "a beautiful sight," a twenty-six-foot cross burning.[38]

It is difficult to assess the level of discrimination that minority Catholics (or Jews and African Americans) experienced in Havenville in that era. Many of the town's key merchants at that time were Jews. Catholics at All Saints managed to build a new school building. In 1922, the year of the cross burning, 40 percent of all families at All Saints included non-Catholic spouses. Across the 1920s, 56 percent of all Catholic marriages at All Saints were to non-Catholics, the vast majority Protestants. While stereotypes of the era picture beleaguered religious minorities hiding in the shadows, something else entirely appears to have happened in Havenville.

This does not mean that the spirit of the era had no impact. One elderly member of All Saints reported that her mother's family, devout members of a small Protestant church, vehemently opposed her mother marrying her father, a Catholic, in that era. Nevertheless, they attended the wedding, her mother in tears. Many of the non-Catholic employees at the factory where she worked also attended, expressing curiosity about exotic Catholic customs.[39] Perhaps more telling, in this era of local and national economic prosperity, the number of baptisms at All Saints shrank. The number of parishioners dropped precipitously in 1926, including a huge drop in the number of mixed families attending. In that same year, however, the parish had three different pastors within a matter of months.[40] At the same time, Havenville's synagogue declined. It went from a high of 137 members in 1907 to 51 members in 1927, closing in the 1930s. Intermarriage may have offered Catholics and Jews the option of defecting to more favorably viewed faith communities. Intermarriage with Christians was relatively common for Jews in small towns of that era, and Jewish scholars believe it may have precipitated the decline of communities such as that in Havenville.[41]

The Social Parish at All Saints, 1940–1981

Like almost all organizations and religious communities, All Saints struggled during the Great Depression. The situation was dire. According to the pastor's report to the diocese, the parish facilities deteriorated through lack of repair with the onset of economic troubles. The parish defaulted on debt. In 1933, a new pastor solicited friends to help make repairs on the physical plant and went into debt himself trying to set things aright. With the bishop's permission, he closed the parish school for lack of funds. A comprehensive religious education program was established in its wake. One man now in his eighties remembers having to serve mass nearly every day; there were so few other altar boys.[42] Yet, in 1937, Hamilton Electric moved to town from another part of the Midwest, bringing 173 employees with it, including many Catholic families. The company expanded over the years until it became the largest employer in town.[43] The company also brought engineers and managers, and employment for them, some of them Catholics. Before that time, Catholics had mostly been factory workers. The arrival of Hamilton eventually became part of a demographic shift for the parish. Almost immediately, the number of baptisms at All Saints rose significantly, and there were many signs of parish life and activity on into the 1940s.[44]

By the early 1940s, with the economic recovery and the war, the parish looked quite different. Suddenly there is record of a great burst of organizational activity, especially focused on the nationally known Catholic societies and organizations. The Holy Names and Altar Rosary societies occupied men and women respectively—the former focused on encouraging responsibility and the judicious use of language, the latter on church cleaning and decorating. The Catholic Youth Organization (CYO), founded earlier in the century in Chicago, organized picnics, bicycle outings, bowling leagues, basketball, drama, and softball. As men left for war, these activities almost exclusively focused on young women. The popular May Crownings also put the focus on women, as they received public honor by representing the Virgin Mary crowned as queen of heaven. The Young Ladies Sodality associated itself with the catechetical efforts of religious sisters offering religious education in the absence of a Catholic school. Even the choir, generally the exclusive province of men, became mixed at this time. The sisters did focus some attention on younger boys, starting a Knights of the Altar organization for altar servers, invoking military metaphors—albeit medieval ones—in an age of war.[45]

Though still a small parish, All Saints was transformed by a decade of industrial growth and social upheaval from the war. No longer focused almost solely on worship, it became what the historian E. Brooks Holifield has called a "social congregation"—a comprehensive community that provides many public services to its congregants.[46] (I adapt the term to a more Catholic-inflected version, the "social parish.") In the late forties at All Saints, for example, a credit union was founded, a fall

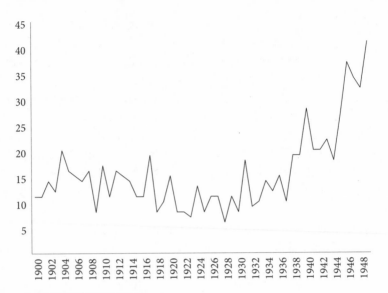

Figure 1.2. Baptisms at All Saints, 1900–1949

festival begun, and a parish library initiated.[47] Holifield notes that, in the nineteenth century, such parishes formed for Catholics in circumstances where, because of anti-Catholicism, they had few other institutions and organizations to turn to. In the postwar period, anti-Catholicism abated nationally. Yet as many local Catholics recall it (and even some Anabaptists), anti-Catholic feeling and religious tension came to the fore in postwar Havenville: a Catholic family from Canada faced housing discrimination in the area in the 1940s; in the 1950s, Protestant families in one neighborhood frowned upon their children playing with the Catholic child on the street; some Protestant teens were not permitted to date Catholics in the 1960s; families on one block in the 1960s met to decide how to handle a Catholic family moving in; a Catholic teacher was informed late in that decade that the district school board would never hire her on account of her religion; 1960s Catholic children were kept at a distance at a local Christian kindergarten. Even in the 1980s, one parishioner found anti-Catholic propaganda placed on his desk at work describing Catholic ceremonies as "paganistic."

Some of the diversity that had characterized the early decades of the city's history disappeared during the twentieth century. The synagogue closed. Although 21 African Americans had lived in Havenville in 1890—still a tiny proportion of the population—there were almost none living there after 1900.[48] By the 1950s and 1960s, the city had become known as a "sundown town," where African Americans had to depart before sunset.[49] One couple reported to me about their 1972 move to Havenville: "The realtor told us they were real proud of the fact that there were no people of color in Havenville." Another (white) woman remembered that, as late as 1989, a black employee of her husband's company rebuffed her entreaty for him to stay the night in town. He told her bluntly that no hotel in town would rent him a room.

As for the Catholic population, it persisted and thrived, but the eventual ascendancy of the town's Anabaptist population seems to have resulted in a surge of anti-Catholicism after World War II. Anabaptist religious language is historically rooted in a radical rejection of Roman Catholicism during the Reformation Era, and Anabaptists recount stories of persecution by Catholics (and Lutherans) from that time. By the 1950s, Anabaptists became the city's "establishment," but Catholics were also becoming numerous in a traditionally Protestant town. With Catholics' growing numbers and economic power, members of Anabaptist churches only partially excluded them from local institutions in this era. As one Catholic man who grew up in the late 1950s and 1960s put it, being Catholic felt more like being an anomaly than being truly discriminated against. Nevertheless, the tension made the complete social environment of All Saints attractive and welcoming. A woman who arrived in 1969 said:

> I know previous to our coming here, All Saints was the core of Catholic activity—the Altar Rosary [society], and everything for the Catholics living here; they didn't belong to other groups like the Elks. Well some [did], I suppose, but it was all All Saints and the activities, and I guess they were very, very frequent, very active.

A local lay leader compared the situation of All Saints among the Anabaptists in Havenville to that of Catholic ethnic parishes in an Anglo-American world—forging identity by defensive boundaries.

This basic pattern of the social parish held and expanded after the war through the decades of postwar economic expansion. A new façade was put on the church in 1948, expanding its seating. In 1949, the school reopened, staffed by another group of religious sisters, and this time the parish charged no tuition. In 1952, the interior of the church was renovated.[50] The roster of activities continued to grow with study groups, a PTA, sports clubs, and scouting for both boys and girls. There were countless socials and dinners, usually prepared by the Altar Rosary women and served by the young women from CYO. A new women's choir became so accomplished that they made a record and took their repertoire of sacred music on the road.[51] By the end of the decade, there was religious education for both grade school and high school students.[52] A particular type of family and home life made possible this energetic pattern of parish life, enabled by the 1950s concatenation of high marriage rates, high birthrates, lower rates of divorce, and women working in the home.[53]

This arrangement (and these activities) continued well into the 1960s. By this time, the larger-than-life Fr. John Nowak had arrived, who was pastor for a quarter century. "He thought we were hicks," one of the older men in the parish told me. He decreed that the small dinners would become large parties. "Smokers," casino night fund-raisers just for men, became so popular that the women demanded their own version. Although Catholic identity remained crucial to Fr. Nowak, and although he favored the social parish model he inherited, he also felt that the time had come for Catholics to engage the local community. The "smokers" brought in hundreds of Protestants. Inducted into the Rotary Club, Fr. Nowak became a well-known figure in the local business and legal community. He made ecumenical connections, developing a lifelong friendship with Havenville's Episcopal priest. And when it came time to build a new church, he insisted on a Colonial design, wanting the church to blend into the largely Protestant environment.

Despite Fr. Nowak's civic and ecumenical openness, he had oft expressed negative feelings about the massive changes in church and society that dominated his pastorate (1957–1981). He especially disliked the transformations around gender roles and family. He railed against divorce and the families of the divorced, prompting at least one family to seek a more welcoming parish in another town. Through most of his tenure, he would not allow female teachers at the school to wear pants. No women or girls could approach the altar except to clean it. Though he implemented the liturgical reforms of the Second Vatican Council, he did so minimally, resisting both the removal of the communion rail—where people knelt to receive communion—and the inclusion of a handshake for the sign of peace. He continued to preach from the pulpit that those who sent their children to public school risked hellfire. On the other hand, with great consistency on this issue, he kept the school tuition-free through the 1970s, a feat of great financial acumen. Nor was he simply a curmudgeon. A daughter of one of the only Mexican families in town remembers him as very kind and encouraging to them, speaking of the struggles of his own immigrant parents.

Without a doubt, Fr. Nowak made his influence felt. In a 1962 parish bulletin, youth who missed high school religious education classes without permission were publicly listed by name. In writing, he referred to himself in the third person as "your pastor" and explained that what appeared to be imposing his will was simply in the best interest of the parish. At times, his forceful style proved advantageous. The parish continued to grow through this era. Five Sunday masses bustled in the old church. Despite substantial opposition, Fr. Nowak (with the parish trustees) was able to acquire new property quickly for expansion of the facilities. He also managed to get convince one wealthy man to donate the entire sum for a new priest residence. As students jammed the school, he mailed out renovation plans, including financial requirements for each family. And they gave.

His decisive, calculating style, however, did not go over with everyone. Despite his strong feelings about Catholic children attending the school, its attendance declined through the 1970s.[54] When Fr. Nowak proposed the Colonial design for the new church, at least one family felt he was charging ahead without sufficient consultation of the parish. A longtime parishioner precipitated a revolt, and Fr. Nowak was forced to resort to more subtle tactics—offering alternative designs he knew people would hate, and holding successive votes with narrower and narrower constituencies until all approved his design. In the end, however, the new church he wanted was built and then paid for within five years.

When John Nowak retired from the pastorate in 1981, it was the end of an era at All Saints. The pastors who followed were more amenable to contemporary changes in church and society. Ultimately, some of those changes—more women in the workplace (with less time to spend at church), less anti-Catholicism, greater economic prosperity, more options for entertainment and activity, and a gradual decease in religious commitment—brought All Saints' life as a social parish to an end. By that time, people were no longer the "joiners" they once had been. All voluntary organizations—not just churches—saw either an outright decline or, at least, a looser style of participation.[55] All Saints certainly became more diffuse and more loosely connected as a parish. The city of Havenville itself became more loosely connected and less centralized. And the most sweeping transformation of all, the influx of thousands of Latin American immigrants, was about to commence.

Parish Life in an Era of Transformations, 1981–2008
The Decentralized City and Parish

"It was a Main Street town," Richard and Helen Klug said in an interview over lunch at the Veterans of Foreign Wars club. They arrived in Havenville in 1950. "Saturday night they used to have popcorn machines and all the businesses were on Main Street." Shirley Alder, a lifelong resident in her sixties, said that when she was young, people took the bus downtown and shopped all day. This centralized image of Havenville not only describes its former commercial heart but also its former demographic concentration. When the Klugs built a house almost a mile from downtown, they found it impossible to secure carpool partners to travel "that far" out of town. Yet transformations were not far off. They described to me what happened in the 1970s and 1980s: "Then out north of town between here and [Brookton] they put in a mall out there. Wal-Mart started going in and they put the mall and the Wal-Mart outside [of town], and all the stores kind of destroyed the downtown business at that time. We used to have four or five drug stores, two or three hardware stores, clothing stores for men and women. All that stuff was back in the—fifty, sixty years ago, even forty years ago it was."[56] The commercial center of gravity for the city shifted to the highways entering town from north and south. An enclosed mall was built between Havenville and Brookton, and in 1989 a Wal-Mart was built south of town, followed by innumerable "big box" stores through the 1990s and on into the early 2000s. The downtown commercial district eventually returned, but now it had a specialized boutique flavor.

Even before this, a similar transition had begun in housing:

Suburban living has steadily increased around [Havenville], especially since the 1950's. There is a wide variety of ranch and other styles of homes in older suburban subdivisions and also in some older neighborhoods. New subdivisions provide a broader style of homes with price ranges that start in the low $100,000 range to several hundred thousand dollars each. Some newer developments have a mix of single family and duplex dwellings and some are comprised of manufactured homes.[57]

Some commuting to the urban center of Port Jefferson emerged (thirty miles away), both for entertainment and for work. Especially after 1970, the town, really now more of a city, spread out horizontally, with more people living on the periphery.[58] This outward movement was facilitated nationally by highway building outside of towns and cities. Even small cities like Havenville moved in the direction of sprawl.[59] In the 1980s in particular, Havenville experienced a growth in per capita income and a rapid increase in population.[60] The net effect was a partial decentralization of the city, something that occurred in similar areas as well.[61]

This local shift, along with larger societal changes around work, child rearing, and gender roles, altered the course of All Saints Parish from the late 1970s through the first years of the twenty-first century. The small-town parish of All Saints, social center of the Catholic world of Havenville, where "everyone knew everyone," disappeared. The new parish that emerged was something of a hybrid, with new thinking and new organizations, yet with parts of the old social parish persisting. Leaders from the social parish era remained influential, and core parishioners from that era continued to socialize with one another for years to come. Yet much leadership passed to a new generation.

A few parish organizations and events continued from the Nowak days, usually with diminishing attendance or altered focus. The Altar Rosary society remains today, but it has no new members and meets on an ad hoc basis for specific projects. The Knights of Columbus, reinitiated late in the social parish era (it existed with tenuous parish connections from 1906 to 1925), is perhaps the most robust organization to persist. Succeeding the Holy Names Society and the Men's Booster Society as the parish's chief men's group, it had its origins as a

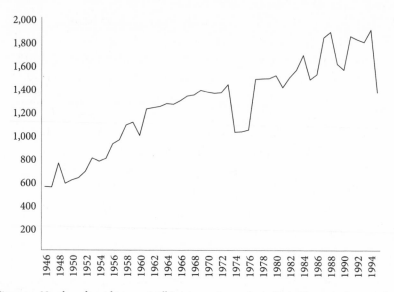

Figure 1.3. Number of parishioners at All Saints, 1946–1995 (as indicated by pastor in annual reports to diocese)

non-ethnically rooted ritual and mutual aid society for men in the late nineteenth and early twentieth century (competing with the histori-cally anti-Catholic Masons). In the post-Nowak era it became more and more associated with event planning, fund raising, and parish building, eventually becoming, in the 1990s, an alternative parish finance system. To this day, it funds and staffs parish pancake breakfasts and fish fries.

As the parish grew even larger (1,550 members in 1983; 1,789 in 1993[62]), and Catholics in Havenville invested in more activities outside the faith community, parish groups and organizations came to be orga-nized by interest rather than purely by gender and age. In the 1980s, Henry and Ellen McKeller initiated small faith communities at the par-ish, allowing people to connect with a small number of people socially and spiritually amidst the larger parish. A weekly group called Rite of Christian Initiation for Adults (RCIA) was begun for those interested in becoming Catholic. In 1987 the parish participated in a bishop-sponsored renewal program that included evening talks and monthly prayer sessions.[63] A handful of parishioners formed a Blue Army group to pray the rosary and honor the Virgin Mary as revealed through the apparitions at Fatima. There was also a Prayer and Share group, dedicated to faith sharing and group prayer. Later in the 1990s, the McKellers also initiated adult education classes on Sunday (taking the Protestant model of Sunday school), and a group of senior citizens formed a group called JOY—just older youth. These distinct groups offered the social and spiritual community the parish at large could no longer provide. Notably missing in this assortment were groups related to the large church movements of the era—charismatic prayer groups, Cursillo retreats, the neo-catechumenate—although Marriage Encounter groups for married couples were active. Havenville still remained somewhat isolated from the larger Church.

Though internal conflict at the parish was not absent during the Nowak years, it intensified in the years after his retirement. Although Nowak slowed the progress of Vatican II alterations and kept the school tuition-free, changes could no longer be kept at bay. The lay teachers now teaching instead of religious sisters required salaries, and this in turn necessitated tuition, something some parishioners still resent. Others objected when the altar was turned around to face the people and the communion rail removed. Some pulled their children from the school over policies instituted by Fr. Nowak's successor and a new principal. Then, in the 1990s, when the pastor balked at buying property for parish expansion, the Knights of Columbus arranged to do so on its own, working with the school principal (now a layman) and diocesan authorities. This was an end run around the customary hierarchical channels of the Roman Catholic Church by a largely traditional organization. During that time, the pastor sought treatment for alcoholism, citing the pressure of finances. The pastor who followed him, Fr. Paul Collins, told me he inherited the facilities debt ridden and in a "shambles." His predecessor was well liked (and highly respected for entering treatment), but, in the words of one parishioner, "Father was a great guy. But he catered to the older persons of the church. Seriously, . . . younger than sixty years old it didn't get a lot of his attention."

When Father Paul, an accomplished fund-raiser, arrived in 1998, he put the parish on a solid financial base after the building expansion. An intensely social man, he threw dinner parties at the priest's residence and networked extensively among the city's secular clubs and key Anabaptist organizations. As he put it to me, in a Protestant environment he wanted to represent the Catholic faith well. When the diocese decided to get involved in "stewardship" as a way of promoting parish commitment, he invited parishioner John Huber to organize it.[64] Stewardship was one answer to the signs of the times. In an era where parishes were larger, with less personal connection than before, where both spouses worked and other commitments competed for time, people tended to have "loose connections" to groups and communities.[65] Stewardship at All Saints aimed to increase people's commitment to the groups and organizations of the parish. John Huber, a highly structured and driven man, gathered a committee and used such tactics as weekend talks and phone banks to secure from fellow parishioners greater commitment to volunteer ministries and weekly collections. The program was massively successful, bringing a new infusion of volunteers and donations, with a highly organized feedback loop so that neither a prospective volunteer nor a potential donation was left uncontacted. In 2006, John stepped down to study to be ordained a deacon.

Immigrants and Transformation, 1995–2007

Even as these changes altered the parish in Havenville through the 1990s, an even greater demographic transition was underway, the result of Latin American migration. The local roots of that migration, however, remain murky. A popular explanation in Havenville was that, in the late 1980s and early 1990s, the area experienced such low unemployment rates that local factories required workers and recruited them from Texas and Mexico. Rumors even surfaced that, implausibly, a local nonprofit social service agency had advertised on billboards on the United States–Mexico border. Truthfully, unemployment was low, below 5 percent from 1986 to 1989 and again after 1992.[66] There is larger evidence of recruiting along the border at the time in the meatpacking industry, which employed many immigrants in other new destination areas of the Midwest.[67] Nevertheless, the situation in Havenville was almost certainly more complex. Most immigrants at All Saints Parish were not from border states but from the interior of Mexico. Also, in many rural midwestern counties, labor shortages were compounded by the out-migration of native young people and the in-migration of retirees.[68]

Researchers have looked at the initiation of migration in analogous situations. One study looked at several communities in Louisiana, communities that also had very few immigrants until a recent influx. Similar to the situation in Havenville, the study found almost no unionization, a proliferation of subsidiary jobs for a key industry (oil, in this case), and volatility in employment levels. Unlike Havenville, most jobs were highly skilled or semiskilled, and employers made use of contract labor. While contract labor may have played a role early on in Havenville, it did not dominate the scene in the 2000s. But in both Louisiana and perhaps in Havenville, employers valued "soft skills"—amiability, loyalty, and reliability—and associated these skills specifically with Mexican immigrant workers. Such workers, in contrast to young American workers, required lower salaries and found the work acceptable in comparison to opportunities back home.[69] This analysis appropriates labor-market segmentation theory, where social stratification interacts with employment patterns and migration.[70]

More certain is the role of immigrant social networks in Havenville. Social networks have long been recognized as a key factor in what is called "chain migration," both in the nineteenth and early twentieth centuries, and especially since immigration law prioritized family reunification in 1965.[71] Others have pointed out how it functions among unauthorized immigrants. Whatever the case, it had a clear impact in Havenville. Large numbers of immigrants in town were from the same three states in Mexico (and often the same areas in those states). A mobile home park consisted of people from the same small town. Such social networks are known to increase social capital—including job opportunities—for immigrant groups struggling with a lack of it. These networks may be strong (family) or weak (acquaintances at work).[72] One All Saints parishioner looking for a safer job than the industrial painting he had been doing did not drive around and submit applications; rather, he depended on his networks of friends and coworkers. The same man introduced me to a lower-cost network of body shops run by Mexicans he knew. Another parishioner's factory supervisor was his *compadre*—his child's godfather—and he held onto his job through difficult times.

The density of these networks tends to create an ever-expanding circuit of reciprocal obligations and opportunities.[73] One study points to the multiple and overlapping social networks that impacted immigrant employment in an Oklahoma town. The primary networks there always consisted of family and friends, but many immigrants belonged to a church network and a contract employee network through the meat-packing plant.[74] At All Saints, most immigrants did not have extended family members living with them. Unauthorized immigrants, of course, cannot take advantage of government family reunification policies. But parishioners did create ties through *compadrazgo*—the social networks of godparentage signified in financial and spiritual sponsorship at baptisms, weddings, and other *ceremonias*. I had particular occasion to witness the stronger ties among active parishioners and leaders, where common participation led to mutual help and stability, as well as marriages.

In any case, word spread, business boomed, and the town filled with immigrants. According to the 1990 census, Hispanics made up a mere 4.9 percent of Havenville's population. By 2000, they were 19.3 percent. According to the American Community Survey estimate, 2005–2007, 23.9 percent of residents were Hispanic.[75] The 2010 census counted 28 percent of the population as Hispanic. Marriage and the arrival of spouses brought the children of immigrants to Havenville. In the 1990–1991 school year, only 7.7 percent of children in the local school district children were from any cultural or racial group other than majority whites. By the 1996–1997 school year, 11.5 percent of children were Hispanic. By 2007 when I arrived, the district was 37 percent Hispanic.[76]

Census numbers from 1990 to 2010 show that the vast majority of these new immigrants were Mexicans, who in the United States continue to disproportionately self-identify as Catholic compared with other cultures.[77] (According to the 2010 census, almost a quarter of Havenville residents were Mexican.) The town already had a small number of residents from Puerto Rico and South America affiliated with Anabaptist churches.[78] Despite this growing presence of Mexican and presumably Catholic immigrants, in 1994 there were as yet no parish services for immigrants at All Saints, the sole Catholic parish in town. A Euro-American parishioner who arrived in town in 1993 said about the parish and Latinos: "When we first moved here, it was like, you didn't even hear about that." Spanish-speaking immigrants who did attend church made the trek to the next county over. Our Lady of San

Juan de los Lagos was a church built in a former car repair garage. Later immigrants were able to attend mass at the parish in Brookton, about ten miles away.

Despite the language barrier, a few Latino individuals and families attended mass at All Saints anyway. Most were migrant farmworkers, some of whom opted to settle in town. They worked at an orchard and in fields owned by the Archer family south of town. James Jonas "J.J." Archer had planted an orchard there in 1922. During the bracero migrations (1942–1964), the Archers began hiring seasonal workers from Texas and Mexico for the apple harvest and other agricultural work, and they maintained housing for them on the orchard grounds. In the 1950s, a Mexican-American family from Texas decided to stay, and two of their children were the first Latinos to be baptized at All Saints.[79] In those days, there were so few Latinos that one member of that family felt that it made more of a difference for the mostly Protestant residents of Havenville that she was Catholic than that she was Mexican. In any case, over the next few decades, housing conditions at the orchard improved, and the Archers found it congenial if some families could stay year-round. Others opted to move into town and seek nonagricultural work.[80]

In the late 1960s, a local poultry processing plant hired a number of Mexican-Americans, establishing housing for them on site.[81] In the intervening years, Latino infant baptisms inched upward at All Saints. In 1969, however, a Mexican worker at the poultry factory died from either an accidental or self-inflicted gunshot wound. Controversy erupted (including a boycott), and eventually local religious groups, including Catholics, joined forces to establish a nonprofit aid organization for Latinos.[82] In the meantime, Latino baptisms peaked at All Saints while a priest from the diocesan Spanish apostolate was in residence from 1974 to 75.[83] In 1978, All Saints pastor John Nowak wrote in his annual report to the Port Jefferson diocese, "Help Wanted: The Spanish Apostolate should do something for the Spanish-speaking people in Havenville and area. Nothing is being done. Yet there are around 100 Spanish speaking families here."[84] By the late 1970s, the tiny church of Our Lady of San Juan de los Lagos was founded about fifteen miles away across the county line, and it attracted most of the Spanish speakers for years to come. Still, a handful of baptisms continued to take place at All Saints through the 1980s, usually performed by Fr. Peter Donders, a former missionary to Latin America and later pastor at San Juan de los Lagos.[85]

In the mid-1990s, however, Father Peter, now in charge of Hispanic ministry for the diocese (and in residence at All Saints), formed a committee of All Saints parishioners, both Latino and mixed Latino-Euro-American couples, and asked them to join him in beginning a ministry to the Latin American immigrants in Havenville. Father Peter and the committee held a town hall meeting of Latinos from the area to make sure there was enough interest to begin ministry. People came from far away to show their support, and the meeting was packed full of people. The diocese gave approval for the ministry, and Father Peter secured the services of a Mexican-American deacon from Texas to work at All Saints. He arrived midway through 1996. (That same year, the Ku Klux Klan came to town from another part of the state to protest the presence of Latino immigrants, sparking a large counterdemonstration from the city's ecumenical organization, including participation from All Saints.) A 7 o'clock Saturday evening Spanish mass was begun, with Deacon Jose Manuel Gonzalez preaching the sermon and the pastor reading through the Spanish text of the mass. One person remembers the pastor trying very hard but inflecting the Spanish with Latin pronunciation. When Fr. Paul Collins arrived as pastor, he moved the mass earlier in the evening; he believed 7 p.m. too late for people with small children. This also moved the Saturday evening English mass to the earlier hour of 4:30 p.m.

Deacon Gonzales—in cooperation with other deacons hired to work in the diocese—organized emotionally charged, charismatic-style retreats. He performed many baptisms, but he became most famous for developing a medical clinic affiliated with a local hospital. There had been little medical care available in town for immigrants. Eventually the clinic received ecumenical support and was moved to an evangelical church. The committee members, for their part, managed to initiate training for ministers at mass and some basic religious education for children and adults. They had few resources and little experience, but they worked hard. The mass and education programs brought in moderate numbers.

Deacon Gonzales left the parish in 1999. After he left, the parish scrambled to find a priest to cover the Saturday night mass. A priest

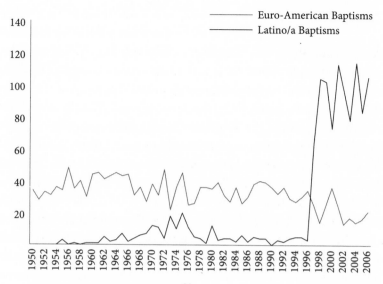

Figure 1.4. Baptisms at All Saints, 1950–2006[86]

doing graduate work at a nearby university began to come regularly. But he could do no more than weekend services. To fill in the gap, Julie Martinez, a Spanish-speaking Euro-American woman married to a Mexican, volunteered to coordinate the day-to-day Latino ministries. Fr. Collins hired her. She had already been working for a year or two with Joanne Joyner, the parish director of religious education, persuading Latino parents to enroll their children in the English religious education program. She attended to parents at evening meetings as well. She coordinated all the religious education when Joanne temporarily retired. Now, as coordinator, she and the other leaders brought in outside experts to do some elementary adult education in Spanish and to train readers and Eucharistic ministers for the liturgy. She and Father Paul spoke to people at national training centers for Hispanic ministry such as the Mexican American Cultural Center in San Antonio, Texas. Nevertheless, as Father Paul sees it, Julie's limitation was that she was "tall and blond"—not Hispanic by anyone's standard. Nevertheless, many years later in 2007, a middle-aged man took me aside after mass to praise Julie, insisting she should not be overshadowed by Deacon Gonzales.

In this interim period, the bishop visited All Saints to see whether a full-time Latino priest was called for. He attended the Saturday evening mass, and they called a meeting afterward. The church was again packed with people. The diocese was in the process of negotiating with a diocese in Mexico for priests to come to the diocese, and the bishop assigned one to All Saints. Fr. Ignacio (Padre Nacho) Barba arrived just before the feast day of the Virgin of Guadalupe in 2000, immediately slipping on the unfamiliar ice and injuring himself. Padre Nacho came to the Midwest in part because of family connections to the area. Initially he lived in the priest's residence (rectory) with Fr. Collins, but soon he moved out to live with relatives.

In the meantime, Padre Nacho set to work at the parish. He discovered many young adults (*jovenes*) in the parish who had never made their first communion, a fact he found disturbing, since it is commonly a rite of initiation for children. He soon set up an ad hoc preparation course meeting three times a week. Joanne Joyner complained that the class was not meeting diocesan guidelines for class meetings (two years for first communion). He felt this was mission work, a pastoral emergency that justified relaxing the rules. And at the rate they were meeting, they would cover the required class hours over a shorter period of time. It is not clear how the conflict was resolved, but the class continued. Joyner confirmed to me that she did not initially agree with Father Nacho's idea of having separate religious education in Spanish but later changed her mind.

The next year, Father Ignacio started a formal program preparing Latino children for first communion in Spanish. He had found only about eight Hispanic children in the English program, and yet he knew many children who had not made their first communion in the community. He could locate no Spanish-language textbooks in the diocese, so he simply met with the volunteer teachers (catechists), and they created lessons as they went along. That first year they held open enrollment, more than 150 children enrolled. This time, according to Padre Nacho, Fr. Paul Collins intervened, unsure if separate classes in Spanish were permitted under diocesan guidelines. Padre Nacho protested that he did not have sufficient catechists who could speak English. Again the issue arose of the length of the program, since it ran from January to April. Again he noted it met on more than one day a week. Record numbers of children continued with the program, yet Father Nacho felt discouraged by the reaction

of his colleagues on the parish staff. In addition, he began to receive complaints from the teachers at the parish school, who objected to the movement of items within the classrooms. Nevertheless, his programs continued and were commended by the bishop and, in the long run, by Father
Paul himself, who said of Father Nacho, "He built a parish from scratch."

Father Nacho's work ensured that All Saints went from being a Euro-
American parish with a small Hispanic outreach to becoming a shared
parish. The recognizable presence of a Mexican priest speaking Spanish at All Saints increased Latino attendance at mass and in parish programs. Padre Nacho lobbied for and organized a second Spanish mass
on Sunday at 1 p.m.; it eventually became the best-attended mass at All
Saints. The English-speaking parish staff members gradually adapted to
the new parish realities. Father Paul went to Mexico to study Spanish for
a few weeks. A part-time secretary was hired expressly for Father Ignacio and the Hispanic ministry. Euro-American parishioners began to
notice the presence of the Latinos and to adjust to their use of the parish.

Increasing numbers of ministries and programming in Spanish necessitated more frequent intercultural negotiations over space between
Latino leaders and parish and school staff. Some of the questions that lay
behind the negotiations, however, did not prove easy to sort out. Where
were all these new meetings going to be held and would they conflict
with ongoing events? Was Father Ignacio observing diocesan guidelines,
engaging in missionary work, or just doing his own thing? Were Latino
volunteers really taking good care of these facilities that Euro-American
parishioners had built and paid for over many years? Were teachers and
parish staff members too hard on those volunteers? What was the right
language of religious instruction? The need for these negotiations came
as a surprise to Euro-Americans, mostly unprepared to share their parish. And the cultural differences between the two approaches to Catholicism were unfamiliar on both sides. The shared parish was underway at
All Saints, but it was inhabited by two separate cultures. Like Havenville
itself, it developed a "bifurcated" identity.

Two Worlds in One Parish

It is difficult to comprehend the demographic transformation at All
Saints without considering what happened to the corresponding social

environment in Havenville. Prior to 1990, Havenville was a relatively homogeneous city—white, working class, and disproportionately of German descent.[87] A decade and a half of Latin American immigration disrupted that cultural consensus. But it did not produce a multicultural city, despite the rhetoric of multiculturalism promoted by both the local college and the city council committee tasked with dealing with cultural diversity. What it produced was a city split in two. Havenvillers perceived their social environment as bifurcated into "Anglo" and "Hispanic," even if the realities were more complex. A local newspaper article summarized the situation simply: "Havenville has two subcultures: The Anglo one that's been here for a long time and the Hispanic one that has its own restaurants and shops."[88]

In fact, each one of these two "subcultures" had not only restaurants and shops but also newspapers, social clubs, hair salons, markets, medical clinics, churches, and automotive repair shops. These institutions frequently existed separately, operating according to different cultural rules and serving different clienteles. A party store that rented space from the owner's godchildren was staffed by their in-laws; they were located in an old furniture store still identified as such and serving Mexican clientele entirely by word of mouth. A diner catering to Euro-Americans had local sports paraphernalia on the walls and giant signs on the main thoroughfare; a hostess greeted you cheerfully. An "Anglo" auto-body shop—on a main street with big windows and signs—offered computerized formal estimates for instance companies. A "Mexican" body shop—on a side street within a corrugated metal building with no windows and little signage—offered cheaper estimates on the spot, providing formal estimates if required in pen stuffed into a blank envelope. Because businesses operated with different wage structures and supply networks, clashes occurred when people decided to wander across cultural lines in search of a good deal. A local Midas auto repair shop had a price match guarantee. When a Euro-American couple decided to test that guarantee out, they found two Latino-run shops at half the price. When the couple called Midas with their findings, at first Midas would not return their call at all. Later they offered to chop two hundred dollars off, but they would not match the Latino shops' price.

In reality, of course, not everything matched this perception of a bifurcated city. A Mexican hairstylist cut white people's hair as well as that of a steady stream of Hispanic patrons. A predominantly Latino Protestant church had Euro-American members, and almost all the Mexican restaurants had a large population of Euro-American customers. The most established businesses and the larger institutions—supermarkets, chain restaurants, government offices, the community hospital, and Wal-Mart—served both communities. Some Euro-American businesses—such as banks and funeral homes—developed niche markets in the Mexican community, especially where Mexicans did not yet have sufficient financial capital or the necessary expertise. One of the local Spanish newspapers was owned by an English daily. There existed more fluidity in the city than one might expect.

Yet the perception was resolutely of two opposed worlds. Part of this was, no doubt, the contrast between Havenville and other cities in the area. Port Jefferson, was multifaceted with a complex mix of cultures, races, religions, and classes. Nearby Brookton had a large swath of upper-middle-class whites, a sizable and diverse African American population, and a multinational Latino population. Havenville was different. There existed less internal diversity within the two key cultural groupings. For example, the city's institutions were dominated by Anabaptists, and the vast majority of Anabaptists were white and of northern European ancestry. The Hispanic population, on the other hand, was largely Mexican, a great number from three states in that country. Thus, both "Anglo" and "Hispanic" had a more monolithic feel in this community.

Sociologists have historically understood ethnic identity either as a naturalistic system of human classification or as the outcome of external (usually economic) processes.[89] In recent decades, however, social constructionism has deftly combined elements of both. Circumstances (social, economic, and cultural) do produce and reproduce ethnicity in a sense, though they do so through a combination of external attribution and internal assertion of identity. The ethnic identity that results, however, is felt by both insiders and outsiders to be natural and persistent.[90] This is just the way we are. Historically, this process is well documented in the development of German ethnicity in the nineteenth-century United States.[91] In Havenville, it was more of a work in progress. The large scale and relatively rapid introduction of migrants from Mexico in the local economy of a largely homogenous area had, in a sense, created a world divided in two. Both sides were in the midst of developing terms and assumptions to describe the other group (external attribution). Euro-Americans in Havenville and at All Saints had started to rely more heavily on the governmental term "Hispanic" to describe the newcomers. This sometimes led to curious turns of phrase, as when a Euro-American couple complained about young Mexican children in the schools drawing the "Hispanic flag." For many Mexican immigrants, the analogous descriptor for whites was *americano,* a counterpart to their self-description as *mexicanos.* Whatever the term, the distinction and significant cultural distance between "us" and this other group were treated as self-evident, as "natural."

Both groups were tentative about the internal assertion of any ethnic identity in contradistinction to that other. Euro-Americans had only begun to think of themselves as a distinct group rather than the dominant culture, and people were often still uncertain with terms like "whites" or "Anglos." Immigrants and their children continued to rely on their nation of origin as a means of asserting ethnic identity. Even those who did use the term "Hispanic" (or *hispano* in Spanish) frequently used it in reference to the entire community of immigrants and services directed to it. They identified institutions such as housing agencies with the term *hispano.* Churches, local government, and businesses used the term "Hispanic" or *hispano.* Those Latinos involved in these local institutions became comfortable with the term *hispano* as a means of self-identification. A local (Mexican-American) woman employed by the college insisted that I use the term *hispano* rather than *mexicano,* seeing the latter as disenfranchising of non-Mexicans. The Colombian woman who edited the Spanish newspaper in town told me she had never known she was "Hispanic" until she came to Havenville. But now she embraced the term in her work to defend the community. All this supports a point about ethnicity made within the new institutionalism in sociology: social institutions—government classification systems, schools, churches, the law, housing markets—remain a powerful factor in shaping both how people attribute ethnicity to others and identify with it themselves.[92]

Like Havenville residents in general, All Saints parishioners saw themselves in terms of these separate cultural worlds. The Euro-American middle school youth were surprised to learn (from me) that their group had a counterpart in the Latino community. A teenager in the Latino youth group found having two communities *raro*, that is, weird. Even though he served English masses and spoke the language fluently (our conversation was mostly in English), he said he did not understand what anyone was saying at those English masses. Interviews revealed people in both communities who had little contact with and no information about people from the other community. The language barrier (relatively few adults spoke both languages fluently) no doubt contributed to that complete differentiation of experience. One thirty-something mother from the Latino community, when asked about the presence of two cultures in the parish, said in a distracted voice, "*No me afecta.*" "It doesn't affect me." Henry McKellar, a longtime Euro-American parishioner in his eighties, summed it up: "We've got two parishes now, one Mexican and one English, and we pray that they can be more combined than they are today."

In a sense, the structure of the shared parish enabled this perceived bifurcation. The Latino parish community had its own priest, two masses in Spanish, a separate bulletin, its own celebrations and fundraising dinners, and twenty distinct ministry programs.[93] All of its leaders except the priest were Spanish-speaking volunteers. The Euro-American community had its priest (Fr. David Adama, the pastor), three masses in English, its own bulletin (professionally produced, with advertising), and about thirty distinct ministry programs.[94] Many of its leaders were hired professionals who spoke only English. The end result was that nearly everyone worshipped, socialized, participated in activities, and even sought the help of leadership according to the customs of their own cultures and in their own language. Curiously, even places and events meant to unite across cultural lines inevitably revealed the separation into two cultural worlds. Leaders at the parish school designed Grandparents Day as a celebration for the families of all students, and both cultural communities patronized the school in large numbers. Yet the event drew many more Euro-American grandparents than Latinos. Latino grandparents were either working in the factories or lived outside the United States.

The bifurcation of the communities downplayed other types of diversity that nevertheless played a role in the parish—those of age, politics, and socioeconomics. In the Latino community, geographical origin within Mexico mattered a great deal, not only in terms of personal identity but also in terms of the relational networks people belonged to. Youth mattered. Teenagers had much stronger cultural ties to the United States, even as some—experiencing discrimination—disavowed these ties and proclaimed their total Mexican identity (in American-accented Spanish). In the Euro-American community, theological differences were significant. At meetings for the Rite of Christian Initiation for Adults (RCIA), a group for those considering becoming Catholic, former Episcopalians disparaged the Episcopal Church for its liberalism. Members of a different group, a small faith community that had met together for many years, praised Anabaptist pacifist theology and talked about their trips to left-leaning Catholic conventions. In truth, this kind of internal diversity remains customary across Catholic parishes of this size with their multiple masses and ministries (even in the same language). Parishes often function like a "community of communities."[95] All Saints parishioners remained aware of these kinds of internal diversity within their own cultural communities, but they did not find them as salient as the distinction between cultural communities. For example, parishioners who took part in a leadership development program in Spanish tended to play down internal differences, emphasized the unity of *la comunidad hispana*, and consistently contrasted their experience with the dominant Euro-American culture.

The language barrier substantially prevented greater awareness of internal diversity across cultural lines. All Saints had a paucity of bilingual adults and bicultural interpreters. This state of affairs contrasted with several local Protestant churches that had Euro-American members with Spanish fluency from overseas mission experiences. One diocesan priest claimed that none of the Anglo diocesan priests in the area spoke Spanish well, and he considered me an anomaly for doing so. Many Latinos spoke at least a little English, but a great many felt intimidated about doing so. Also, at least initially, insufficient institutional resources existed to help them improve (for example, the church's English-language classes were overcrowded and staffed by untrained volunteers). In the absence of direct bilingual communication, people on both sides created and put faith in stock generalizations to explain cultural and other differences they could not understand. Virtually no one had good information to contest them.[96] What emerged as salient to both communities were the larger and baffling cultural differences between them.

Cultural anthropologists have long noted that this bifurcation of culture often occurs during the early years of intercultural encounter. Joan Comaroff and John Comaroff refer to the "working essentialisms"— provisional stereotypes—that persons from different cultural experiences put together as they attempt to make sense of the differences they encounter.[97] Unfortunately, at All Saints, these provisional stereotypes were hardening into persistent and oppositional generalizations. In the perceptions of both sides, Anglos were rich while Hispanics were poor; in fact, most people in both communities were working class. Anglos were seen as speaking English and Hispanics spoke Spanish, though, in reality, second-generation Hispanics spoke both, and most were more comfortable in English. Culturally, Anglos were seen as more distant and Hispanics more friendly, with no accounting for personality differences. Anglos liked bland food and Hispanics liked spicy. Anglos had spare, whitewashed churches and Hispanics had baroque churches (at least back home). These oppositions rarely became more nuanced over time.

The oppositions were exacerbated by populist anti-immigrant discourse. I heard frequent unattributed and unsubstantiated stories about abuse of the system by Latino immigrants—not paying hospital bills, refusing to speak English, being unwilling to play by the rules. I heard and read several negative tropes over and over again (such as "illegal is illegal," they don't want to integrate, they don't want to learn English, they're freeloading).[98] Cultural anthropologist Leo Chavez sees such tropes and stories as constructing a negative social imaginary, a "Latino threat narrative" shaping the popular Euro-American understanding of Mexicans and Mexican-Americans without reference to actual data or direct experience.[99] The threat narrative set up a tidy contrast with Euro-American conceptions of American culture, self-conceptions that Latinos had little power or opportunity to contest.

Thus, if Latinos were seen to game the system, Euro-Americans saw themselves as belonging to an especially law-abiding community. They consistently wondered why Mexicans could not just obey the rules, presuming that they themselves did so consistently (even as a host of common traffic infractions suggested otherwise). They saw "the rules" as culturally neutral, including, for example, parish rules for use of rooms and spaces. Yet members of the Euro-American community had set up those rules according to their own cultural standards of fairness and organization. Latinos had to learn and practice these standards, even if they did not always appreciate or own them.[100] Father Nacho on many occasions pleaded that his parishioners obey the parking rules so that they not incur the wrath of the *americanos*, potentially limiting their ability to conduct ministry.

In truth, no level playing field existed on which the two sides could comfortably dialogue in order to dispel stereotypes. Stereotypes—either of one's own group or the other—frequently served as the most salient resource members of the groups used to make a point. The less powerful group often had to contend with negative stereotypes, while the more powerful group worked with positive stereotypes.[101] We can see this in the "law-abiding" self-stereotypes some Euro-Americans used to condemn the habits of Latinos. And even when Latinos defended themselves against certain negative stereotypes (for example, bad parking habits and dense housing arrangements), they frequently deployed other stock generalizations ("Mexicans are oppressed and exploited" or "Latinos always want to be together"), as if stock generalizations were the only legitimate means of discourse. Indeed, postcolonial theorists of culture hypothesize that "working essentialisms" easily turn into "oppositional discourse" when one cultural group dominates the power structure.[102] Positive self-stereotypes and negative stereotypes of the other take root. "The politically stronger group gets to impose its essentializing definition on others, a definition that disparages their inventiveness and historical agency."[103]

As should be clear by now, despite this dramatic social construction of bifurcated worlds, the two communities at All Saints never truly existed as fully separate and distinct. Intermarriage and cross-cultural friendships existed, though in small numbers. Ironic juxtapositions abounded. I visited a Mexican restaurant with a Euro-American man who vociferously objected to the use of the Spanish language and the spread of Mexican culture. Moreover, structurally, All Saints *was* one parish. It had one set of administrative records and one pastor. Perhaps most significantly, all parishioners shared the same church buildings and other facilities. As Matthew Campbell, a Euro-American man whose wife, Daniela, was Salvadoran, noted, "I just think that there is a long way to go, but I think the fact that [All Saints] is a building that kind of is drawing people together, that is also an important thing. . . . That space is used by a variety of different people. Different people, different cultures, different economic status." Another key facility was the parish school. Approximately 36 percent Latino, it hosted Mexican cultural events for children and parents of all communities, such as the Christmas custom of the *posadas*.[104]

During my parish year at All Saints, the parish also hosted a regular bilingual mass on Sunday evening. That practice was difficult to keep up (neither priest had strong facility in the other's language), and Father David discontinued it after about eight months. The parish had other, longer-running bilingual events, including Holy Thursday mass and a summer parish picnic. The parish council had several Latino members, though not yet proportionate to the demographics of the parish. The Home and School Association[105] also had a significant history of Latino membership (usually English-speaking), as did the stewardship committee (usually just one). In addition, over the ten months I spent at All Saints, I observed members of the two communities in intercultural negotiations over various aspects of parish life—parking, room use, and so forth. These negotiations probably best encapsulate what made All Saints at the same time a single parish and two distinct cultural worlds. I will treat them in more detail in a later chapter.

The Transformed Purpose of a Shared Parish

This chapter has given us detailed insight into the historical and cultural context of All Saints Parish. We have heard about its growth from a tiny Roman Catholic community in a Protestant town into a comprehensive social community and then a decentralized parish. This chapter has also described the making of the shared parish, how that came to be in an already pluralistic and decentralized context. Thousands of others stories like it could be told for thousands of other parishes, each one unique, with its own historical context, communities, and cultural story. The parishioners of each one would have to ask, "How did we get to where we are now?" But for almost all, the answer would include some tale of dramatic demographic transformation. Such transformation requires great adjustment in parish life. There may be resistance to change on the part of the cultural community already in place. They may grieve what they have lost. Arriving communities may feel disoriented and unwanted. They may feel defiant in the face of resistance. Yet despite all this, the parish develops some kind of renewed parish life, a new sense of purpose. This transformed parish life and purpose at All Saints forms the substance of the next chapter.

2

Making Sense of a Changed World

The Strategies of Shared Parish Life at All Saints

Church kitchens lend themselves to household metaphors. Standing in the small kitchen in the church basement at All Saints, an elderly Euro-American first communion teacher named Diane offered me her rendition of what had happened with the demographic transformation at All Saints Parish. It had all worked like a marriage where the daughter-in-law moved into her mother-in-law's house. Initially, the son's wife is forced to abide by the mother-in-law's rules and is none the happier for it. She paused. I weighed the analogy in my head. It did seem to capture the strong sense many Euro-American parishioners had of having others now living in a house they had managed for many years. It captured the Latino community's frustration over having to live under someone else's rules. Finally, there was an implicit acknowledgement that both parties had a right to live there. But I still worried that the generational element left all the authority in the mother-in-law's (thus, the Euro-American community's) hands. But Diane continued. Ultimately, she said, both have to learn from each other. The mother-in-law has to learn some of the daughter-in-law's ways too. She then smiled a mischievous smile I have seen before—when older people know they speak controversial words but have confidence that age and experience will permit them to get away with it.

On another occasion, I sat in a family's kitchen listening to another household analogy for the parish. Octavio and Petra Fernández, a retired couple originally from the Rio Grande Valley in Texas, had lived for decades in Havenville. They remembered well when they were

among only a handful of Latinos in town. We sat there drinking cof-
fee while they reminisced about the old days for my audio recorder.
Octavio, a former maintenance man and an author of children's books,
became philosophical speaking about the parish after the influx of
immigrants. He compared the tensions and conflicts that emerged at
All Saints to those within a family household. "The larger the church,"
he said, "the more the conflicts. If there are two cultures involved, that
too. Just as in a married couple there's a lot of disagreement. Imagine
if there were some five hundred families?" He smiled, content with the
metaphor.

Of course, not everyone at All Saints subscribed to domestic metaphors to make sense of the transformations I described in the previous
chapter. Some immigrants, trying to avoid dealing with a dominant culture they experienced as racist, would have disliked a story that related
them so closely to Euro-Americans. A few Euro-American parishioners
would have winced at the use of such an intimate metaphor to describe
their relationship with unwelcome strangers. In fact, a small number of
Euro-American Catholics would go as far as to use metaphors of threat
to describe that relationship, such as the threat to good citizens posed
by foreign invaders. There were other narratives and metaphors. A
leader in the Knights of Columbus relied on a familiar American story
of religious competition—Evangelical and Pentecostal proselytism
would claim Hispanic Catholics if Euro-Americans did not roll out the
welcome mat. Not a few people on both sides looked to extended metaphors of hospitality, commenting back and forth on the proper behavior of hosts and guests. And some got no further than slogans: "Illegal
is illegal." In some way or other, however, almost everyone fashioned
some sort of language to make sense of the dramatic changes still happening all around them.

Within this chapter, I report on four strategies parishioners at All
Saints consistently used to make sense of parish life in an era of transformation: (1) through frameworks for social order, though articulated
from clashing perspectives; (2) by asserting identity through correct,
that is, properly regulated worship; (3) through popular religion reimagined and adapted to a different context; and (4) via evangelization
as a narrative of conversion. The next chapter will tackle a fifth way—
constructions of intercultural unity. The first two "ways"—social order

and correct ritual—occupied both cultural communities in a significant way. The second two—popular religion and evangelization—served the Latino community, engaged as they were in a more dramatic process of adaptation and change. All four strategies functioned as lenses for observing, understanding, and taking part in the transformed parish environment. They provided focus for both beliefs and practices. People saw them as representative of the evolving purpose of their life together as a parish. Through them, people at All Saints responded religiously to the historical, cultural, and ecclesial context in which they found themselves, especially to the juxtaposition of two cultural worlds within the one city and parish.

Social Orders in Conflict

In 2007 when I arrived in Havenville, All Saints remained at an unsettled moment in its history. The demographic transformation had left both city and parish rent in two. Euro-American parishioners routinely pointed out how the arrival of immigrants had radically changed their community. Latino parishioners, on the other hand, worried intensely about the insecurity brought to their lives by Euro-American opposition to immigration and the possibility that they or people they knew would be deported. In both communities, people worried about the dangers posed to their children by local gangs. A "discourse of alarm" about illegal immigration on television and radio exacerbated these tensions. By the middle of 2008, the housing bubble had burst and recession set in. Economic uncertainty and increasing unemployment provoked anxiety anew.

Against this great tide of insecurity and anxiety, members of both cultural communities consistently focused attention on a social order in and for the parish. Many practices reinforced and reflected the focus on order. Parishioners remained constantly attentive to doing things in the "right way"—the proper way of receiving or not receiving communion, of saying the rosary, of leading the Stations of the Cross. People argued in minute detail over the proper amount of wine to prepare for mass. Both communities scrupulously followed the liturgical calendar of the Roman Catholic Church—Advent, Christmas, Holy Week. Members of both communities considered the church to be sacred space (using altar, tabernacle, statues and images, pews, and doors to mark it off). Both communities recognized a host of proper procedures for ministries. This was true for every ministry group, from the highly regulated (English-speaking) Knights of Columbus to the looser structure of the couple who led marriage preparation in Spanish. Curricula guided religious education for children in both languages. Parishioners followed common norms regarding the celebration of mass and the sacraments. At first communion, there were carefully ordered lines and processions, syncopated photography, neatly pressed dresses and ties.

In other studies of Catholic parishes, sociologists have found a different reality—parishioners objecting to too much standardization or "orderliness." Jerome Baggett argued that in this way parishioners negotiate a "dilemma of administrative order," that is, navigate between the need for administrative order and an "over-elaboration" of that order.[1] Baggett's study took place in the San Francisco Bay Area, a highly urbanized region of the country with a decades-long history of dramatic demographic and social changes—population growth from industrial ship and munitions production during World War II, the rapid growth and rising influence of gay communities after the war, free speech and various power and liberation movements in the 1960s and 1970s, the incorporation of millions of Asian and Latin American immigrants across the decades, environmentalism, and economically powerful entrepreneurial movements around information technology. Havenville, on the other hand, was historically a small town in the rural Midwest—a socially conservative, reserved, voluntaristic, and culturally homogenous region of the country.[2] It should come as no surprise if parish communities there steered more closely to the need for order rather than objections to its overelaboration.

On the other hand, while everyone seemed to value social order, the two cultural communities at All Saints had dramatically different perspectives on that order. Coming from distinct cultural milieu and responding to distinct challenges, each community accessed its own cultural resources in order to construct and maintain a social order. Indeed, culture seems to work like a "tool kit" or repertoire of resources that people appropriate in order to respond to the context in which they live.[3] Some resource choices appear obvious or self-evident, while others remain almost literally unimaginable.[4] Faced with the question of how to keep the social order, each cultural community at All Saints worked with their own cultural tool kit, bringing forth different resources—narratives, ideologies, assumptions about reality, norms, and practices—that fit their historical and contemporary dilemmas around social order.

In the Latino community, for example, Father Nacho's ideological discourse around the "new evangelization" helped make a difficult transition to a new social order intelligible. Latino immigrants had left behind the customary order of their families and cultures at home. Many spoke limited or no English, the language of commerce and government. A large number had no legal papers. Some used false ones to find work. People had to live with the constant stress of being discovered and deported, potentially breaking up their families (indeed, this happened to at least one family from the parish). The mainstream culture of their locality was unfamiliar, confusing, even shocking. In short, they lived in a crucible of stress. Not surprisingly, people spoke to me of loneliness (*soledad*), marital problems, alcoholism, and drug abuse in their community. As will be noted in the last section of this chapter, regular parishioners easily accessed Father Nacho's "new evangelization" ideology. Like most ideologies, it had cohesiveness and countercultural power. Deeper involvement in church and a greater awareness of Catholic teaching would keep the chaos associated with the secular culture of the United States—excessive drinking and drug use, family disintegration, overemphasis on material possessions—at bay. In other words, it provided people with new strategies for action in a strange land—frequent church attendance, commitment to ministry training, a suspicion toward proselytizing evangelicals, and a focus on social networks within the parish.

In contrast, Euro-American community members continued to access longtime cultural resources whose usefulness in terms of keeping the social order appeared self-evident to them—a form of common sense. Thus, most appreciated the pastor's ability to finish mass in fifty minutes or less, an efficient use of a structured and allotted chunk of time. They sat in customary pews. They parked in open spaces and drove further to a distant lot if they could not locate one. If controversies arose at the parish, they expected these to be resolved through the equitable enforcement of preestablished rules. When books in the school library were tampered with, the librarian checked with the parish receptionist to see what group had met in the library the night before. The receptionist called the leader of that group to ask that such tampering be prevented in the future. If such rules proved insufficient, the pastor, Father David, devised more. When the gym door was left open one night, he added additional steps to the room reservation process.

Accordingly, some Euro-American parishioners professed bafflement when others did not act in ways consonant with these established norms and customs of order. A few consistently made negative moral judgments about the Hispanic people who seemed not to abide by them. Longtime parishioner Peggy Johnson could not understand what she was observing at church, especially after the English mass:

> I don't know if [Hispanic parishioners] have religion classes or what, but I mean, they are parked any which way and park you in, there's just such a mess of people coming and going, it's just—somebody's going to get hurt some time—but they don't seem to care a whole lot for being very orderly, a lot of them. It's like: we're just get here and get in. And you want to say, hey, think about others too. . . . You want to offer opportunities for their events and things to do. But with that comes responsibility, and they haven't always taken up on their end of that. If they see something, they think it's for everyone to use. They take advantage sometimes.

Irritated by this "taking advantage," one man in his sixties described immigrants as "scofflaws." He felt that they "thumb their nose at the country," take advantage of the system, and have no regard for the way things are done here. Parishioner Joan Bucher said, "It's not acceptable to go to an insurance office and say you're not going to take that car to Mexico. And you trust that person and they did [take it to Mexico]." A cultural norm violation that frequently elicited moral judgment was not speaking English. Joan also said, "It is not acceptable for you to not take advantage of all these English-speaking free classes available. . . . If they're going to be here, they have to learn the language; they just have to. It's just not right."

The bafflement over the violation of cultural norms perceived to be self-evident matches the expectation that, in settled times, cultures provide a repertoire of relatively stable cultural traditions from which people choose strategies of action to guide them in everyday life.[5] The Euro-American community at All Saints was settled—residentially stable, culturally comfortable, and relatively economically secure. The vast majority were born and raised within the state. Some families had been in Havenville several generations. They easily went about their daily activities with minimal thought to what they should do. Even when the immigrant community arrived, that did not alter the most basic patterns of their lives. Their institutions and social codes were not yet significantly altered by the experience of cultural diversity. They simply found it disorienting to be confronted with a large community who did not think and act as they did. As Joanne Miller, a fourth-generation parishioner, said, "I think we're still topsy-turvy here, trying to deal with both the Hispanic and Anglo communities." They felt confusion about the presence of a distinct culture in their midst, yet their motivation to change to accommodate them was low. As sociologist Ann Swidler writes, "Culture's influence in settled lives can be observed in what is usually called 'cultural lag,'—the reluctance to abandon established strategies of action. People do not readily take advantage of new structural opportunities that would require them to abandon established strategies of action."[6]

Thus, in settled times, the power of culture comes not from its pronounced influence over people in terms of specific ideas, traditions, or ideologies but from its unconscious pervasiveness.[7] In the settled lives of Euro-American parishioners at All Saints, I rarely found rigid consensus around a strict vision of how things ought to be. People were opinionated but ad hoc in those opinions. The punch of Euro-American culture came instead through the way Euro-Americans found it baffling that Latino parishioners seemed to deviate from established ideas and practices. Some of this operated through "common sense," what everyone assumed to be so. Common sense has been said to function like an ad hoc cultural system characterizing the immediate world by what is perceived to be natural and practical. Of course, what people perceive as "practical and natural" is actually not given but something people assign meaning to depending on their circumstances—a social construction.[8] But almost by definition, people remain unaware of this.

At All Saints, "common sense" prevailed in Euro-American parishioners' articulations about norms and rules. Several parishioners agreed in interviews and informal conversations that the law—ecclesial or civil—preserved social order among diverse individuals and concerns. As one woman admitted, "[Even] if I disagree with a given law, I believe I still must obey it until it is changed." A fifty-something woman, long divorced and remarried, never presumed for one moment to break church law and go to communion, even though she believed the Church should change its rules and allow for her to do so. Euro-American parishioners saw order as precarious in a chaotic world, a product of purposeful social arrangements, both in society and church. It is possible that this focus on the elaboration of rules increased in more recent unsettled times, but this is not clear from historical data.

Of course, Americans have long believed that a robust sense of the "rule of law" makes order out of chaos. The New England Puritans (along with most eighteenth and nineteenth century Protestants) believed in the total depravity of human beings, that nothing we accomplish on our own could be good. This left them with a precarious sense of the social order, always ready to fall into chaos without God's direction. We directly trace our American notion of government to the concept of the social compact as articulated by political writers of the British Enlightenment. Thomas Hobbes famously imagined human life as originally "solitary, poor, nasty, brutish, and short."[9] Only the agreement of individuals on strong authority could prevent constant, selfish warfare. Though John Locke imagined human beings as naturally independent and equal, he insisted on the need for law even in the state of nature and the importance of government as a social contract among individuals.[10] As to the contemporary United States, several sociological studies have emphasized how Americans perceive their world almost exclusively in terms of autonomy and individualism.[11] In this context, social connection functions as a voluntary act rather than as intrinsic to human identity. In summary, whether a Hobbesian tendency toward chaos without laws and government exists or not, Americans believe order to be held together by social agreement on the "rule of law." Even many American social scientists, such as Talcott Parsons and Clifford Geertz, looked upon chaos as impending without the intervention of cultural ideas, norms, and values.[12]

In contrast to this reliance on long-articulated traditions and on rules and norms perceived to be common sense, Latino parishioners had to fashion order in a more conscious and purposeful way. The Latino community at All Saints was largely composed of younger people who had arrived in the United States within the last fifteen years. In order to guide their actions, they found themselves depending on re-created Mexican cultural resources they had to apply in a radically different environment. For example, as in most parts of Mexico, the community organized time through the Christmas season using the Mexican cultural tradition of the *posadas,* where for nine days people follow the journey of Mary and Joseph seeking hospitality in Bethlehem. But Father Nacho and a group of parishioners reworked this celebration so that it could occur in the warm confines of the church instead of a wintry exodus door to door through potentially unwelcoming neighborhoods. Refreshments followed in the parish hall instead of at a neighbor's home.

At other times, no cultural resources came close to addressing the unfamiliar environment. This especially rang true around the organization of Latino ministry at All Saints. Interviewed parishioners saw their style of organizing ministry at the parish as unique. One man drew proud attention to the neat black and white garb of the catechists and liturgical ministers. Leaders and ministers in the parish clearly distinguished themselves from those churchgoers who simply "warmed the pews" (*calentaban la banca).* An outside church consultant came to help ministries grow even more efficient. The head usher, Francisco Martinez, summarized the situation, calling attention to "the organization that . . . has been given to the priest and has made him able to carry on his ministry, and he has carried it on with integrity." Both the involved parishioners and Father Nacho saw their local system of order as different from that of parishes in Mexico. Indeed, visiting churches in the Mexican states where All Saints parishioners came from, I found most of the lay leadership invested not in committees but in older women and a few older men recognized by the community. But few older people had migrated to Havenville. Another form of church organization in Mexico was neighborhood or village base communities, usually led by trained catechists.[13] This also did not exist in Havenville, where most parishioners lived scattered about the town.

Instead Father Nacho and lay leaders created a highly organized network of ministries, bound together by the priest's vision of the "new

evangelization" and creating order through the decisions of a committee of ministry heads. In unsettled times, people consciously and frequently think about what they will do. They negotiate with traditions
and create new strategies of action, often using recently constructed
ideologies such as the new evangelization ideology of Father Nacho.[14]
At All Saints, members of the Latino community cleverly combined
the new evangelization ideology Father Nacho learned at seminary in
Mexico with a committee-based organization strategy. While a committee-based strategy may seem to emerge from American cultural
traditions of voluntarism, in fact traditions of voluntarism also exist in
Mexico, especially represented in the era after single-party rule through
labor, cultural-educational, professional, and church associations and
movements.[15]

In marked contrast to the Euro-American community's common-
sense notions about rules and norms, the Latino community at All
Saints did not see order as necessarily contingent upon norms and laws.
Society was not seen as a diverse and potentially contentious group of
individuals held together by social contract. Instead, Latino parishioners emphasized relationships and social networks as constitutive of
the social order at the most basic level. Public speeches (such as homilies) and informal conversation focused attention on marriage, family,
loneliness, and the internal unity of the Latino community. A young
woman summarized the situation when she told me that the Mexican
community valued law a great deal, but that law should serve justice,
not order. Thus, when unauthorized immigrants found, contradicto-
rily, that the local economy desired their participation even as the law
did not permit them any status, they procured false papers as a stopgap
measure.[16] When unauthorized immigrants found themselves unable
to acquire driver's licenses, they opted to drive anyway, but they were
careful to avoid routinely policed roads. The parish cancelled a Latino
community dance to avoid even the chance of people being stopped or
arrested and deported. Overall, most people in the Latino community
had a pragmatic approach to law. They viewed the contradiction of economic demand but no legal status not as a moral problem (as the Euro-
American community did) but as a series of practical problems—how
to evade the police when driving, how to acquire new false papers if the
previous ones brought problems—and not infrequently the source of

humor. One father joked to me that the only papers his family had were in the bathroom.

This is consistent with sociological literature on Mexican immigrant cultures. The extended family, not the individual, is seen as the basic unit of society in the cultural imagination of most Mexican immigrants.[17] We have already seen how crucial social networks are to Mexican immigrant life. Even Mexican popular religion is seen as a network of relationships—with Jesus, the Virgin Mary, and other saints.[18] Moreover, Mexican politics, especially since the 1910 revolution, has not sustained much trust in laws and norms. Theoretically, the revolutionary one-party state has served as agent of the people integrating both workers and peasants into a justly structured society.[19] In practice, one-party rule has engulfed that state in corruption and cronyism.[20] Confidence in government has been and remains low. In a 2008 survey, less than a quarter of Mexicans thought their country's democracy worked better than that of other Latin American countries.[21] As one man in the state of Puebla emphasized to me, social connections to the powerful trumped both education and merit on the job market. Mexicans particularly lament the corruption of the police and judicial system. A friend in Guadalajara wondered what I would do if I encountered an emergency walking along. When I suggested I would call the police, she replied, "Not if you lived here you wouldn't." Of course, Mexicans living in the United States sometimes have reason to alter their views over time. Many at All Saints acknowledged that the laws worked reasonably well in the United States and were grateful for a predictable social order. Nevertheless, because so many people in their community had no legal status and no promise of obtaining it, they could not view a social order based simply on the law as functional and just. Too many people had to improvise their relationship to the law from day to day.

Most Euro-American parishioners had little understanding of this history and dilemma, and the presence of so many people without papers irked them. Even people sympathetic to the plight of undocumented immigrants agreed that being in the country without legal papers was morally wrong. At dinner one night at a Euro-American couple's house, the husband told me he disagreed with his in-laws' desire to deport all the illegal Mexicans, since they are Christian brothers and sisters; still, he could see how people thought it was morally

wrong—it is wrong, he said. "That's why they call it illegal." At a parish
school festival filled with members of both communities, a middle-aged
father said matter-of-factly that immigration was fine as long as people
were legal and the town was not "overrun." It seemed self-evident to
people. In their conception, anyone could see it was morally wrong.
A parishioner who was a sheriff's deputy did not worry that members of his department acting as immigration agents would disrupt the
Mexican community's trust (as has been argued by many urban police
chiefs). After all, they had violated the law. He vetoed the idea for practical reasons—the federal government could not be depended upon to
pick up immigration suspects once the sheriff's department had appre-
hended them.

For some cultural anthropologists, this powerful distinction between
"legal" and "illegal" in the United States can be explained in part by the
distinction cultures make between purity and impurity.[22] Mary Douglas decades ago observed a connection between perceived disorder in
society and social judgments of impurity or pollution. Culture offers
us public classification systems that differentiate and make order out of
the world. Whatever does not fit in those classification systems—what
Douglas calls anomalies—registers as polluted, dirty, and even dangerous. "Our pollution behavior is the reaction which condemns any
object or idea likely to confuse or contradict cherished classifications."[23]
Anomalies become emotionally laden symbols of impending chaos.[24]
This initially seems helpful in understanding the Euro-American community's unambiguous moral categorizing of illegal immigrants. "Ille-
gals" *were* seen by some as polluting the environment, though this point
of view appeared more widespread in unattributed editorials in the
local newspaper and Internet forums than in general conversation. For
most, legality served as a self-evident arbiter of moral soundness rather
than a marker between purity and pollution. And there often existed
only an indirect and often opportunistic connection between what read
as immoral and what read as polluted.[25]

We might find a more adequate explanation for the tension between
Euro-American and Mexican attitudes toward the law in Clifford
Geertz's understanding of common sense as a cultural system.[26]
Although both cultural groups at All Saints saw their view of the law as
self-evident, the two views remained incompatible. Ann Swidler writes,

"Those who have no occasion to speak to one another may have incompatible forms of common sense without being aware of it."[27] In other words, specific cultural perspectives shaped their common sense on the issue even as each group presumed that any rational human being would share its view. Thus, Euro-Americans saw an immoral slide toward chaos implicit in lawbreaking, and this helped them explain the tension they felt over the demographic changes wrought by unauthorized immigration. On the other hand, what many Euro-Americans viewed as immoral lawbreaking, Mexicans saw pragmatically as leaving cities and towns plagued by underemployment in order to work where there *was* work. Local factories wanted their labor. Merchants took their money. All kinds of people patronized their fledgling restaurants and businesses. In that context, the legal complications looked like governmental hypocrisy, not unlike the corruption they had experienced back home. Both of these perspectives seemed self-evident. Both groups would have to become more aware of their own cultural assumptions about the nature of social order—for example, whether order lies in relationships connecting people or laws restricting them—before they could imagine the possibility of any other rational perspective.

The Catholic Mass as Identity Marker at All Saints

In spite of deep differences between the two cultural groups at All Saints around issues like social order and the law, parishioners from both communities engaged in religious practices that were formally identical—saying the rosary, baptizing children, kneeling on one knee upon entering the church (genuflecting), asking that masses be offered in remembrance of a deceased relative. The most salient of these common practices was attending mass. Hundreds of Catholics did so every weekend in Spanish and English. Half of all English-speaking parishioners interviewed identified the mass as the most important thing going on at All Saints. Several Latino parishioners attended both Spanish masses many weekends, serving in some liturgical role Saturday night and then bringing their children to sit with their religious education classes at Sunday mass. A middle-schooler from the Latino youth group went out of his way to tell me he came to mass even though his parents did not. One Friday afternoon, I encountered the Euro-American young adult group at the Spanish mass. None of them spoke Spanish; they "just wanted to go to mass." Two students from the sixth grade English religious education class asserted that the whole reason the Church exists was for people to take an hour out of their week to be with God.

This is not to say that no one contested the focus on this practice. One parishioner described this focus on the mass at All Saints as excessive. Many children in the youth groups and religious education classes admitted to coming to mass only because they were forced by their parents, and many people did not come during the summer months when the parish held no religious education classes. Nor was it difficult to find Catholics in Havenville who never attended mass, including people who sent their children to Catholic school or to religious education. Even those who did regularly and enthusiastically attend mass admitted various and contested meanings for the practice. Some Euro-American parishioners commented that they felt the mass served as a kind of foundation, either for faith, for the other ministries of the parish, or for the community that gathered around it. Other people from both communities mentioned the importance of the sermons preached by the two priests, how they made them think. Frequently people noted the importance of the mass without elaborating on how or why. Still, for a large number, attending mass constituted a foundational structure of life in the shared parish, though, as we will see, the way it constituted such a structure differed for the two communities.

The centrality of the mass traces its roots back to the identity-marking Sunday commemoration of the Last Supper among the early Christians, and especially to the further elaboration of that commemoration during what church historians call the Patristic Era (from the second to the fifth century). In medieval western Europe, that commemoration came to be known as "the mass" (Latin *missa* from the words of "sending forth"), and during that time mass continued to be celebrated in Latin even as Latin no longer served as a vernacular but as the elite language of theologians and church leaders. The medieval mass thus became the domain of the clergy—who sometimes celebrated it alone—while ordinary Christians observed from a distance a ritual increasingly felt to be transcendent and otherworldly. The Protestant Reformers deliberately contested that split, and they insisted on the simplification of the ritual, its translation into vernacular languages, and a shift in focus from the clergy's participation to that of the laity. While there was some initial interest in such reforms among Roman Catholics, the polemical debates and wars of the Reformation era provoked a holding fast to the Latin mass as a sacred experience that could only be conducted by ordained clergy and that uniquely made Christ present in the bread and wine. In the 1960s, the Second Vatican Council broke with that strategy, looking back to the early Church's experience. The mass was to remain a unique, sacred, and awe-inspiring experience, but it had to occur in the vernacular and it would require "fully active and conscious participation" from the lay faithful.[28] A great deal of Church controversy since then has centered on how the mass should be celebrated in the wake of those dramatic changes.

Much social scientific research on the Catholic mass in recent years has focused on quantitative data about the declining impact of mass on Catholic people's lives. Researchers have especially argued over mass attendance and the level of belief in Eucharistic doctrines.[29] At least one qualitative study has looked at how Catholic worshippers interpreted and experienced the changes of Vatican II.[30] Less examined is what Catholics actually do and what they make of what they do, including its emotional resonance for them. Observation of the mass at All Saints raises interesting questions, most beyond the scope of this study. At Easter mass, a Euro-American woman complained bitterly to the usher when the lay minister of communion did not, as prescribed, make the sign of the cross and offer a verbal blessing over family members who opted not to receive the host.[31] Why did that bother her so much? When dipping their hands in the holy water font, Latino parishioners would not only make the sign of the cross over themselves but enthusiastically rub holy water on their necks as well. How did Latinos interpret this practice (and Euro-Americans their more physically restrained version)? When, at the bilingual mass on Holy Thursday, Father David washed twelve parishioners' feet in commemoration of Jesus washing his disciples' feet, several Latino children wandered up the side aisle to get a closer look at the very physical ritual. Some parents held up their children to see. Some Euro-Americans liked this and others disliked this. What was this all about? Sociologist Meredith McGuire argues for the importance of attending to what people do with their bodies around religion. "Religious ritual is like a chain of such embodied practices," she writes, "each link having the potential to activate deep emotions and a sense of social connectedness, as well as spiritual meanings."[32] McGuire follows Emile Durkheim in emphasizing the importance of the emotional evocation of community through the practices.

At All Saints, parishioners in both communities paid particular attention not only to these embodied practices but also to the "correct" performance of them. Priests and laity spoke frequently about the way liturgical guidelines—real or imagined—established boundaries around "proper" and "correct" worship at All Saints. Fr. David Adama, the pastor, insisted on the proper interpretation of Vatican-issued rules for worship, and he described himself with partial irony as a "liturgical nazi." At the bilingual confirmation mass, he persuaded the bishop that church rules required that the Eucharistic prayer be all in one language. He once asked the associate pastor, Father Ignacio, to ensure that the Latino community knelt throughout the Eucharistic prayer, as is required by the U.S. bishops.[33] He worried about how the local practice of having two Easter Vigil masses abrogated church norms. Father Nacho's response, perhaps fighting fire with fire, was that the bishop had explicitly given permission for a distinct Vigil mass in Spanish some years back. Padre Nacho also had his own opinions about liturgical rules, some rooted in his experience back home in Mexico. For example, he insisted that Saturday evening masses, customarily celebrated as a Sunday mass in the United States but infrequently in Mexico, were not really proper Sunday masses.

Yet it was not only the priests who asserted the importance of liturgical norms for creating correct worship. Longtime parishioner Richard Klug told me how he once remonstrated with the curmudgeonly former pastor, Fr. John Nowak, over rules for worship. Nowak repeatedly complained about the norms the bishop had introduced for implementing the Vatican II reforms of the liturgy, such as those encouraging people to share a handshake at the exchange of peace. Richard grew tired of Fr. Nowak's complaining and resistance to this and told him that the ministry of a bishop must be difficult, having to "rein in" some priests and "drag the others along." Most lay people at All Saints routinely expressed ignorance of church matters before the priests' superior knowledge, but that did not prevent them from instructing the priests on proper liturgical practice. Doña Claudia Salazar gave me extensive instructions on the proper way to clean chalices (communion cups) after mass. Elizabeth Renford, a retired Euro-American woman, complained that Padre Nacho did not participate more in the annual bilingual Holy Thursday mass, though she allowed that perhaps "rubrics"—guidelines in liturgical books—might not permit this. On the night of Good Friday, several members of the Latino community told me that on this holiest of days, only I and the other priests could go into the sacristy where the Blessed Sacrament was being kept, a rule not found in the liturgical texts (and not really observed at All Saints). People sometimes took guidelines designed for mass and generalized them to other practices. In a gesture of goodwill, the local Protestant college asked a Catholic student to preach at their weekly chapel service. He declined, citing that only priests and deacons could preach. This is, in fact, a norm in canon (church) law, but there it applies exclusively to the homily or sermon during mass.[34]

The late Catherine Bell is recognized for her pioneering work in overturning old assumptions about the meaning and practice of such attention to ritual. In her estimation, scholars have too frequently defined ritual in terms of preexisting and uncritically appropriated categories.[35] She argues for considering ritualization as a strategic social activity:

> Viewed as practice, ritualization involves the very drawing, in and through the activity itself, of a privileged distinction between ways of acting, specifically between those acts being performed and those being contrasted, mimed, or implicated somehow. That is, intrinsic to ritualization are strategies for differentiating itself—to various degrees and in various ways—from other ways of acting within any particular culture.[36]

To Bell, the Catholic mass distinguishes itself from an ordinary meal (and from other everyday activities) by its distinctive features as enacted bodily by participants—its frequency and timing, amount of food, manner of eating. As Bell herself notes, such an understanding reverses the order of things in the tradition of ritual interpretation initiated by Emile Durkheim. Instead of ritual being defined by its orientation to the community's experience and judgment of the "sacred" and beliefs about it, ritual actually creates and reproduces categories like the "sacred" and "religion."[37]

The continuous looking to norms and rules of ritual at All Saints confirmed that parishioners associated the category of "Church" with authorities and symbols that went beyond the local parish. They indicated their acceptance (sometimes grudging) that Vatican and diocesan authorities legitimately served as arbiters of correct ritual, establishing boundaries between proper and improper practice. Of course, the Vatican and other church leaders have had their own purposes in establishing such guidelines. Pope John Paul II himself urged priests to ensure the proper celebration of the mass: "It must be lamented that, especially in the years following the post-conciliar liturgical reform, as a result of a misguided sense of creativity and adaptation, there have been a number of *abuses* which have been a source of suffering for many."[38] While the pope is never specific about the suffering (or the abuses) he mentions, he clearly felt that certain kinds of liturgical experimentation promoted erroneous liturgical practice and teaching. In the same encyclical, he worried about "confusion with regard to sound faith and Catholic doctrine concerning this wonderful sacrament."[39] The Congregation for Divine Worship and the Discipline of the Sacrament echoed the sentiment: "In the end, they introduce elements of distortion and disharmony into the very celebration of the Eucharist, which is oriented in its own lofty way and by its very nature to signifying and wondrously bringing about the communion of divine life and the unity of the People of God."[40] Distortions in practice were seen to alter or damage the creation of sacred experience that should inspire awe and respect among the faithful. It was the job of bishops and the Vatican to evaluate such potential distortions and to root them out lest the mass lose its character as a transcendent experience.

Many parishioners, however, accessed liturgical guidelines according to their own perspective on the "sacred." They interpreted church norms on their own, a few individuals remaking the wording or design of the official norms in the process. Nevertheless, however they accessed such norms, many saw them as ensuring respect for transcendence in Catholic worship. For them, liturgical norms and customs offered structure and boundaries to establish and handle something precious and holy entrusted to them. This fits with Jerome Baggett's observation about a very traditional parish in California. In particular, parishioners there felt that celebrating the Latin mass preserved the reverence missing from the usual Catholic worship and indeed from American life.[41]

At All Saints, I was told repeatedly that only the Roman Catholic Church had the sacraments and the real presence of the Body and Blood of Christ in the Eucharist, even though the position of church authorities is actually considerably more nuanced.[42] Such an absolute distinction is reminiscent of Reformation polemics between Catholics and Protestants. The long period of Christian religious reform in the late medieval and early modern period—"the Long Reformation"— altered European practice and understanding of faith. Before the Reformation, Christians engaged in a diversity of local practices that all signified Christian identity. "Rather than focus on what people believe, by contrast late medieval religion privileged practice, not only in the ideals for religious virtuosi but also in the expectations for ordinary laypersons. Being a 'good' Christian was defined in terms of a few prescribed occasional practices such as properly observing certain holy days."[43] After the Reformation, people made much more of the boundaries of religious identity established by correct belief:

> Although there had been efforts to denounce heretical teachings since the early centuries of Christianity, earlier disputes over boundaries had been generally confined to teachers and theologians. Along with the shift to emphasizing belief over practice, church authorities during this early modern period of transition turned the focus of heresy examinations to ordinary church members. It was no longer sufficient that Christians simply engage in certain core religious practices; if they also held unorthodox beliefs, they must not communicate them to others.[44]

Accordingly, Catholic and Protestant reformers began to limit worship to approved zones supervised by the leadership. Popular magic and miracles became suspect. For Catholics, the sacraments and sanctioned devotions became the only "real" worship.[45]

Distinguishing between "real" and "unreal" worship suggests a focus on boundary maintenance and negotiations in order to establish and reinforce identity in a contested environment. We know who we are by distinguishing that from who we are not. The divided cultural and religious environment of Havenville gave specific content to the articulations of how worship marked off identity. In Jerome Baggett's study of parishes in Northern California, he attempted to listen to the "conversational shards" Catholics employed as they attempted to distinguish and cultivate a sense of identity for the self in a rootless world.[46] My observations and our team's interviews constituted a similar process of listening to the distinctions made negotiating identity. For example, I heard the former pastor at All Saints saying that his mission as pastor had been to represent the Catholic faith well in a Protestant environment. Many Euro-American Catholics explicitly argued that distinctive Catholic worship helped them reinforce their religious identity in a largely Protestant environment. They noted how Catholic worship was structured very differently from the simple, music-centered worship of the Anabaptists, the largest local denominational group. Catholic worship celebrated multiple sacraments, images, and religious practices. On feast days it drew attention to the Virgin Mary and the saints. And unlike in the fast-growing Evangelical churches, there were no rock bands, TV screens, or focus on the language of a "personal Lord and savior." Catholic worship was purposefully—one might even say transcendently—unlike all other activities. In short, the mass reminded Euro-American Catholics how unlike other churchgoing Euro-Americans they were. And Havenville, at least according to popular reports, was a church-focused town.

Members of the Latino community also looked on Sunday worship as a space and time set apart, but worship for them brought to light a somewhat different process of identity distinction. In interviews, most Latino parishioners did not highlight the mass in itself as Euro-Americans had. After all, in a majority Catholic country like Mexico, the customary practice of the mass does not indicate a distinct religious identity. Everyone knows about it. And mass within parish life has even less salience for identity. Shrines and famous chapels rather than parishes serve as markers of regional and national Catholic identity. And both in Mexico and in the United States, popular religious practices in the home and neighborhood—not parish worship—reproduce Latino Catholic religious identity in a foundational way.[47]

But in the United States, mass in *Spanish* does have a powerful impact for at least some Latino Catholics in helping to negotiate identity. Far from home, feeling alone and disoriented, immigrants longed to attend mass together and pray in their own language. They develop what one man called a "thirst" for attending mass. As Doña Claudia Salazar, a prayer leader or *rezadora*, told me, "The most important thing is, after all, that we have a priest that speaks our language and that can listen to God in our language."[48] A member of the choir noted that he felt empty when he had only English masses to contend with. A research team member agreed with that assessment, and another told the story of a woman visiting from another city where there was no mass in Spanish. She wept with desperation after mass at All Saints, telling local parishioners they did not appreciate what they had.

This was a deeply felt sensibility, a powerful emotional experience created by hearing one's own language used for public prayer in a foreign land dominated by a different language. This experience was made more precious to people by the presence of anti-immigrant sentiment. They knew that many Euro-Americans wanted no Spanish in the city or the parish. In newspapers and online forums people objected to Spanish signs and phone messages. A child playing outside the church one Sunday said his teacher forbade him to speak Spanish at recess. Some Euro-Americans noted their opposition to having separate Spanish masses at All Saints, feeling that it divided the community. Such a divided and socially insecure environment made the assertion of Latino Catholic identity through the mass in Spanish all the more important.

Popular Religion Migrates

Aside from the mass and formal sacramental worship, another sort of worship formed a part of the way Latino Catholics at All Saints asserted a distinct identity in response to their culturally bifurcated environment. Here I use the somewhat controversial term "popular religion" to describe these worship practices, mostly because people at All Saints used that term.[49] The corpus of theological, sociological, and religious studies writings on Latino popular religion is vast, and I do not intend to wade into the numerous discussions and controversies about it here.[50] I simply note six key clusters of popular religious practices in the Latino community at All Saints: (1) praying the rosary; (2) veneration of the Mexican image of the Virgin Mary of Guadalupe, including a dramatic representation of her story on December 11–12; (3) building an altar in remembrance of the dead for *el Día de los Muertos* (All Souls Day or the Day of the Dead); (4) the Christmas *posadas,* a communally sung reenactment of the pregnant Virgin Mary and her husband Joseph searching for hospitality in Bethlehem; (5) the *acostar al niño Dios* (*acostada*) ceremony for resting a lifesize infant Jesus statue in a replica of a manger on Christmas Eve; and (6) various Holy Week customs, including the *Via Crucis* or Living Way of the Cross and the *Pesamé de la Virgen* or Rosary of Condolence to the Virgin Mary.

Members of the Euro-American community also engaged in periodic popular religious practices—the rosary, Eucharistic adoration, flowers delivered to the Virgin Mary at weddings, and house blessings. Yet these scattered practices did not have the scale or commitment of the Latino community's involvement in popular religion. For Mexicans in particular, popular religion marked off the church year more recognizably than official church liturgies. The most important event in Holy Week was the popular *Via Crucis* procession, not the official masses and liturgies. The masses that hosted the *representación* (dramatic reenactment) of the story of the Virgin of Guadalupe on December 11–12 were the most crowded church events of the year. The Christmas *posadas,* though less well attended than these other celebrations, functioned within the Latino community as a more visible sign of the imminent coming of Christmas than the official church preparation season of Advent in which they occurred.

These popular religious practices drew crowds and marked off the church year. Immigrant people consciously identified them with the cultural heritage they had left behind. But that did not mean that Mexican Catholics at All Saints enacted or interpreted popular religion in a standardized or univocal way. Shaped by custom rather than official rubrics, popular religious practice at All Saints reflected a plurality of interpretations and practices. Sociological literature on the subject suggests that such variations remain a part of Mexican Catholic popular religion wherever people practice it in the United States: "It would be a mistake to comprehend these expressions of 'popular religion'—Mexican American traditional practices—as a unitary phenomenon. While popular religious traditions have some historical coherence, individuals draw on them selectively and creatively."[51] Certainly in Havenville, popular religion served as a marker of home country identity amidst the tribulations and dislocations of migration. But economic transformations back home and migration to the United States had also changed the practice and understanding of it. It represented both a preservation and an alteration at the same time.

One of the most common stories told to me by migrants in Havenville was about the loneliness their arrival engendered. People very close to their families of origin and enthusiastic about their neighborhoods and friends had left everything, and many had not seen their loved ones for years. When I brought back photos from a research trip visiting families in Mexico, they were received with tears. Theologian Daniel Groody describes loneliness as a common aspect of the psycho-spiritual alienation of immigrants. "Loneliness is a heavy burden and one of the most unrecognized aspects of the immigrant's pain."[52] Groody describes how many look to the church as a salve for their loneliness. In Havenville, church served as a place to find companionship. As a man back in Mexico told me, *there* (in the United States) you feel lonely and empty, and you fill it up with the church.[53]

Popular religion provided an emotionally powerful embodied enactment of religious practices people connected to homeland and cultural identity. Thus, reflecting on the dramatic Guadalupe *representación* or the Good Friday *Via Crucis,* Latino parishioners did not hesitate to describe their experience enthusiastically, and often with emotionally expressive language. Yet these events were more than discrete individual experiences of being moved. The sustained attention of the congregation, the bursts of applause, and communal shouts of joy suggested affective reactions shared by the whole community. Anthropologist Richard Flores suggests that such a popular religious performance creates community bonds through its invocation of reciprocal relationships with divine persons, a point also made by theologians Roberto Goizueta and Orlando Espín.[54] On Good Friday at All Saints, Domingo Salazar, a seminarian and the son of Doña Claudia, reminded me that the *Via Crucis* actually brings people together in community. The simultaneous engagement of their bodies and emotions offers powerful remedies for a people suffering from isolation and cultural disorientation.

Domingo and others on Good Friday also reminded me of the role of memory in popular religion. In discussions about the *Via Crucis* and the Christmas *posadas,* people emphasized the importance of carrying on Mexican traditions in the United States. The children especially needed to know who they were, and where they came from. Large numbers of Latino parishioners saw popular religion as a cultural marker par excellence. Part of this was no doubt the long association of Our Lady of Guadalupe and other customs (such as the Day of the Dead) with the Mexican nation and nationalism. But perhaps, paradoxically, it was also the way in which most Mexican popular religion has a geography to it, a localism. Cities and towns have a patron saint (and corresponding fiesta); shrines and pilgrimages have a regional character; legends grow around places; and regions and states have their take on holidays and festivals. Some scholars even prefer to think of popular religion as local religion.[55] Differing opinions at All Saints over how to conduct, for example, the *posadas* or celebrate the Day of the Dead reinforce this notion. On a research trip to various states, cities, and towns in central Mexico, I discovered both consistencies and diversity in religious practices. Again, identity formation is in part a process of negotiating boundaries. Migrants do that—in part—by asserting the memory of their former home while living in their new home. What makes someone a migrant (rather than a native with "heritage") is the specificity of that memory. Local religion is specific.

At least it is for a while. A woman from the Mexican state of Puebla told me how she tried to continue with popular religion as they did in Puebla as much as possible, reciting to me the entire calendar of popular religion there, month by month. And she was able to while I was there, living in a trailer park with many other *poblanos*—people from her state. Yet many of her fellow parishioners were not from Puebla. Moreover, the separation of All Saints into two cultural worlds—Mexican and Euro-American—tended to emphasize Mexican national identity rather than local identities. Meanwhile, economic transformations and migration diluted people's sense of local religion. On my Mexican research trip, people complained to me about the vulnerability of popular religious customs due to changing industrial habits and anxiety about work and money. In Havenville, migrants expressed the same worry as it related to the displacement of migration. Some admitted that, back in Mexico, their parents never taught them about such practices in the first place. Many other things seemed more pressing, such as finding adequately paying work. But in a foreign land without such customs, it became crucial to re-create and assert popular religion as a means of negotiating identity. Historically, the celebration of St. Patrick's Day remains a bigger event among Irish-Americans than it ever has among Irish in Ireland. People select and reshape popular religious practices in a new landscape.[56] In Havenville, dislocation created a strong need to assert an identity over and against the unfamiliar culture of the new country as well as in reimagined continuity with the home country.

The loss of popular religious practices and their subsequent reinvention was inevitable considering the demographics of migration in Havenville. Transmission of popular religious practice depends on intergenerational contact. All Saints lacked persons from the older generations, what Mexicans call la tercera edad—the third age. One of the few persons of la tercera edad in Havenville was Doña Claudia Salazar, who lived there with her husband Don Alberto and some of their children.[57] I visited Doña Claudia's on Christmas Eve, and I watched her instruct a younger woman from her hometown in the art of serving as madrina (godmother) to the niño Dios (infant Jesus) statue for the acostada ceremony, where one lays him in the manger.[58] For her knowledge of such prayers and traditions, the other people from Puebla called Doña Claudia a rezadora, or folk prayer leader. Yet I rarely saw this kind of intergenerational instruction in the homes of the All Saints community.

Indeed, much of the popular religion at All Saints had apparently changed locations. In Mexico, popular religion takes place in neighborhoods, schools, and homes. The clergy—educated in the official tradition—does not always support or encourage it at church. In Havenville, however, much popular religion took place within the church building. There were no processions or festivals in the streets, no neighborhood posadas.[59] Most people offered practical explanations for this. The cold weather precluded outdoor events; processions required complicated arrangements with the police; people were all Catholic back home but not here, precluding public demonstration of the faith.[60] All of the explanations sounded plausible. It was also true, however, that the parish facilities functioned as a safe community gathering space in an environment perceived as unfamiliar, even occasionally hostile. There

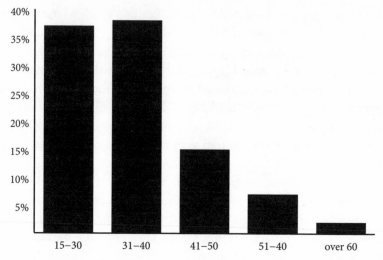

Figure 2.1. Age groups in the Latino/a community

people could pool their limited expertise and create something sustaining for them.

There were benefits and costs to this move to the parish. The parish provided a centralized site for identity making and cultural preservation in an environment without abundant Mexican Catholic resources and where the people sometimes faced discrimination for their identity making. The church was also space watched over by a priest relatively friendly to popular religion. Father Ignacio offered leadership, encouraging popular religion generally, drawing connections between its stories and the suffering immigrants endured. In his view, he could use popular religion to catechize people.

Yet another member of the community wondered if his exclusive championing of Mexican customs discouraged any openness to Catholic practices from the new country. Perhaps this was so. On the evening of December 11, Padre Nacho shouted to the people, "*Viva Mexico*," and they responded joyfully, "*Viva!*"[61] The following night, the actual feast of the Virgin of Guadalupe, he had me, an Anglo priest, concelebrating by his side. Perhaps out of consideration for me, he added a salute to my country. "*Viva Estados Unidos!*" he shouted.[62] The invitation fell somewhat flat and provoked giggling. Perhaps more seriously, Father

Ignacio's leadership may have "re-gendered" popular religious practice. McGuire writes, "Women are frequently respected religious specialists in Latin popular traditional practices."[63] This was certainly so in home practices and some parish practices at All Saints. But the charismatic priest's leadership sometimes overshadowed the leadership of lay people, especially women, over popular religion in the parish. Moreover, for Padre Nacho, popular religion was just one piece of a larger project of parish-based education in the Catholic faith, a project rooted in his vision of ministry as an expression of the "new evangelization."

Evangelizar: A Narrative of Conversion

Francisco Martínez, a middle-aged man from central Mexico, was disoriented and lonely when he arrived in Havenville. Having mistaken the courthouse for the church (as I described in the introduction), Francisco checked with a friend to see if there were churches in Havenville. His friend guided him to All Saints, and in time Francisco started attending a Bible study class offered by Father Nacho. He described what happened there: "One day God removed the blindfold from my eyes, and I could discover the truth. It was for me very beautiful, for me that at that time I began to weep because I had remained in the shadows and the Word of God made it so my life was given expression." Francisco went on to describe his increasing involvement in learning at All Saints, and how grateful he is for the opportunity, how he hopes lots of young people will also experience what he did in the Bible.

Many people involved at All Saints offered a similar narrative of a life of loneliness or loss altered by involvement in some form of religious education at the parish. Difficulties and disorientation were overcome through learning more about the faith. In many interviews, parishioners from the Latino community related how they had understood very little about their faith in earlier days, many having done little aside from attending church (many used the Spanish verb phrase *calenté la banca*—they had merely "warmed the pew"). Now they felt they really understood. Some described how this faith formation process helped resolve instability, lack of life focus, marital problems, and temptations toward addictions and other social problems. Jesús Domínguez, a fifty-something man everyone called Don Chuy, told me that loneliness, bitterness, and misogyny had once characterized his life. Now everything was different because of what he had learned at church. The young mother Paulina Delgado admitted that she was depressed and bored when she arrived in the United States, going every day from the confined factory where she worked to her cramped house. Now she was involved in a bigger world, teaching the children with several other catechists. "*Nuestra familia es más grande*," she said. Now our family is larger.

An even greater number of people recommended such a narrative of conversion through education in the faith as the solution for *other* people's problems. The young widow Adriana Garcia wanted people to learn more about their faith so that they could be converted in their lives. Maria del Pilar, a young mother, saw that parish programs could help a lot of people who did not know God or had a different conception of God. Antonio Nuñez believed that ignorance of the Catholic faith made people turn to Protestant groups, and he thought a deeper understanding of their faith would enable people to defend it against Protestant arguments. The serious young usher Miguel Fernandez thought that the parish's mission should be to form people in their faith so that they might become better people—better Catholics, better citizens, and better professionals. Whether described in their own lives or prescribed for others, this common narrative spoke of a process of religious conversion spawned by parish efforts to educate, form, and deepen people's faith.

Both Father Ignacio (Padre Nacho) and parishioners summed up the common narrative using the Spanish verb *evangelizar* (to evangelize). Influenced by the evangelical tradition, people in the United States often associate this word with preaching and proselytizing. For these Mexican immigrants, it had more to do with learning about one's Catholic faith and then sharing with other Catholics what one had learned. Jorge Alvarez, a young adult leader at All Saints, articulated it like this:

> The most important thing is that each person feels the need and has the
> interest to do what they can to evangelize [*evangelizar*]. Sometimes we
> are limited by the lack of people who are well educated, but from the
> same people comes the desire to get ahead. And they start to investigate,
> to go to courses, to go on retreats, to go to classes. And in this way we are

continuing to evangelize. This is what I see as the most important thing in our people, the desire to share what they have learned or what they are learning.[64]

The former head catechist for the children, Manuel Nieves, agreed, but he focused his attention on the need to learn enough so as not to have one's faith disturbed by Pentecostal and Evangelical preachers and evangelists. Manuel said that the parish existed "to evangelize, evangelize. The sects and Protestantism are gobbling up the one we send out there, and we are staying behind." His worry came up frequently in conversation with others, and several Latino Evangelical or Pentecostal churches did dot the Havenville landscape.[65]

The psychologist Lewis Rambo and the theologian Charles Farhadian argue for seven common phases in narratives of internal spiritual change (conversion) like the *evangelizar* narrative at All Saints. Context factors influence the need for or any resistance to such change, the major contextual factor here being migration. A crisis or rupture in the internal logic of experience facilitates a quest for some solution to the rupture. At All Saints, loneliness, alienation, and instability spurred a quest for a religious identity largely taken for granted back home. In Rambo's model, a quest precipitates some encounter with a change agent who proposes a different perspective. In most of the stories I heard, Padre Nacho served as such a change agent. Intense interaction with the change agent helps the converting person develop the new perspective. His interaction with new parishioners encouraged them to engage in a process of deepening their faith through some form of religious education. Finally, there is a commitment to the new perspective followed by the comprehensive consequences of the change.[66] Those who did engage that process of deepening their faith reported changes in their lifestyle and social networks.

As Rambo recognizes, there are always difficulties in attempting to reduce the complexities of human experience to a model, even an interdisciplinary model like his.[67] Rambo and Farhadian's model does remind us how a particular narrative often looks and sounds like other religious conversion narratives. But there is also value in listening and understanding the particular narrative template of the *evangelizar* narrative at All Saints. This is not to suggest that the narrative template perfectly reflects the psychological experience of spiritual change lived by migrant parishioners at All Saints. It may or may not. A narrative is as incomplete a guide to human experience as any psychological model. But parishioners at All Saints themselves used this narrative template to frame their religious experience, and that framing itself shaped the experience.

The cultural anthropologist Sherry Ortner terms such narrative templates "cultural schemas": "A cultural schema represents a hegemonic selection, ordering, and 'freezing' of a variety of cultural practices into a particular narrative shape, by virtue of their representation in cultural stories—myths, legends, folktales, histories, and so forth."[68] It may seem excessive to describe the *evangelizar* narrative as a hegemonic cultural story like legends or folktales. At the same time, it did possess tropes and vocabulary repeatedly expressed through personal stories and Father Nacho's teaching and preaching. It was remarkably precise, as if everyone were reading from the same playbook.

That playbook framed not only conversation but also the shape of parish ministry in the Latino community at All Saints. Great attention went to educating people in their faith as a means of conversion. The children's catechesis program—oriented to the sacraments of first communion and confirmation—was accompanied by biweekly mandatory talks by Padre Nacho for the children's parents. The catechists themselves met twice a week outside class—once to share ideas and learn together and on another night to prepare lesson plans. A weekly Bible study on yet another night drew a lot of catechists and other leaders as well. The young adults met on Saturday evenings, one group member exploring a theme from scripture or Catholic tradition for the sake of all. The former head catechist began a weekly apologetics class, teaching a group about how to use the Bible to defend against common Evangelical or Pentecostal objections to the Catholic faith. Lengthy preparation classes were offered for baptism, *quinceañera* celebrations, adult confirmation, and marriage; those for the latter two met every week for months. There was also an intensive Latino lay ministry training institute that met at the parish once a month. About thirty parish leaders attended.

And there was the mass. Padre Nacho was well known—some said infamous—for giving lengthy catechetical homilies. Many of them, especially on major feast days, addressed marriage and family issues. But even outside the homily Father Ignacio engaged the congregation as a teacher. Especially, but not exclusively, on celebration days, he would stop the mass (or other sacraments such as baptism) to offer commentary on everything from another priest's homily to the meaning of Christmas to the diocesan collection to the palms of Palm Sunday. He even stopped midway through blessing the ashes on Ash Wednesday to explain that this was a blessing over the people and not just the ashes. Padre Nacho took every opportunity he had to teach.

And there can be no doubt that the *evangelizar* narrative at All Saints originated with Padre Nacho. People quoted him directly (for example, when they used the expression "warmed the pew"). He himself focused his attention on education in the faith, describing it as a tool for personal conversion and the betterment of relationships. He frequently emphasized the need for a faith perspective on marriage and family issues in his catechetical talks and homilies. He told me that he first chose this path after discovering in 2001 that many people in his new parish had not received their sacraments. He realized he wanted All Saints parishioners to truly understand what they heard, practiced, and believed. He negatively compared this to his experience as a priest in Mexico, where he presided at multiple masses and sacraments where people constantly came and went. He declared that he would rather spend a couple of hours teaching the parents of children in religious education classes than celebrate any number of masses on Sunday.

Naturally, such a consistent and complex narrative did not emerge only from the head of Father Ignacio. We can trace his narrative template to what Latin American Catholics call the "new evangelization paradigm." For decades, Latin American Catholic clergy have had concerns about church attendance, religious literacy, and Protestant competition.[69] In 1983, Pope John Paul II coined the term "new evangelization" in a speech to Latin American bishops at Port-au-Prince, Haiti. He saw traditionally Christian lands like Europe and Latin America as requiring a renewed commitment to the Christian faith. The pope further developed this paradigm in a 1990 encyclical letter, *Redemptoris Missio*. In Latin America, the new evangelization has privileged spiritual development and resolving marriage and family problems over the political and economic analysis of the formerly ascendant liberation theology.[70] In their 1992 meeting at Santo Domingo, the Latin American bishops' conference promoted it for the entire continent. Anthony Gill compare their subsequent efforts to the struggle of a corporation for market share; he sees the Church as having streamlined its structure and improved services in order to compete more efficiently against Pentecostals and Evangelicals.[71] Alexander Zatyrka, a theologian from Mexico City, told me that the new evangelization paradigm dominates the ecclesial culture in central Mexico and no doubt influenced much of Father Nacho's training at the seminary.

The new evangelization narrative has its critics. Protestant theologians complain about its polemical tone vis-à-vis Protestants.[72] The U.S. Catholic biblical scholar Jean-Pierre Ruiz agrees that the paradigm unnecessarily creates a negative "other" out of Latin American Protestants.[73] Other scholars draw attention to the way in which the new evangelization directs Latin American Catholics away from direct political engagement.[74] In reality, the new evangelization is a mix of things, concerning itself with some of the politically charged issues of liberation theology (social injustice, option for the poor, empowerment of the laity) but also co-opting them to reinforce clerical authority and compete with Protestant evangelists.[75]

Padre Nacho himself defended the *evangelizar* narrative in practical terms, referring to the many cases of marriage and family problems people brought to his attention. He shied away from explicit political statements or economic analysis—that was not his area. He did draw constant attention to immigrants' experience of oppression and exploitation. Yet he could not see the advantage of, for example, publicly addressing the occasional immigration raids; only rumor and panic would result. Few interviewees at the parish, in fact, thought that the parish or church should work toward legalization or help deportees, though nearly everyone in the Latino community worried about immigration crackdowns. The political machinations over immigration policy seemed like distant negotiations to them, taking place in another universe they could not hope to influence. As parishioner Cesar Gutierrez said:

> I think that all those that are here and attend the church are praying to God so that an agreement come together in this country and allow us to

work peacefully without worry of this, without worry that you are going out into the street and . . . God only knows if you are going to return again home or if they are going to grab you and send you back to Mexico.

What they could influence was a world of spiritual development, personal virtue, and family discipline as they hoped for a better world for the poor. Perhaps such a focus drew their attention away from common political action for change in, say, immigration law. But the involved immigrant parishioners at All Saints saw the *evangelizar* narrative as a personal tool for liberation in a world seemingly set against them.

Boundaries and Identity in a Diverse World

At the beginning of this chapter, I noted how the change to a culturally bifurcated social environment at All Saints provoked different attempts to explain or understand what had happened. Various metaphors and stories came forward as lenses through which to view the demographic transformation. People imaged the parish as a marriage or family, or they saw it as an event where visitors needed to be welcome. A few looked to negative metaphors like that of invasion. In truth, there were almost as many explanations as there were parishioners. Still, four strategies stood out in the dozens of interviews and hundreds of observations conducted during my year at All Saints. Through these four strategies parishioners in the two cultural communities made sense of a demographically altered social environment: (1) both cultural communities elaborated (competing) conceptions of the social order; (2) both asserted Catholic identity (or specifically Latino Catholic identity) through focus on a correct practice of the Catholic mass; (3) Latino parishioners adapted Mexican popular religious practice from its original context in the neighborhood or home to parish life; and (4) Latino parishioners articulated their experience of church involvement after migration through a conversion narrative rooted in the Latin American language of the "new evangelization." All of these strategies focused their attention on negotiating identity in a culturally (or religiously) diverse social environment.

Members of both cultural communities had focused little attention on negotiating cultural identity before they came together starting in the

1990s. Euro-American Catholics had more experience with negotiating religious identity. But cultural identity remained largely unexamined in the more stable and homogenous cultural environments both groups enjoyed before the onset of migration. "In settled lives . . . culture is ubiquitous, yet it is difficult to disentangle what is uniquely 'cultural' since culture and life experience seem to reinforce one another."[76] As we saw in the first section, both groups regarded many of their culturally rooted assumptions about life as simply common sense, "assumptions so unselfconscious as to seem a natural, transparent part of the structure of the world, objectively real and needing no explicit support or elaboration to be true."[77] Once both groups found themselves in a changing and heterogeneous social environment—unsettled times— they were forced to take a conscious look at their cultural identity and articulate its importance.

A conference I once attended on cultural and racial diversity in the Catholic Church is instructive. Attendees were divided up into groups based on their "cultural family," that is, according to the standard racial-ethnic classifications of the contemporary United States: white, African American, Latino, Asian American, and Native American. Most of the Euro-Americans or whites had never experienced classification as a group over and against other groups. They had been taught to think of their group as the norm. The sociologists Stephen Cornell and Douglas Hartmann write, "Most racial categories . . . have been constructed first by those who wished to assign them to someone else; race has been first and foremost a way to describing 'others,' of making clear that 'they' are not 'us.'"[78] At this conference, however, a large group of Euro-Americans, classified as just one group among others, struggled mightily to understand who they were as a group. What was their identity if not the norm? Who were they in this new situation? What did they all have in common with one another?

People from the dominant culture do not generally think much about their identity as a group, and both immigrants and Euro-Americans had started off as part of a dominant culture. The cultural dominance of Euro-Americans had not disappeared in Havenville, but both cultural groups now had to reflect on their identity in the altered environment. They became surprisingly articulate about the expectations of social order, whether realistic or not. They thought about their central parish activity, worship, as producing and reinforcing their identity over and against other groups—English-speaking or Protestant. They laid down firm boundaries such as that signified by having or not having legal papers. Members of the Latino community renegotiated their sense of communal purpose or mission in ways that made strong distinctions between one's old life and one's new life, between Catholic and Evangelical, between those truly committed to the Church and those simply "warming the pew." It was a virtual flurry of boundary-marking activity. Most of the identity making focused on buttressing the internal identity of a group, using socially constructed distinctions with the other group as a tool.

Sometimes such a flood of boundary marking occurs over and against groups of "others" who are actually more imaginatively than physically present. For example, in the late 2000s some states, such as Oklahoma and Indiana, attempted to erect strict legal barriers between the status of unauthorized immigrants and everyone else, but in reality these states had relatively few such immigrants in their population. On the other hand, California and Arizona had significant immigrant populations when they did the same thing with laws passed in 1994 (California state initiative proposition 187) and in 2010 (Arizona SB 1070). The boundary-marking activity described in this chapter occurred at a time when different groups did physically coexist in a proximate area. Some of these groups (Euro-American Catholics and Euro-American Anabaptists) had very mild tensions in the present day, though they remembered tensions from the past. Latino Catholics experienced some tensions with another distinct group with whom they shared the city, that is, Latino Evangelicals and Pentecostals. But the largest tensions surrounded the way in which Euro-American and Latino Catholics had to relate to one another within the city and the parish. Sharing a city and a parish forced them to keep working out the practice and meaning of this relationship.

3

Being Apart Together

Sharing the Shared Parish

During my parish year at All Saints, I attended two distinct Easter Vigil masses on the same night, one in English, immediately followed by one in Spanish. The Easter Vigil is a unique mass celebrated annually on the night before Easter Sunday (Holy Saturday—*sábado de gloria*). It includes prayers and chants around the lighting of the Easter fire and (Paschal) candle, a retelling of the biblical accounts of the foundational narratives of Judaism and Christianity, and the baptism or confirmation of adults who wish to become Catholic. Many Catholics consider it the high point of the official liturgical calendar; St. Augustine called it "the mother of all feasts." Church law actually discourages more than one Easter Vigil mass at a parish, but All Saints had been celebrating dual services for some years.[1]

The English mass began at twilight. I stood beside Father David on the front steps wearing a white chasuble (a decorative outer tunic for liturgical use) that matched his own. He lit the Paschal candle from a little fire of wood branches in a broad-brimmed bowl of black metal. There were patches of snow on the ground around us. We moved inside where those assembled filled about two-thirds of the church. All of the biblical readings, the prayers, and the songs occurred in English, and the vast majority of people present were white. A first-time visitor might have assumed that the parish had few nonwhite parishioners and no services in languages other than English. After the homily, a group gathered around the baptismal font near the entrance, and Father David baptized three people, including one woman in her early thirties who was a municipal judge. Two men who had been baptized in other Christian denominations were received into the Catholic Church. After mass, the choir sang the "Hallelujah Chorus" from Handel's *Messiah* accompanied both by organ and a small, talented group of young people on brass instruments. Afterward there was a small feast in the parish hall, and the jocular man in his sixties who had taught the new Catholics handed out white lilies to each of those baptized or received into the Church.

While the feast continued in the parish hall, parishioners from the Latino community began to arrive and prepare for the Easter Vigil in Spanish—the *vigilia pascual.* Now even casual visitors would have noted that the parish had different cultural groups; they would have seen Euro-Americans driving out of the parking lot as Latinos arrived. In the sacristy—a small room off the sanctuary where priests put on their robes (vestments) and other ministers make logistical preparations—Padre Nacho recommended I wear a chasuble for warmth, whether or not it matched his. We repeated the ritual with the fire on the front steps, Father Nacho pausing to explain about the ritual phrases that accompanied the lighting of the Easter (Paschal) candle. His desire to teach manifested itself throughout this most solemn of services. Inside, the church was filled with people, all of them Latinos; a handful had to stand in the side aisles. Designated readers (lectors) began to read the dramatic biblical stories associated with this mass—the creation story in the first chapter of Genesis, the testing of the patriarch Abraham, the exodus of the Israelites from slavery in Egypt. Each of them chanted an accompanying passage from the Book of Psalms after the reading.

During the readings, we witnessed an unmistakable sign of the fact that two different cultural groups were negotiating their sharing the parish for the night. While I sat next to Father Ignacio in wooden chairs to the right of the altar, both of us vested in white, a middle-aged Euro-American parishioner tiptoed into the church from the side door and approached me in my chair. He whispered that the social next door had come to a conclusion, and someone had emerged to find his car blocked in by a car from the Spanish mass. He handed me a slip of paper with the license plate of the car. The Spanish Easter Vigil mass would go on for at least another hour and a half by my calculations, so I handed the paper to Father Ignacio with my own whispered explanation in Spanish.

During a pause between the readings, Father Nacho got up and read the license plate number, asking that the car be moved. He sat back down. A short time later a different Anglo parishioner returned with another slip of paper. Again I handed it to Padre Nacho, who read out the license plate between readings and asked for the driver to move his or her car.

No more slips of paper came after that. Just before the New Testament readings and the homily, the choir lead the congregation in the singing of a piece of liturgical music called the "Gloria" (named for the Latin of its initial line, "Glory to God in the highest"). People banged their hands against the wood of the pews and rang bells in celebration. During the homily, Father Nacho preached that Jesus's resurrection instruction to his disciples not to be afraid applied to this congregation; they should not even fear *la migra*, that is, the immigration authorities. One adult and three children received baptism after the homily. Their names were announced for everyone to hear. After the baptisms, Father Nacho blessed a number of bottles of water and images of saints that people left near his chair by sprinkling water from the baptismal font upon them. Later the wife of the head Eucharistic minister told me this happens every year. The service ended with the minor-key drama of "Resucitó," a famous Spanish hymn to the resurrection.

*   *   *

In the preceding chapter I recounted four major strategies by which parishioners from the two cultural communities at All Saints made sense of parish life in a world demographically transformed by immigration. The stories illustrating these strategies, however, focused mainly on how each community made sense of the world on their own. I noted how their notions of the social order arose separately and clashed. The mass that proved so important to their identities occurred in distinct languages at different times. Popular religion was a phenomenon mostly practiced by Latinos for their own reasons. Members of the Anglo community knew nothing about the *evangelizar* narrative of conversion; indeed, their lives embraced a relative stability that made such a narrative difficult to fathom. If All Saints functioned through the paradoxical combination of diverse groups sharing a parish while worshipping and ministering separately from one another, the stories behind these four strategies came from a place of separation. Indeed, psychologists refer to such an isolation of perspectives, where members of socially disconnected groups judge all things by their own cultural perspective and have trouble identifying or understanding the perspective of members of other groups, as "cultural encapsulation."[2]

Encapsulation actually helps distinct cultural communities to adjust to changed demographic realities. Immigrants have opportunities to socialize, work, and worship in familiar ways. A distinct worshipping community offers them a safe space to express themselves in their own language and according to their own culture. They escape the world of work and commerce dominated by others. They worship in a language they understand and to which they affectively connect. They talk openly about issues citizens do not see or understand— the differences in power and privilege between communities, cultural expectations of family and social life, the difficulty of negotiating the immigration system, and, for some, the necessary duplicity created by the simultaneous presence of a demand for labor and a lack of government authorization to fill it. In other words, they develop together what sociologists term "bonding social capital"—internal social networks that help them succeed in work, feel safe, buttress their sense of cultural identity, and reform experience of community surrendered in migration.

On the other hand, cultural encapsulation also helps longtime residents, who generally already have developed the social networks that give them social capital. Encapsulation instead allows them to gradually adjust to demographic change. They gain an opportunity to grieve the loss of a world they had to themselves. Their distinct worship and socializing affords them space to reflect on their cultural identity in a world inexorably altered. Even though they are not forced to do so, some use such space to collaborate on a more hospitable relationship to the newcomers without the immediate frustrations of face-to-face cross-cultural interaction.

Still, despite the advantages of cultural encapsulation, no cultural world in a multicultural society can remain completely independent of other cultural worlds. In Havenville, the two communities still had to share the city and the parish. They had to negotiate with one another constantly over the shared spaces, and this social fact felt like an interruption to the relative comfort of otherwise encapsulated lives. Sharing a church in particular, as the tale of the Easter Vigils demonstrates, required interaction across cultures even at moments that appeared completely separate. In this chapter then, we address that required interaction, the reluctant process of sharing the parish. We look at the perspectives and practices that arose in the encounter between the two cultural groups, an ongoing encounter that included both avoidance and embrace, appreciation and resentment, assertion and resistance, cross-cultural insight and painful culture clash.

Not surprisingly, the two distinct cultural communities reacted and made sense of this ongoing encounter in markedly different ways. In general, Euro-American parishioners tried to make sense of the experience of sharing through a discourse of unity. This talk about unity, however, had only a thin relationship to any practical forging of cross-cultural bonds. As the longtime resident group, Euro-Americans generally engaged the Latino community on their own terms—in English and through the local structures of work and commerce they were long accustomed to. The Latino community, however, had to engage Euro-Americans mostly within the Euro-American world—at work, in stores, through nonprofit and government agencies. Feeling themselves at a disadvantage in a land unfamiliar to them, they made sense of the sharing of their town and parish in more cautious, even defensive terms. They made more of their own intracultural quest for strength and unity. Yet even as these two communities looked at the sharing differently, they had to engage in the actual intercultural negotiations that concretized their sharing of the parish. This chapter examines the process of intercultural encounter through both the two communities' talk about it and the practices in which they engaged to embody it.

Talk of Unity

Strikingly, almost all Euro-American parishioners at All Saints appeared preoccupied with the unity of the two communities within the shared parish. Fifteen out of the eighteen in-depth interviews in that community included some expression of concern about the lack of integration between the two communities. Jami Potts, a young mother who works for the school system, called the coming together of cultures the most important thing about All Saints: "I would say [it's] the mixing of cultures, honestly, because I don't really see it happening outside—other than the education system." An elderly couple, the McKellers, former adult education leaders in the parish, simply wanted the cultures at the parish "more combined." A local college student, Joanna Hogan, called overcoming the obstacles that separated the two communities "the most important thing that is going on at All Saints." Fr. David Adama, the Euro-American pastor, declared the "unification of the two communities" part of the central mission of the parish. It was a common topic of informal conversation, and it reflected similar concerns in the broader Euro-American community in Havenville.[3] Most pointed to the demographic transformations of the previous decade and a half as having created the need for unity. As Joanne Miller, a fourth generation parishioner, said, "I think we're still topsy-turvy here, trying to deal with both the Hispanic and Anglo communities."

Placing this desire for unity in a context of upheaval and adjustment suggests that the quest for unity by the Euro-American community should be seen less as an attempt to integrate Latino parishioners—it seldom resulted in concrete initiatives to do so—than as the desire of Euro-Americans to understand their place in a changed world. Parishioner Mary Kruk framed the question thus:

> The most important thing that happens at the parish now, I think, is resolving the feelings perhaps in both communities . . . to have an explanation of "what unify the communities means." It sounds good, it's a nice phrase, but what does it mean and what are the perceptions on both sides?

The need to rearticulate identity in a culturally changed world accords well with intercultural communication theory. Theorists in this area of study generally argue that contact across cultures disturbs the psychological equilibrium of persons involved. Intercultural encounter creates both uncertainty and anxiety.[4] We might even say that intercultural encounter upsets the security of a person's identity. Because identity is inherently relational, contact with "people like me" increases the security of identity while contact across cultures creates vulnerability around identity. Intercultural communication then constitutes a process of identity negotiation.[5] I would argue that the talk of unity at All Saints in the Euro-American functioned as a process of identity negotiation. This is why such talk was emotionally intense but usually not pragmatic. It was largely an internal conversation about adaptation to a new reality. Actual rapprochement with Latinos proved much more difficult because of significant language and cultural differences.[6]

Identity negotiation requires a marshalling of resources, and those resources generally come from people's own cultural backgrounds.[7] At All Saints, Euro-American Catholics laid claim to a discourse of unity that they constructed from different sets of cultural resources, hoping this talk of unity would help them adapt to the new demographic situation. Below I discuss these different types of talk of unity. Some accessed the traditional American language of assimilation to work this problem. They assumed that the Mexican community would (or should) come into conformity with American cultural traditions of Catholicism. Their own adaptation would thus be minimal. Others worked with a language of love and relationships to develop unity, a somewhat vague discourse that required something of both sides but often remained romantic and idealistic. Still others admitted they did not know how to reach for unity but felt it had to happen. I term their approach "bridging without blueprints."

The Persistence of Assimilation

Because culture remains a powerful influence in a person's life, assimilation into a different culture rarely occurs as an immigrant's first choice. But it does occur. For example, before 1990, the few Mexican immigrant families in Havenville really had no choice but to assimilate, that is, to draw more or less exclusively on Euro-American cultural resources in order to adapt. They had nothing else. There were few Spanish-speaking families, almost no one from their own culture to consider as a potential mate. Their friends, schools, churches, banks, and stores all operated in English with Euro-American cultural assumptions. When I asked one Mexican-American woman in her late fifties about the other Hispanic families in town during her youth, she described her experience:

There wasn't any. There was a couple other families that I went to school with that were Hispanic. They were just like we were; we're more Anglicized, I think, than the average, just because we weren't around any of the other things. We didn't have a lot of choice. We really didn't . . . I just never—there were just so many things that I learned from the deacon— who was the deacon that started our Hispanic ministry here about ten years ago—about a lot of the customs—Día de los Muertos, that was new to me. So many different things, the novena to our Lady of Guadalupe, the posadas, the mañanitas.

After 1990, a critical mass of migrants created a new ethnic enclave in Havenville. They brought thick cultural resources with them in the process. So even as they adapted some Euro-American cultural resources for their use, they retained many resources from home to help them slowly adapt. Spanish remained a lingua franca in certain quarters of Havenville. The situation was quite different from that of years past.

Some whites in Havenville strongly disliked that development. Bothered by the cultural intrusion of the Spanish language and Latin American customs, this group found assimilation the only possible alternative in their cultural repertoire of responses to the situation. After all, they reasoned, they themselves had not moved to a new country. The migrants should adapt to their world, not they to the world of the migrants. "They are coming here and bringing their country with them," said Bernie Wilkinson, the Catholic half of a mixed Catholic-Protestant couple. Bernie felt that Latinos had obstinately refused to assimilate into American culture, not learning English and hanging on their home cultural identity. Other Euro-American parishioners agreed that unity and peace between cultures could only come through Latinos leaving behind Spanish and Latin American culture in order to embrace Anglo-conformity. Matt Hauser, a parish leader in his early thirties, said:

I mean are we helping the Hispanics to be able to live in our culture and get along side by side in a non-political manner and be able to greet friends and do everything that the parish has set for us to do—which is the Eucharist and spreading the gospel? We can all do it together, but do it as one body. Until that language barrier [is broken down], it's never going to happen.

Bob and Shirley Jones, a couple in their sixties, agreed. Shirley even invoked the authority of the pope to support this position:

> A mass is a mass no matter what language it is set in and if you can't understand it then you obviously don't have too strong of a religion if you can't figure out where the mass is at . . . so if you are saying mass in English I do feel these people should be understanding because the mass is the mass. If I go to—wherever I go—I prefer to go to Rome and hear it in Latin because I like the old Latin mass, or if I go to Germany and it's said in German or whatever, I'm going to still understand the mass. So it makes no difference what language it's set in. Therefore, I do think the Hispanic people, if they are going to come to mass here—most of the mass here should be said in English because the pope has said in this country we say mass in English so let's say it in English.

The pope had not done this, but Shirley may have inferred this from the gradual approval of English translations of the mass and sacraments for use in the United States by the U.S. bishops and the Vatican in the wake of the Second Vatican Council's encouragement of the vernacular.[8]

At All Saints, a handful of Euro-American parishioners consistently invoked reference to successful ethnic assimilations of the past in describing why they thought Latinos should move toward Anglo conformity. Bob Jones said to the team member who interviewed him:

> If we are going to be a true Catholic church we need to stop having Anglo masses and Hispanic masses and bring them together. Even when they had the old ethnic parishes, they brought people together. At one time, maybe, once a month they would have a German mass or a Polish mass or something like that. But to have two separate masses, and then we end up with two separate churches. That is not going to help bring the people together.

In reality, most ethnic parishes in the nineteenth and early twentieth century Midwest had weekly mass in Latin but with sermons and devotions in languages other than English. But immigration scholars routinely note how nostalgia for an imagined past of quick Americanization plays a significant role in assimilationist perspectives: "Forceful assimilationism does look at the past but less to find the origins of contemporary immigrant flows than to search for ways in which prior waves were separated from their cultures and integrated into the American mainstream."[9] Assimilationists tell a compelling story about the past less to understand how immigration works (or has worked) than to demonstrate that their present desires for assimilation are reasonable. Thus, such invocations of past assimilation often contrast the cultural conservation of contemporary immigrants with the rapid process of change in the experience of European immigrants of the past.

As noted in chapter 1, however, many European immigrants of the past also held to their language and culture of origin, sometimes more tenaciously than contemporary immigrants do. Contemporary assimilationists have to reengineer the immigrant cultural expressions of their ancestors to appear more superficial than they actually were. As Bernie Wilkinson said,

> When the Germans came here and they still made their German food, they still spoke the German language in the house, but they came here to America, they learned English, they learned American language. And they worked American jobs. And they still maybe had the odd piece of clothing, the hat, or perhaps the jacket that was definitely distinctive from their culture, but they still became Americans who just happened to speak German or just happened to speak Portuguese, or just happened to speak Polish . . . When the Hispanics come up here, they don't necessarily want to become Americans because they don't have to. Because this country has bent over backward to get their money, they speak Spanish everywhere so that we can make it easy for them to spend their dollars.

Assimilationist discourse often relies on idealized portraits of the immigrant past, to the point of obscuring the generations-long struggles of previous immigrants. We might think of this as a kind of "immigrant amnesia."[10]

Historical inaccuracy does not represent the only challenge in the discourse of assimilation, however. Immigration scholars, for example, sometimes describe it as "forceful assimilation," drawing attention to the pressure required for people—especially people surrounded by other immigrants from their own nation—to utterly reject their home culture in favor of Anglo-American ways. The means of exerting such pressure vary. One common element in contemporary assimilationist discourse is a desire to ban public use of languages other than English—the so-called English only movement. Another is opposition to the formation of ethnic enclaves. Again, assimilationists justify this opposition with a look back to an imagined immigrant past:

> The nation's success in absorbing so many foreigners in the past is attributed to its relentless hostility to the perpetuation of cultural enclaves and the immersion of foreign children into an English-only environment that made Americans out of them in the course of a single generation. Assimilationists want the future to mirror this past as a proven way to restore cultural unity and peace.[11]

In reality, cultural enclaves have persisted in American history, and children of immigrants rarely found themselves immersed in an English-only environment. More importantly, the expectation of full assimilation within the immigrant generation fails to appreciate the formative strength of culture in the life of a human person. Adult immigrants spent most of their young lives acquiring the habits, symbols, practices, and patterns of action embedded in their culture. They cannot jettison these completely, especially not over the course of a few years, as some assimilationists expect. For this reason, immigration scholars remain blunt about the improbability of assimilation over the course of a few years, past or present: "Assimilation as the rapid transformation of immigrants into residents 'as American as everyone else' has never happened."[12]

To be fair, most Euro-American parishioners at All Saints did not engage in the romanticizing of the immigrant past or advocate the banning of Spanish or Latino cultural expressions. Only a small cross-section of Euro-Americans at All Saints called for this kind of forceful assimilation of Mexican migrants. In a parish survey, only 15.5 percent of Euro-American parishioners thought that having church with both cultural communities would work only if people spoke English and learned American customs. Moreover, though 27 percent of Euro-American responses from the survey came from people forty-years-old or under, only 5.5 percent in that cohort agreed with that statement.[13] This suggests a possible "cohort effect." Because those under forty either grew up or lived through their twenties in a Havenville characterized by the presence of the Latino community, they found Spanish language and Mexican customs unremarkable. More people over forty, however, found it unusual, as they remembered the city more clearly as it was before.

Relational Language and Unity

For Euro-Americans seeking to adjust to their new multicultural environment, assimilation had the virtue of being a clear path with low cost to themselves. Yet not a few Euro-Americans at All Saints found fault with that clarity and low cost. Several appreciated the hold culture had on immigrants. They saw it as unrealistic to expect a complete movement from one culture to the other. Some had immigrant relatives who had kept home country customs and spoke the language, and they had a keen sense of how difficult adaptation could be. Some simply empathized with the challenges implied in leaving one's home and family. Still others thought the very one-sided nature of assimilation made it untenable. It asked nothing of them personally, and that did not seem "fair." In general, the assimilationists at All Saints did not believe that the culture of the newcomer had anything to teach them. But most Euro-Americans had at least some passing interest in or felt some responsibility to learn about the culture of the newcomers. They visited Mexican restaurants; a few came to Spanish masses; some appreciated bilingual worship.

Among those Euro-American parishioners who rejected assimilation, a number used the language of love and relationships to reconcile themselves to the changes in their parish and city brought by the growth of the Latino community. The music and liturgy director, Joseph Davis, said, "I think [the mission of the parish] should be to promote or facilitate better relationships between the Hispanics and Anglos. I think that should be done with relationships, not just setting up a bilingual mass or program execution. Actually have meals together, games together, do things together." I have already mentioned the first communion teacher who compared the two communities' relations to that of a mother-in-law and daughter-in-law. Most, however, had no metaphor or particular plan for the relationship between the two communities. They just found the terminology of interpersonal relationships a satisfying way of talking about the two cultures in the shared parish. During the English morning mass on Mother's Day, a twenty-two-year-old woman and her mother were in the church basement heating up a bottle for the infant of the former. The daughter told me that she simply likes having the Latino parishioners around. Her mother agreed. Pressed for an explanation, the mother told me that, like her daughter, "I'm a lover." Joe Grabowski, who brings communion to nursing homes, hoped that Latino parishioners felt accepted in the parish: "You don't want them to feel uneasy. That's the last thing you want the Hispanics to feel. . . . And if you can't speak English, well then that's fine. At least we want them to know that." One of the teachers at the parish school also used the interpersonal language of acceptance, "I think as a community we need to be accepting of the Hispanics also, as far as a community." She appreciated the generosity of gestures she saw in the Latino community, such as the demanding job of making of tamales for parish events. She was learning to be comfortable when she ended up being the minority at parties and events.

A few Euro-American parishioners went beyond the language of relationships and actually worked at developing cross-cultural relationships. One research team member, a parishioner in her seventies, talked about what she had learned in her decade-long friendship with a Mexican-American couple in the parish. A parishioner who is an official with the national Catholic men's organization the Knights of Columbus intentionally partnered with Latino Knights he knew to promote the formation of Latino Knights of Columbus councils across the state. The Latino men would take the lead on this, but he accompanied them and supported them in it. He thought some of his most effective support was serving as a "lightening rod" when Euro-American pastors or parishioners resisted the idea of a distinct council for Latinos. Other parishioners' efforts to form relationships were simpler and more discrete. For example, one evening the Euro-American young adult group attended the Spanish mass and afterward invited a cadre of Latino young adults to dinner, using me as a translator.

What then should we make of this nebulous use of the language of relationships and love to speak of the two communities at All Saints, talk that occasionally turned into concrete action? We need first to understand better how Euro-Americans customarily use this language. In the 1990s, sociologist Ann Swidler did an extensive study of the way middle-class white Americans talk about love.[14] Though she looked at narratives of romantic love, her conclusions have some bearing here. She also found people vague and indeterminate in their use of the language of love, though she managed to ferret out two different discourses of love at work among her suburban Northern California subjects. One she called the "mythic view of love," that is, love as intensely emotional, a clear and enduring choice, unique to each couple, and transformative through various obstacles.[15] She contrasted this with a "prosaic-realistic view of love," where ambiguous relationships grow over time, require commitment and hard work, are not unique, do not depend on one's emotions, and can come to an end. Swidler argued that the institution of marriage has given rise to both of these narrative frameworks, and that both support it. The mythic view as a cultural narrative powerfully facilitates courtship, in part because American life has no strong institutional structure for courtship, such as arranged marriage.[16] The prosaic-realistic cultural narrative, on the other hand, helps people to maintain already established marital relationships.[17]

While Swidler writes primarily about the way the institutional structure of marriage shape the narratives of a culture, her theoretical construct applies by analogy. For many Euro-Americans at All Saints, the attractive cultural narrative of love and relationship provided a resource for bridging the gap between cultures that Euro-American parishioners found so troubling. Instead of marriage, the institution the narrative surrounded and supported was the shared parish. Though it had much less influence in people's lives than marriage, the shared parish was an institutional arrangement that structured people's lives and expectations. It created requirements for cooperation—primarily the need to negotiate sharing the parish spaces—and it generated expectations about each community's adaptation to the other's presence. At the same time, it did not generate firm institutional structures to facilitate that cooperation or adaptation. There existed a kind of gap, and Ann Swidler argues that the elaboration of culture often occurs in the gaps between institutional structures. Moreover, this cultural elaboration fit well with general practice in Euro-American culture, putting the onus on individual action and choice.

Additionally, the language of love and relationship at All Saints seemed to have "mythic" and "prosaic-realist" strains. Few of the people I quoted above who spoke of a relational strategy had much experience with actual cross-cultural relationships, and consequently they remained perhaps a bit idealistic about the power of personal connections and the subsequent possibilities for intercultural reconciliation. When asked why she appreciated the presence of Hispanics and wanted to reach out, the mother simply said, "I'm a lover." The older man active in the community hoped that hospitable outreach would ease the transition for newcomers. "We don't want them to feel uneasy," he said. But those who did have more extensive cross-cultural experience were much more likely to acknowledge the complex challenge of a relational strategy. It was work. The teacher told a story about being the only white mother willing to come to a Hispanic family's birthday party. The Knights of Columbus official went as far as to strategize cross-cultural relationships. He built up multicultural teams of Knights who would make the pitch to pastors for the creation of Hispanic councils. He encouraged the Hispanic men to do the talking while he would step in to support them and accept any negative feedback from the pastors.

Addendum: Bridges without Blueprints

Most Euro-American parishioners did not have a consistent way of talking about unity like those who used either assimilation discourse or the language of love and relationships. But they still thought about unity as important. A local college student, Joanna Hogan, called overcoming the obstacles that separated the two communities "the most important thing that is going on at All Saints." But she admitted this was her first experience with such a parish, and she knew little about it. On the other hand, the veterinarian Peggy O'Brien had once seen the separation between the communities as a problem only assimilation could resolve. But she had softened as she saw the priests working more smoothly back and forth, and she hoped for a similar cooperation between the two communities.

Some of the majority group had practical ideas for building bridges between the two communities, even though none of these ideas amounted to a coherent, shared discourse of unity. Liliana Blount saw the mission of the parish "to move forward and to build a strong bridge between the Anglo and Hispanic communities." She hoped more people would attend the bilingual masses, and she felt the English as a Second Language classes helped. She also felt it would help if people learned some Spanish. Don Terembula thought Father David's leadership was crucial and already had made a difference. The Catholic convert Earl Fanucchi agreed: "I also like about how [Father David] includes the Hispanic ministry—their activities, particularly their traditions, what they do at Christmas time, when the young girls are recognized [as] adults [at the quinceañera ceremony], and when he includes Father Nacho up there, and how he compromises with him, so that he's more a part of the mass than just being up there as a kind of lame-duck." The Potts, on the other hand, believed that simply recognizing the two communities' common Catholic faith could accomplish things. The Spanish mass was a help, not a hindrance. They also felt that the parish could function as a leader for the Latino community and a negotiator between the two communities in the city. Vince and Ann Connor, members of the liberal-leaning small faith group, suggested joint social activities as well as activities like music that did not require conversation. Few of these parishioners had opportunities to put such ideas into practice. Perhaps the most impressive example of action came from Tony Marcusi, chair of the stewardship committee, who passionately wanted to integrate his committee. Not wanting only token representation, he first got the feedback and support of Latino members of the parish council. Then he made an appeal before the Latino ministry heads committee, which was the real power center in that community. This bought him a lot of goodwill as well as substantial cooperation in the stewardship program. Eventually the two communities hosted a joint "ministries fair" advertising all their good work to the rest of the parish.

Enacted or not, an ad hoc quality surrounded this group's proposals, an open-ended creative pragmatism not unlike that which created the shared parish in the first place. This discourse of "building bridges without blueprints" should surprise no one. The parallel track structure of the shared parish meant most parishioners had only occasional and cursory interactions with people from the other major cultural group. Thus, many parishioners appeared game to try a variety of things, but they had few opportunities to test their ideas. None of the community members except Tony Marcusi were leaders with sufficient social capital and commitment to see their proposals through. Yet most of them were quite creative with good social skills. It would be interesting to revisit them in ten years to see if their ideas had coalesced around certain frameworks or proposals. Their proposals might well one day be part of a parishwide effort to bridge the communities.

The Latino Community: Unity and Power

One day Latino Eucharistic ministers (lay people who distribute the host at mass) gathered for a meeting after the Sunday Spanish mass. An impassioned discussion emerged around two issues: people not showing up on scheduled Sundays and too much wine left over after mass. Some of those present framed both issues not as practical but moral issues—proper commitment to a valued ministry, on the one hand, and proper attention to sacred ritual, on the other. An opposing faction worried that they had drifted over into excessive criticism of others rather than humility. No resolution seemed likely. Finally, a young mother pointed out that the purpose there was not to point out people's errors but to ensure unity (of practice) in the community. The coordinator affirmed that, as adults, they could disagree with one another and still maintain unity. The episode illustrates both the factional disagreements that sometimes shook the Latino community—and the Anglo community, for that matter—and the way in which unity within *la comunidad* proved a preoccupation of Latino parishioners.

In interviews, Latino Catholics at All Saints echoed this sense of the crucial importance of unity within their own community, more so than across cultural lines. The Delgados, for example, worried about the rupture between the relatively unified group involved in ministries and the vast number who "only" attend mass. Pilar Herrera, the young mother and parish teacher of religious education (catechist), said, "[The important thing is] the growth of the community in general, although we are of different [Hispanic] races, mestizo race [*la raza*] is that which unites us; the activities [of the parish] are like droplets of water and that grow and become a rain of which unites us to Jesus."

The Morenos, who served the Latino community as head catechist and youth minister respectively, described the priority of internal unity directly. They thought it should be the primary mission of the Latino community within the parish. Youth minister Gaby said:

> First that as Hispanics we must unite, that is to say, that we unite first because you cannot—you cannot—as the saying goes, you cannot rip open one hole to cover up another. . . . First we seek the way to unify ourselves among Hispanics and seeing that accomplished, we find a path . . . we go by another path and seek to unify ourselves with the Anglos. Because how will it be if some unite with the Anglos and where then are the rest who remained?

Her husband Javier, the head catechist, added:

> The mission should be the same for everyone, should be Jesus, that is, how to love one another. . . . so I believe that this is the search to love one another—I say the same as [my wife]—how am I going to love the Anglo person when I cannot love someone from my own race?

Javier went on to note the cultural differences among Mexicans, usually because they came from different states in Mexico. He urged more unity without "disregarding the Anglo" or suggesting that all the focus be on internal unity and only then afterward on unity with the Anglos.

Subtly operative in this dilemma were old and sometimes stereotypical worries about the fractiousness of Latin American communities.[18] But even more so, this focus on internal community unity emerged from the larger asymmetrical power dynamics of the parish. Euro-Americans sought cross-cultural unity, but they sought it from an unconscious position of strength. Their culture indicated the terms under which the institutions of the city, the economy, and the parish operated. On the one hand, this does not equate to an intentional abuse of power. The Latinos were newcomers to a world of established institutions, and some Euro-Americans did strive to equalize the playing field by learning about Mexican food, language, and customs. Nevertheless,

Euro-American parishioners had been formed in a social context where power-differentiated conceptions of race impacted culture and institutions.[19] Historically, they and their ancestors enjoyed better socioeconomic status and greater influence over political and economic institutions. Culturally, it felt "normal" to them to have social advantages. But this racial privilege remained largely invisible to Euro-Americans; many bristled at even the suggestion that they had some sort of power advantage. Other researchers have also noted the invisibility of asymmetrical power relationships to dominant groups in churches: "This was a common misuse of power that I observed in multi-racial congregations—the power to declare that power imbalances do not exist, are off-limits, or will not be addressed."[20]

Latino parishioners had an acute awareness of the asymmetrical power situation they had entered. In comparison to the Euro-American community's socioeconomic diversity, residential stability, U.S. citizenship, English fluency, and cultural and racial privilege; the Latino community was disproportionately poor and working class, majority immigrant with few adult U.S. citizens, culturally socialized elsewhere, and was racially "other" in this historically white part of the Midwest. They knew they were outsiders without the advantages that longtime residents had. Jerome Baggett's research on multicultural parishes in California noted a similar awareness among people of color there: "Members of these multicultural parishes perceive community through the lens of their outsider status and, accordingly, employ narratives of difference in conceptualizing it."[21]

Still, several Mexican parishioners at All Saints expressed gratitude that the Euro-American community permitted them—a group of outsiders—to worship there at all. While this might sound like a "colonization of consciousness," an internalization by the subaltern group of the dominant group's perspective, it often occurred alongside more critical analyses of Euro-American power and privilege at All Saints. Indeed many scholars caution us against prematurely equating an acceptance of disadvantage by the subaltern group with a situation of total and unfettered domination. Discourses of resistance often coexist with discourses of domination, often in internal dialogue only intelligible to the dominated (what James Scott calls the "hidden transcript").[22] At All Saints, Latinos knew they had little control over the larger power arrangements under which they lived, let alone the terms of intercultural encounters within the parish. Yet, out of earshot of Euro-Americans, one Latino leader complained that any bridging of the communities always involved her going to the meetings of her counterpart in the Euro-American community, never vice versa. Sardonic humor about the relative privilege of Euro-Americans emerged in everyday conversation in Spanish.

In any case, given the context of asymmetrical power, Latino parishioners wanted to retain control over what they could control—the community's distinct space for ministry, mass, and leadership. Protecting a "safe space" for Latino ministry—maintaining separate ministry offices, supporting mass in Spanish, sustaining religious education in Spanish, keeping distinct ministries going—retained a higher priority than any intercultural dialogue over which, in the end, the dominant Euro-American community had greater control. Thus, for example, a catechist confided to me his hope that the opening of a new Hispanic ministry building would obviate the need for more intercultural contact.

In spite of this understandable urge to protect safe space, a minority of people in the Latino community saw building bridges with the Euro-American community as crucial to parish life. Some of them were the same people who expressed strong caution about such unity. In part, this indicated the simple hope for better relations in the future. One man said he remained hopeful that faith could bridge misunderstanding, despite his own negative experiences of Anglos in the past. In other cases, leaders saw that the practical dilemmas of sharing a parish demanded some intercultural dialogue, a situation we will explore in the next section. Finally, I should note that many of the most serious promoters of unity with the Euro-American community were younger men. Omar Cervantes, a young single man (and research team member) who read at mass and trained the altar servers, had Euro-American acquaintances at his job, and he appreciated opportunities for the two communities to get together. An usher friend of his made a point of thanking Euro-American ushers at the end of the Sunday bilingual mass. Omar's friend Jorge Alvarez, who was bilingual and attended secondary school in the United States, hoped that more knowledgeable intermediaries could help with the crucial task of bridging the two communities. Another young man, Juan Carlos Estevez, called the two cultures being together "nourishing."

Many of these men worked side by side with Euro-Americans in factory jobs. They shared tasks and the same supervisors. Both Jorge and Omar had Euro-American guests at their weddings. In short, these men had less asymmetrical power relationships with the Euro-Americans in their lives than others in the parish did. Not surprisingly, this had a major effect on their perspective. One of these men explained, for example, how the bilingual Sunday mass had changed his mind about cooperation. It put the two communities on a more equal footing; he got an opportunity to meet Euro-Americans who welcomed worshipping together instead of looking upon Latinos merely as "strange people" (raros). This suggests that fomenting more equal power dynamics could create the possibility for more openness to intercultural cooperation and unity. Much of the structure of life in Havenville made this difficult. Latinos remained overrepresented in menial service jobs and whites in professional jobs. Shared parish life, however, could provide greater opportunities for side-by-side cooperation—service projects, parish beautification, various committees, perhaps even a bilingual or bicultural retreat. Parish leadership would need to initiate and coordinate such efforts.

Intercultural Encounter and Grief

Up to now, I have focused attention on the *talk* within the parish about the relations between the two cultural communities. This reflects what I and others observed during my year at the parish. Neither community at All Saints placed a high value on the planning or managing of concrete intercultural encounters. In fact, the institutional structure of the shared parish more or less restricted the amount of intercultural contact. Parish life occurred in two relatively encapsulated spheres of operation—distinct masses, separate religious education, multiple ministries catering to one community or the other. This structure permitted the Latino community a culturally distinct parish life less encumbered by the asymmetrical power relations within the political and economic institutions of the locality. The shared parish structure allowed the Euro-American community to maintain previously established patterns of parish life. As a result, most parishioners spent most of their time in distinct worlds. And when those distinct worlds did collide, it felt like something out of the ordinary, a departure from customary practice.

For many Euro-Americans in particular, demographic change felt like an experience of loss. Joan Bucher, a middle-aged Euro-American who sang in the choir at All Saints, told the story of such a collision of worlds at a meeting she had organized in the church basement: "I got down there, and [the Latinos] were all over the place down there. . . . [The parish secretary] told me that they would be down there, but they would be winding up. But they have the whole basement of the church." Joan tried to find someone to talk to about this, but she spoke no Spanish and the people she encountered kept saying, "No English, no English." When she secured someone willing and able to speak with her in English, she found the Latino group more than willing to move across the floor to accommodate her group. Yet she remained annoyed, even weeks later as she told the story. She ended her account of the incident noting, "I've supported this parish for forty-some years, not tremendously financially, but I've been a big part of it, I've tried to put myself into it, and I should count for something."

Why did Joan Bucher take an event that ended relatively well so personally? True, language and culture gaps inevitably make for a certain degree of frustration. Yet Joan immediately interpreted the situation in terms of the ascendancy of Latinos and the demise of her significance in the parish. From my own outsider perspective, however, she *did* "count for something" in the parish. She was friend to the pastor, coordinator of a high-profile event, and she was later appointed to a major leadership position. Moreover, the still-large English-speaking community had twice the number of ministries the Latino community had, and it held on to more positions of authority in the parish. Yet her deeply emotional plea echoed comments by other Euro-American parishioners, people who also worried about the ascendency of Latinos and their own descent. The parish RCIA director worried that All Saints would become like two other parishes in the diocese where Latinos now formed the overwhelming majority and occupied most of the pastor's attention. A man sitting next to me on a plane even spoke of "El Havenville," as if Latinos had already "taken over" the city.

To some extent, intercultural communication theory explains well this fearful overestimation of the strength and influence of a different cultural community. After all, intercultural encounter naturally breeds anxiety and uncertainty. "Social anxiety occurs when we are motivated to present a particular impression in our interactions, but we doubt that we will be able to present that impression."[23] Simply put, we do not know how to predict the responses of a culturally different stranger. The kind of everyday conversation that most people perform without thinking begins to provoke angst. We lose confidence in our ability to interact with others.[24] Above a certain threshold, anxiety and uncertainty overwhelm us and make communication supremely difficult. Clearly Joan Bucher had reached this threshold. And Catholic pastors and pastoral theologians acknowledge a need to attend to the anxieties of Euro-American parishioners during periods of demographic change.[25] Yet Joan's reaction suggests more than just anxiety; it indicates an experience of perceived diminishment, grief, and loss.

One pastor of another midwestern shared parish, Fr. Stephen S. Dudek, emphasized to me that Euro-Americans in his parish experienced this kind of loss and grief as the sights, sounds, and smells of their neighborhood changed dramatically. Instead of jazz or rock 'n' roll, they heard *ranchera* music bursting forth from car and home stereos. They smelled the fixings for tacos cooking in restaurant and church kitchens. They heard Spanish on the street, a language they could not decipher. At the same time, the immigrants themselves experienced this kind of grief, having lost their homeland and families, unable to return for family funerals, watching their children develop into people culturally unrecognizable to them. He called the shared parish a "crucible of grief."[26]

Grief classically manifests itself with emotions like anger. The social world of Euro-Americans at All Saints was altered without their permission, without any recourse, and within a relatively short period of time. Frustration and anger were natural responses, but Euro-Americans in Havenville did not necessarily recognize or feel empowered to direct their anger toward those who had brought on the changes, such as the local factory owners who hired or even recruited immigrant workers. Sociologist Arlie Russell Hochschild notes:

Insofar as anger is deflected at all from its "rightful" target, for example, it tends to be deflected "down" into relative power vacuums. So anger is most likely to be aimed at people with less power and least likely to be aimed at people with more power. Anger runs in channels of least resistance. The pattern is clearest in the case of the *expression* of anger, but I think in a milder way it is there also for the very experience of anger.[27]

Euro-Americans did not get angry with the factory owners, over whom they had little influence, but they did at times get angry with the Latinos who lived in their neighborhoods or worshipped at the mass after theirs.

The anger of grief can also get suppressed rather than deflected, especially in environments like Havenville that emphasize emotional reserve. Robert Wuthnow, in his book on the midwestern states, writes of the unspoken norms found in midwestern towns:

A farmer described the prevailing sentiment this way: "When we have problems, we don't publicize them. We don't advertise them. The community is small enough that people know when members are in need and will make their donations or provide their labor." It was his view that neighbors more often provided labor than money, not because they were "tight-fisted," but because they recognized one another's pride and "don't want to step on that."[28]

Accordingly, at All Saints we saw much frustration and occasional flashes of confused anger (like that of Joan Bucher) but few overt and dramatic expressions of loss. People kept it in.

Joanne Joyner, the head catechist in the Euro-American community, was perhaps one of the few who could articulate the loss and frustration people felt in response to the demographic changes:

What frustrates me if you want to hear my frustrations . . . is just that [change] is happening. And that could simply be that I'm old-fashioned. The fact that the midwestern face is changing; I don't like it. I want it to be like it was in the fifties. I don't like to see things changing to the point, I don't like to see—it just is the wrong mix to go down Main Street and see so many stores that have Spanish on the front of them. I don't want to sound like I am prejudiced; it's not that, it's just that it's not Midwest America to me because I'm older. . . . But I may as well get over it. As well as should the rest of my friends.

Fr. Tim Bacik, a priest who did training for the lay ministry training institute that met at All Saints, noted that it had taken decades for Catholics to "become like everyone else," especially in an intensely Protestant town like Havenville. Then thousands of poor Mexicans moved into town. They had not only broken down the homogeneity of the previous cultural environment, they had disrupted the dominant Catholic cultural narrative: former immigrants who had long ago made good. As if to echo Bacik's point, one of the few upper-middle-class parishioners at All Saints blamed immigrants for the more working-class orientation of the stores in the area: "I think that everything is driven now by the immigration . . . I think if you look at the kinds of stores we have, and I think our economic base is lower middle class here, I feel like when we go into Kohl's, even the styles that are in the store are the kinds of things that I see the Hispanic girls wearing. So I just think that it's all driven, or basically driven by that."

Thus, having previously been the sole inheritors of Catholicism in Havenville, Euro-American parishioners now lamented a cultural narrative and a world lost to them. More accurately, given their emotional reserve, they struggled with lamenting it. The Catholic feminist scholar Marian Ronan has argued that suppressed mourning has become a major theme for Euro-American Catholics in the post–Vatican II era. Euro-Americans have watched the twentieth-century triumphs of Catholicism—the Neo-Thomist revival, middle-class success for the descendants of former immigrants, high mass attendance, large numbers of priests and religious sisters, the hope for a modern Catholic Church expressed at Vatican II—dashed by internecine battles within Catholicism, continued anti-Catholicism in U.S. society, and a wretched sex abuse scandal. Yet they have felt unwilling or unable to grieve these losses. Bringing feminist psychoanalytic and poststructuralist theory to bear on the subject, Ronan argues that the inability to mourn results in rigidity and an intolerance of heterogeneity: "Mourning and the inability to mourn thus have to do with people's ability or inability to tolerate difference and change. In many respects, the post–Vatican II Catholic fixations on abortion, contraception, homosexuality, clergy sex abuse, and women's roles in the church function as a similarly rigid defense against mourning."[29] Although Ronan's sympathies lie with liberal Catholics, she worries about rigidity, intolerance, and "near-totalitarian law-and-order rhetoric" on both sides of the ideological fence. She cites liberal Catholic demonization of the Vatican and a general unwillingness to consider the humanity of any priest sex offender.[30]

Whether or not there is a connection between the inability to mourn and rigidity, certainly pastoral work that focuses on helping people mourn and deal with the transition ultimately aids the practical work of unity and integration at shared parishes. In his interview with me, Fr. Stephen Dudek recommended periodically commemorating the parish's past to honor that grief. Indeed, we found that the exhibits we prepared on Havenville as a city and on the history of All Saints as a parish drew a great deal of interest and appreciation from Euro-American parishioners. People feel better when the past does not simply disappear without a trace but is somehow included in the present. Many Mexican parishioners also showed interest in the parish's past. It enabled them to compare with their own histories, deepening their appreciation for local Euro-American experience and for the city in which they had begun to lay down roots.

Intercultural Encounter as Negotiation

Not all parishioners at All Saints—Euro-American or Mexican—looked upon intercultural encounters in the city or parish as occasions for grieving. In fact, much of the time parishioners approached such encounters pragmatically—they constituted necessary negotiations for a shared social environment. Especially for parish leaders, negotiating to share the parish became an ordinary facet of parish life. Some of those negotiations had become institutionalized. The leadership of both cultural communities submitted calendar requests to the parish office in order to reserve meeting rooms for different ministries. They usually did this months ahead of time so that all requests could be accommodated without conflict. Over time three Latino parishioners and Padre Nacho served on the parish council, which advised the pastor for the entire parish. One Latino leader had for years been liaison to the

stewardship committee; its program had at least some annual procedures in place for both cultural communities.

Most intercultural negotiations at All Saints, however, actually
occurred in an ad hoc manner outside these limited institutionalized
settings. On any given day, for example, there arose the simple practical dilemma of how to greet or say hello to parishioners from the other
cultural group (in Spanish the *saludo*). Intraculturally, Mexican parishioners tended to shake hands with or acknowledge in some way each
person upon entering a room, but Euro-Americans often greeted just
those immediately in front of them. The differences were rarely resolved
totally successfully. Antonio Nuñez complained that Euro-Americans
ignored Mexicans, that in "their house," it was their responsibility to
reach out. Many people on both sides felt afraid to reach out because of
the language barrier, to which they made constant reference. But this
avoidance had become a kind of intercultural negotiation in itself. As
a Mexican woman in her early twenties put it to me, each side waits to
have the other talk to them first, so no one talks at all. Naturally, individuals on both sides did push beyond this and made meaningful efforts.
One elderly woman said, "All of the Hispanics that I approach going
in and out of church, they always smile. I always say, 'Good morning,
good afternoon, good evening.' I don't know if they understand what
I'm saying, but they will smile. And I know their smile means they are
acknowledging you. They are being respectful."

Greeting, of course, presented only the most elementary practical
dilemma that occasioned intercultural contact. More complex intercultural negotiation surrounded, for example, the religious education programs. Father Ignacio had created a parallel religious education program
in Spanish after he arrived in late 2000. Padre Nacho's program functioned differently from the already established English program, which
had to contend with parents struggling with Catholic identity and had
to compete for attendance with multiple extracurricular activities—soc-
cer, baseball, birthday parties. Padre Nacho, on the other hand, worried
less about conflicting activities and more about religious literacy and
people's lukewarm commitment to the official Church. Accordingly, he
had designed a program with strict attendance requirements, biweekly
classes for the parents; all religious education children were required to
sit together with their catechists at the 1 p.m. Spanish mass every Sunday.

By 2007, the coexistence of two programs occasioned repeated, sometimes tense intercultural negotiations. One presenting issue was Latino children laterally moving to the English program. When this happened, the monolingual Joanne Joyner, head catechist in English, hoped parents would continue to attend Padre Nacho's parents' meetings anyway, since she had difficulty communicating with them. Soon it became unclear whether parents were attending required meetings of either program. Father Ignacio grew impatient. He implied at a staff meeting that Joanne should prevent Latino students from going to the English classes entirely, since their families' real intention was to shirk their commitment to the Church by accessing a program with easier requirements. From Joanne's perspective, families were acculturating to the United States, preferring English for their children. Both heard the other's position on the matter but neither seemed to take it seriously, and they contented themselves with a kind of détente at the staff meeting.

Religious education was symptomatic of the most common form of intercultural negotiation at All Saints—the aforementioned need to work out the sharing of community space, including both parish rooms and parking outside. A disproportionately young Latino community with more children and a growing number of groups and ministries clearly needed more space.[31] Furthermore, in the early years of the twenty-first century, the Euro-American community had just finished paying off a 1990s expansion of parish facilities and parking lots. Now they found themselves negotiating over space they had never foreseen they would have to share with anyone.

Concretely, some parish staff members and teachers from the parish school (where the Spanish religious education classes were held) complained about missing items in the parish rooms and school supplies left out of place. Different Euro-American parishioners took hold of the idea that Latinos did not take proper care of the rooms they used and were not orderly. Rumors probably increased sensitivity regarding infractions. Accusations irritated Father Ignacio, who felt Latinos were being held to an unfair standard (especially with many young children underfoot). Manuel Nieves, who had been the head catechist of the Spanish religious education program, complained to me that school personnel asked him about the whereabouts of every pencil, so that he found it expedient to buy extra pencils rather than launch into another investigation with his catechists. On a parallel track, negotiation over parking came to a head after the late morning (10 a.m.) English mass, as English-speaking mass goers were leaving and Latino parents were entering the parking lot to drop off their children for religious education classes. If the mass ran just a bit over, the negotiations could become quite intense.

As in the case of greeting one another, negotiation did not always occur in a way that privileged face-to-face engagement. There was great risk in direct intercultural engagement, especially with the two distinct cultural worlds and a language barrier between them. Most Euro-Americans had no experience in a non-English-speaking environment, and many found the language barrier anxiety producing in the extreme. William Gudykunst argues, "One of the behavioral consequences of anxiety is avoidance. We avoid strangers because it allows us to manage our anxiety."[32] The risks of intercultural communication, however, took on more immediacy for Latinos, who remained acutely aware of possessing less influence. Miscommunication could lead to further restrictions on activity or the deepening of antagonistic stereotypes. Many had no legal papers to work and live in the United States, giving daily life a precarious edge in an era of raids and deportations. In fact, anxiety about legal status has been shown to affect not only immigrants but their native born family members and friends as well.[33] Under these circumstances, it was natural that people sought to avoid anything that might lead to conflict of any sort.

Avoidance seemed like a safer strategy, and it was rampant in Havenville and at All Saints. Families whose young children had once played together failed to acknowledge one another in the street. Even when specific invitations were given out by one community to attend an event of the other (such as the Christmas *posadas*), few came. Euro-American parishioners told me that the solution to parking negotiations was to park on the street or get out quickly after mass, avoiding the issue entirely. At a Saturday morning workshop, I heard Father Ignacio give very specific instructions about parking as part of his welcome, remarking that all must follow them to the letter in order to counter the preconceived notions Euro-Americans had. Both communities submitted their room requests months or even a year in advance. In fact, I found the calendar of room requests the most organized element of life at All Saints, clearly designed to avoid confrontational intercultural negotiations on site.

Negotiating Committees and Worship

Despite these constant efforts at avoidance, face-to-face intercultural negotiations did occur. A small number of these were spontaneous, sparked by simple coexistence. A mother in the Euro-American community reported that friends of hers had found that someone had double-parked behind them at Sunday mass. They went from classroom to classroom through the parish school that morning, asking for English speakers in each Latino religious education class, hoping to find the family who had blocked them in. But most often face-to-face intercultural negotiation took place at events that deliberately brought together parishioners from both cultural communities. At most shared parishes, these events include parishwide social events, the meetings of a handful of joint parish committees, and bilingual or multilingual masses.[34] Parish social events generally draw a large group of parishioners, but parishioners at those events often socialize separately. Few such social events occurred at All Saints, a prominent exception being an annual Halloween Party fund-raiser for the parish school.

Joint committees at shared parishes—such as the parish or pastoral council, the liturgy committee, or the school board—draw a select group of parish leaders, who may become more accustomed to intercultural contact than most parishioners. These committees function either entirely in English or with ongoing translation. Limiting meetings to English may mean that parishes have trouble gathering a representation for joint committees that accurately reflects the demographics of the parish. For example, at All Saints, all of the Latino members of the school parent-teacher association were fluent English speakers. But fluent English speakers at All Saints often presented a different cultural and socioeconomic profile from the majority of the immigrant factory workers who formed the Latino community at All Saints. They might be factory supervisors or merchants, often born in the United States. Such committees might also have trouble recruiting Latino members. At All Saints, the committee preparing the parish photo directory had one Latina representative, a woman who—unlike most Latinos—had grown up in Havenville, spoke perfect English, and had married an Anglo man.

That same parish directory committee later got embroiled in a complex controversy over failed attempts to obtain photos from the parish's Latino ministries. The uproar occurred principally at the meeting of another joint committee, the parish council. Made up of ten parishioners (including three Latinos) and the two priests, the parish council met monthly. Business was conducted in English, but a secretary often translated for the associate pastor. At one meeting, one of the Latino members, Javier Moreno, brought up the lack of Latino photos in the directory. Though he normally spoke at the meeting in English, he carefully planned out his remarks in Spanish and asked me to translate. Looking at the parish directory, he said, you would think there were very few Latino ministries in the parish. He gave the group a full report on the Latino ministries of the parish, enumerating the participants in each ministry. He seemed to want to present a complete and professional accounting of things, but this more formal approach put off the Euro-American committee members, who had never seen him behave in this manner. They tried unsuccessfully to interrupt him. When Javier had finished his remarks, the council president noted that she had served on the directory committee. She explained that that they had consulted with Padre Nacho's part-time secretary to help them get photos but they never received any. In the heated discussion that ensued, Father Nacho pointed out that he knew nothing about this, and Father David inveighed against the "Monday morning quarterbacking" of complaints about the outcome of meetings no one would volunteer to attend. Finally, it became clear that Father Nacho and the committee of Latino ministry heads were the proper "go-to" people for such matters. If they had been involved, the directory committee would have gotten its photographs. Yet that structure of decision making had remained unknown and invisible to the Euro-American leadership. This demonstrated to me that the aforementioned patterns of avoidance exacted a certain cost whenever the two communities sorely needed to communicate clearly in order to negotiate sharing the parish.

*   *   *

In the end, committee meetings drew only a small number of leaders into the arduous process of intercultural encounter and negotiation at All Saints. Shared worship, however, is the one intercultural event that draws a wide array of people together at any shared parish. Bilingual or multilingual masses usually occur on major feast days at shared parishes—All Saints Day, Holy Thursday just before Easter, and Christmas midnight mass. They often involve a coterie of Scripture readings, liturgical music, and prayers in the different languages. Choirs or cantors will lead some bilingual songs, a number of which now populate Catholic liturgical music collections. The sermon is often given in a combination of both languages or in sequential halves in each language. Prayers are pronounced back and forth in different languages.

Bilingual or multilingual worship almost always creates tensions in shared parishes. The Catholic mass involves long-familiar prayers, music, and ritual action. Parishioners know them almost unconsciously through long experience. The negotiation and compromise of shared worship means each group loses some of their familiar words and actions, replaced by a parallel set of words in a different language and actions in the style of a different culture. A priest from my own religious community once told me that only bilingual people like bilingual masses; everyone else is confused. Invoking the infallible barometer of the collection basket, a Jesuit pastor in California noted that bilingual masses inevitably result in lesser donations. None of this should surprise the attentive observer. People at All Saints felt no different. Joanne Miller, a musician at the parish, summed it up, "I personally feel that when we try to do the bilingual things . . . you don't feel like you're part of either one." Not everyone felt that way. When Father David set up a regular bilingual mass at All Saints, a small number of parishioners from both communities did like it. But it taxed the musicians and priests with their limited bilingual resources and language skills. The mass was discontinued after a few months.

Bilingual masses most often occur on some of the most beloved annual celebration days, such as Christmas or the Holy Thursday commemoration of the Last Supper just before Easter. This can prove emotionally challenging. On the very days when people look forward to hearing particular and traditional words and music, and seeing particular and traditional actions, strange forms appear. People await "Silent

Night" or "Hark the Herald Angels Sing" and instead hear "Noche de paz" or "Vamos a Belén." On Holy Thursday, Spanish speakers expect to hear the gospel reading (John 13:1-15) begin with the words, "*Antes de la fiesta de la Pascua, sabiendo Jesús que había llegado la hora de pasar de este mundo al Padre, habiendo amado a los suyos que estaban en el mundo, los amó hasta el extremo.*" But instead they hear: "Now before the feast of the Passover, when Jesus knew that his hour had come to depart out of this world to the Father, having loved his own who were in the world, he loved them to the end." Theologian Allan Figueroa Deck has written dolefully about Latinos losing their distinctive Holy Week traditions as parishes press for multilingual liturgies.[35] The Jesuit sociologist John Coleman argues that bilingual masses work best on occasions other than the most emotionally resonant feast days—Pentecost and Thanksgiving Day rather than Christmas or Holy Week.[36] Unfortunately, church norms emphasize the need for a single parish celebration on the biggest feast days.[37]

At All Saints, a number of Euro-American parishioners expressed sadness at losing the distinct cultural rhythms and expressions of the Holy Thursday service as it became a bilingual celebration. Thirty-something parishioner Courtney Houser was one of them: "I can't look forward to going to Holy Thursday when I know it is going to be bilingual. What am I supposed to do when they are reading the gospel and my head is in the clouds because I have no idea what they are saying unless I am following along on my own." Joanne Miller agreed, "On Holy Thursday, I feel detached and I feel bad about that." Others felt ill at ease at Holy Thursday on account of confusing intercultural negotiations over the details of the shared mass. Padre Nacho noted that Latino liturgical ministers had come to previous Holy Thursday masses confused as to what they were to do. In one of those previous years, Father Nacho learned at the last minute that he had to offer a short homily. During the year I was present, a musician from the English-speaking choir lamented the confusing negotiations between the English and Spanish choirs over their shared musical duties. The two choirs had planned to sing together a bilingual hymn written in the United States, "Pan de Vida." At rehearsal, however, the Spanish choir members—who sing and play by ear and did not know the song—struggled with it. At the mass itself, they opted out and sang a different, lengthier song in

Spanish instead. The ritual the song accompanied ended, and the English choir did not have time to sing an old beloved favorite in Latin, "Panis Angelicus."

Nevertheless, the reports from the Holy Thursday mass were not uniformly negative. A Euro-American college student appreciated the mix of languages. Even though she could not speak Spanish, she felt she could follow the parts in that language. She loved that Father David pushed himself to preach part of the sermon in Spanish. Several Mexican parishioners agreed with her. Perhaps even more important, the bilingual celebration on Holy Thursday offered unique opportunities for gestures of reconciliation at All Saints. A handful of parishioners from both communities told me the story of offering the handshake of peace across cultural lines, some attempting the greeting of peace in the other person's language. In one case, this provoked a shared moment of laughter as each struggled to pronounce it to the other. In another case, a Euro-American pronouncing "*La paz de Dios*" provoked astonishment in a Mexican parishioner.

But a more public gesture of reconciliation caught the attention of several parishioners from both communities. The Holy Thursday mass traditionally includes a commemoration of Jesus washing his disciples' feet—a gesture associated with humble service. On that Holy Thursday in 2008, Father David washed Father Nacho's feet as well as those of several Euro-American and Latino parishioners. Javier Moreno noted, "In the twelve years that I have been living here in this area, in Holy Week, on Holy Thursday, the day of the washing of the feet, I have never seen an Anglo priest wash the feet of a Hispanic priest. I also mentioned this to another person from our parish. That family has been living here in the community more than thirty years. She has never, never seen that."

Shared People in the Shared Parish

Father David's washing of Father Nacho's feet made an impression on account of a concatenation of factors—the emotional resonance of a liturgical action traced back to Jesus himself, the public nature of that action, and the background of asymmetrical power relationships between Latinos and Euro-Americans. It also mattered that the liturgical action involved the two priests, each a leader who publicly represented one of the two cultural communities. Especially for members of the Latino community, the liturgical gesture of foot washing registered not as an interpersonal act of two individuals so much as the public act of two symbols of their respective cultural communities. They acted as intermediaries, performing a drama of humble service on behalf of the communities they served.

A parish shared by two or more distinct cultural communities always needs persons to act as intermediaries on behalf of and between those communities. Not everyone has the opportunity or the skill to navigate across language barriers and cultural differences. That is to say, a shared parish needs some shared people. The two priests at All Saints functioned in this way, usually in a more mundane and practical way than they did within the drama of Holy Thursday foot washing. For example, each solicited information about the other community's activities to help avoid conflicts of schedule. They negotiated on behalf of parishioners in conversations with parish school personnel, with the two religious education directors, with the parish musicians, with the bishop and diocesan officials, and even with local civic leaders at times. Because the two priests had decision-making power within the parish and social influence inside and outside the parish, they generally functioned effectively as intermediaries. But they were not the only "shared people" in the shared parish. In fact, parishioners often did not want to "bother" the priests. Some were intimidated by men they perceived to be highly educated or holy. And others just did not know when or how to get hold of a priest. Thus, the most common intermediaries at All Saints—and arguably at most shared parishes—were not the priests but the parish secretaries.

During my year at All Saints, two different women worked as parish secretaries, one full time and the other part time, both bilingual Latinas. The part-time secretary had come to the United States as an immigrant, though she had grown up in a large city back home and had a relatively high-status job at a bank in Havenville. Though she was a registered member of the parish and attended the Spanish mass regularly, she admitted to a lack of familiarity with the details of ministry and Catholic parish life in the United States. Despite her best intentions, this resulted in some miscommunication when she acted as intermediary. She often had to ask for clarification about religious vocabulary and parish procedures. We have already seen that she was unable to connect the parish directory committee with the leaders in the Latino community who could actually provide them with photographs. The full-time secretary, on the other hand, knew parish life very well, having worked at the parish for decades. She was American-born, raised in Havenville. Many of the Euro-American parishioners had known her and her Euro-American husband for years. Many Euro-American parishioners saw her as so like themselves that they would unguardedly communicate to her their negative feelings about immigrants and immigration, unaware of the cultural solidarity she felt with Mexican immigrants. On the other hand, her fluent Spanish and childhood immersion in Mexican culture gave her credibility in the Latino community, especially among Spanish-speaking parish school parents who relied on her. She herself identified with their struggles, having suffered some bias and prejudice as a young person. Yet she was not fully integrated into that Latino community. She attended mass more or less exclusively in English, and not a few in the Latino community saw her as culturally different from them—as really *americano.*

Sitting in the office and interfacing with parishioners, both secretaries became privy to a great deal of information about parish life. Both remained discreet about the private things they learned about parishioners. While their connections and knowledge often proved helpful to the priests, it did not always work out thus. As administrative support staff members who directly reported to the priests, they did not always wish to share information directly with the priests. Both found it difficult to convey information that included implicit criticism of the priests or potentially offensive words or stories. In my presence, they altered or sanitized their translations of others' words to avoid using harsh or angry language, even when the source people had used such language purposefully. This problem seemed more acute when they addressed the Mexican associate pastor. Although he insisted on accurate messages and interpretation, the relatively greater "power distance" in the Mexican community between priest and people often inhibited the women from communicating the blunt opinions of Euro-American parishioners and parish leaders.[38]

Parishioners called upon the services of other intermediaries at All Saints, though some functioned better than others. One day at a parish party, Father David rejoiced in meeting a Latina woman who spoke fluent English and worked in the local college and to whom he easily related. He hoped that she might serve him well as an intermediary with the Latino community, but she participated in fewer social networks in the parish than others in the Latino community. She could not help him much. As one of the few fully bilingual adults at All Saints with ties to both communities, I was frequently drawn into serving as intermediary in intercultural negotiations. On the key Mexican feast of Our Lady of Guadalupe, a Euro-American committee arrived half an hour before the Spanish mass had concluded, intending to decorate the church for the Advent season. When the service finally ended, they expressed to me some impatience and asked if I would intercede with Father Ignacio so they could begin their work. I went to Father Nacho and explained the situation, and he had no objection to them starting right away.

Other intermediaries operated in a more informal way at All Saints, sharing knowledge they had acquired to smooth out the sharp edges of cultural misunderstanding. For example, after a meeting of the Knights of Columbus, a complaint erupted about Mexican immigrants not learning to speak English. Two men chimed in, each noting that the first generation European immigrant ancestors of local whites had likely never learned to speak English. One of them, a parishioner in his sixties who owned fast food restaurants, described how his Mexican employees remain intimidated about speaking English lest they be criticized or misunderstood. He added that they were hard workers, despite stereotypes he hears about laziness. This mostly informal sharing counteracted a dangerous but very human tendency in a bifurcated cultural world like All Saints: to speculate in the absence of knowledge.

However well they function, intermediaries serve an important need when people share a social environment but do not understand one another's languages or cultures. The perception of bifurcated cultural worlds in a place like Havenville makes communication across cultural lines even more intimidating, as people feel the differences almost like a wall or gap in the earth. A young man in the Latino community at All Saints put it this way:

> We need more people to give us instruction and enlighten us in order to
> see how we can understand the other culture or they can understand us.

> Perhaps people that serve as bridges that speak with one culture as well
> as with the other so both cultures can understand each other, and be one
> church, and do things in the name of God.[39]

This is easier said than done, since bifurcated cultural environments usually involve highly asymmetric distributions of power. Intermediaries have to perform a delicate dance between official representatives with institutionalized power (like the two priests), influential representatives of the dominant group, and leaders in the less powerful group who nevertheless possess significant influence within it. We have already seen a bit of this dance in the reluctance of the parish secretaries to convey difficult messages to the priests, even when Euro-American leaders and the priests themselves insisted that they do so. Ann Neville Miller has found that the most appropriate intermediary depends on a confluence of factors, including placement in the cultural ecology and levels of authority.[40] The secretaries at all Saints had a favorable niche in the cultural ecology but they often lacked authority to facilitate the successful navigation of cross-cultural dilemmas.

Historical research helps us understand the delicate dance of acting as intermediary between communities (or cultural broker, as historians term the role). Historical research into the work of intermediaries between indigenous Americans and their European colonizers illustrates these complexities. Like the secretaries at All Saints, these cultural brokers had access to both cultural worlds—whether via language, mediating institutions such as government or church, or by growing up bicultural—and they used this access to negotiate the practicalities of daily life between two groups of unequal power sharing the same social environment.[41] Tales of the native intermediaries of colonial Oaxaca, Mexico, are instructive. These intermediaries or cultural brokers held together a precarious cultural and political order. They worked hard to maintain social networks and credibility in the colonized communities they served. Yet they also gained privileges, and often substantial power, through their participation in the colonial institutions of the Spanish. Similarly, the parish secretaries had to maintain language skills, cultural affinities, and social ties with the network of leaders in the communities they served. They gained status from their access to the priests and others' reliance on them, but that also put them at a distance from other community members. Like the Oaxacan intermediaries, they were perched precariously on the cultural boundary line.[42]

Not infrequently I myself felt that precariousness, perched as I was on the boundary between the Euro-American and Latino communities at All Saints. In order to conduct the research, I needed the trust of people on both sides of the cultural gulf. If I lost it in any permanent way, the project would be lost. I had to listen and attempt to understand, even when testimonies contradicted one another, when people spread misinformation, or even when individuals lobbed hostility at the other group. At the same time, easy empathy or apparent agreement with polemical positions—total rejection of any use of Spanish, perception of all whites as racists—could make me appear duplicitous, also destroying trust. If I never intervened in the face of false information (for example, that local gangs were brought in from Mexico or that white parishioners were members of the Ku Klux Klan), I would have exacerbated misperceptions that increased local antipathies. It was a delicate dance.

A final word is in order about the role of intermediaries as translators or interpreters. The work of translation or interpretation at All Saints was generally ad hoc. Secretaries interpreted at meetings and translated documents in the office. So did I. Children interpreted for parents. Even passersby sometimes got involved. Despite this informality and spontaneity, many of those who did translate or interpret recognized the subtleties involved and actively shaped their interpretations as a result. The full-time parish secretary admitted to me what I had observed, that she routinely softened or omitted the bluntest comments of Euro-Americans for the more indirect and formal sensibilities of Mexican culture. She saw this positively, as an intervention intended to minimize misunderstanding and create a more irenic environment between cultural groups. When I myself translated Javier Moreno's intervention about the parish directory at the parish council meeting, I felt the need to follow up after the meeting with an explanatory e-mail. His formal style of speech was seen by some Euro-American parish council members as haughty or intransigent, when in fact Javier aimed to be thorough and professional. I tried to underscore the difference in my e-mail.

Scholars of translation have long recognized the perilousness of interpreting someone else's words in a different language. Linguists

Eugene Nida and Charles R. Taber wrote, "The translation of a text with significant cultural differences is like a juggler trying to toss and catch a variety of objects at the same time."[43] Recent translation theory acknowledges that the meaning of a translation does not simply depend on the adequacy of the words used:

> The point is worth repeating: what an utterance means to its utterer and to the addressee of the utterance does not depend exclusively on the meaning of the words uttered. Two of the key determinants of how an utterance conveys meaning (and of the meaning that it effectively conveys) are these: the situation in which it is uttered (the time, the place, and knowledge of the practices that are conventionally performed by people present in such a time and place); and the identities of the participants, together with the relationship between them.[44]

The translation scholar Susan Bassnett argues that translators have always shaped the interpretation of original words, and we should not necessarily see this as negative. She argues instead for more reflexivity and transparency in the translation process.[45] Jewish studies scholar Naomi Seidman has written eloquently about the intrinsic power negotiations involved in language translation, intended or not.[46]

From All Saints Back to the Parish in General

In this chapter and the two that precede it, I have aimed to present a complex picture of the cultural transformation of All Saints' parish. I told the history of the parish and explained its bifurcated cultural context today. Next I organized the story of the transformation of All Saints into a shared parish around several prominent themes—struggles over the meaning of the social order, the interplay of identity and worship, and the role of new evangelization theology in the Latino community. I expanded on that in this chapter by drawing attention to the complexities of both perceptions and occasions of intercultural contact between the two communities at the parish. Now the specific story of the shared parish at All Saints needs to be put in the larger sociological context of the Roman Catholic parish in the United States. Telling the story of a single parish, after all, is not enough. We need a theoretical context to understand a widespread institution like the contemporary shared parish. That theoretical construct, however, has to be nimble enough to explain the particular dynamics of sharing encountered at All Saints. I turn to that challenge next.

4

Theorizing the Shared Parish

I began this study of All Saints in Havenville by characterizing it as a shared parish. I created the term to try to make theoretical sense of a double reality at the heart of this and almost all of the Catholic parishes of this type. On the one hand, All Saints functioned administratively as one church; it had one pastor recognized by the bishop, one set of administrative records and procedures, and a single campus with one church and one parish school. On the other hand, All Saints was two distinct cultural communities operating in parallel—English and Spanish, Euro-American and Latino, each with its own masses and ministries. The structure of the parish encompassed both aspects, often combined in an ad hoc manner. The church lawn boasted statues of the *Pietá* and of the Virgin of Guadalupe, both in a similar style. Inside the church, side-by-side laminated paper signs instructed people in English and in Spanish not to chew gum inside the church. The signatures of the two priests were affixed to both signs.

But making sense of this arrangement requires some work. Even the most involved All Saints parishioners strained to understand it. When I or a team member would ask people about the experience of sharing the parish with another cultural group, we could almost always see the respondent trying to work it out in his or her head even as he or she spoke. One fifty-something couple, Joe Grabowski and his wife, Rachel, initially claimed they did not know anything about the sharing of the parish, even though Joe as a daily mass goer and sacristan probably had more contact with people from the Latino community than most Euro-American parishioners. He began, "We don't see it a lot because—" He paused. Rachel completed the thought, "We normally go to our Anglo mass." Then they noted the "special occasions" when they did see the Latino parishioners—Holy Thursday and Christmas in particular. But then Joe went on, weighing it out as he spoke:

> I really don't consider this two different churches—the Anglo and the Hispanics. I guess I do consider it two different, because of the word "Anglo" for us and "Hispanic" for them, but it is one church. It is hard to explain, but I don't, you know, there's no conflict involved. But I really don't have a sense of a real togetherness mainly because of the difference in the language.

Joe then gave up trying to explain and instead related an anecdote about a Mexican man who attended the English mass and had recently begun to approach Joe and shake his hand for the sign of peace.

I believe that the term "shared parish" helps in trying to make sense out of this odd structure in which All Saints and other parishes like it function both as a single parish and as two distinct faith communities. I chose the term deliberately, but I also recognize that it departs a bit from accepted terminology. Sociologists of religion and congregational studies scholars tend to describe all local faith communities as congregations. In part this emerges from popular usage of the term among mainline Protestants, Evangelical Christians, Pentecostals, Buddhists, and Jews. But it also draws attention to existing sociological theory about how contemporary local faith communities in the United States, including Catholic communities, tend to take the institutional form of the "congregation," that is, the voluntary gathering of believers. Sociological studies of distinct cultural communities that share the same church building then become tales of "parallel congregations."[1] I agree that congregational voluntarism shapes Catholic communities in the United States. And the terminology of parallel congregations accurately captures the way two different cultural communities function at once independently and in parallel. But the term also obscures the administrative unity important to understanding a Catholic parish like All Saints, and it shortchanges the everyday process of negotiating the sharing of parish facilities that I described in the previous chapter.

Moreover, for many Catholics, "congregation" signifies vowed religious communities of nuns, brothers, or priests. Finally, historians of Roman Catholic faith communities almost always use the term "parish."[2]

Historical Trajectories

The word "parish" comes from the Greek *paroikia* related to the Greek term *paroikos* meaning "sojourner" or "resident alien" (a seemingly ironic use since *para-oikos* literally meant "next to the house," or, essentially, "neighbor"). Since resurrection rather than mortal existence was thought to be Christians' ultimate destiny, the double meaning made the term a suitable word for local Christian communities as early as the second century.[3] By the seventh or eighth century, faith communities had developed away from the urban *episcōpos*, the overseer or bishop. Each community had a presbyter or pastor, something like our concept of a parish or congregation today. These local leaders served communities in multiple contexts for multiple reasons. Thus, in Europe, rural faith communities developed their own churches because they were far from the bishop in the city; east of the Mediterranean and in the British Isles, monasteries began to form congregations for people who lived nearby; closer to the Mediterranean, shrine churches developed around sites honoring martyrs and saints; and by the ninth century in Germanized areas, the *Eigenkirchen* (private churches) served landowners and the populations of their estates.[4]

The highly structured and geographically oriented Catholic parish system familiar to Catholics today, however, dates to economic changes in Europe during the High Middle Ages. An agricultural revolution allowed peasants to live farther away from their manors in villages and towns with their own parishes, and a diversification of labor created larger cities with multiple territorial parishes. Ordinary people had a stronger relationship to their parish as a community, and the formal sacramental and penitential systems more closely organized their everyday lives.[5] Accordingly, the Fourth Lateran Council (1215) established requirements for annual confession and communion, church marriage, tighter observance of clerical celibacy, and better training of parish priests. During the Reformation, the Council of Trent (1545–1563) addressed corruption in the clergy and thus indirectly, the parish.

It required the establishment of clear boundaries between parishes. Priests had to live within those boundaries. Trent also obliged priests to preach and teach every Sunday.[6] The Councils of Trent and Lateran IV, while casting light on clerical abuses, had the side effect of canonically establishing the territorial parish system of the Roman Catholic Church. The territorial system not only addressed the reality of clerical corruption and battles over local power, it also contrasted Catholic practice with the Reformation Churches' theological idea of the church as a congregation, a gathering of the faithful (in Luther's German, *Gemeinde*). Reasserting the medieval geography of Christendom amidst the rise of the modern nation-state, it bound pastors to serve all people within the parish boundaries. The focus was on sacramental life administered by the priest as a means of eternal salvation.

This concise history of the origins of the parish as a structure and institution may give the impression that, for centuries, one kind of parish dominated the Catholic world. While the Tridentine decrees and the subsequent centralization of canon (church) law in the twentieth century (1917) reinforce this idea to a certain extent, the impression oversimplifies reality. Even when parishes possessed identical juridical structures, vast differences in culture, politics, and environment across time and space informed their everyday function and purpose. For example, in Spanish Latin America of the mid-sixteenth century, churchmen began to set up a European-style parish system. Coterminous with the *encomienda* system, it allegedly saw to the conversion and sacramental care of indigenous peoples commended to the "care" of the *encomenderos* or land grantees, that is, given to them for work.[7] Yet many of these parishes—aside from a few run by highly motivated mendicant orders—baptized many but catechized few. They defended even fewer from colonial cruelty.[8] Three hundred years later in Ireland, the long-established European parish system faced abysmal participation rates. And then 20 percent of the population died or emigrated during the potato famine of 1845–1850. In the wake of that disaster, the cardinal archbishop, Paul Cullen, became determined to transform and renew religious practice. He found the powerful wealthy farming class cooperative in that venture. In order to keep their considerable land holdings undivided and productive, they wanted to keep most of their children unmarried, chaste, and at home, and the strong patriarchal authority and sexual restraint of the Church assisted them.[9]

These two examples demonstrate the abiding challenge in understanding Roman Catholic parishes throughout history. Centralized authority with its universalized structures and law must be reconciled with the way in which historical and cultural context shape the varied functions, operations, and interpretations of such structures and law in the concrete. Put another way, a Catholic parish feels like something very fixed with clear boundaries and rules, while it functions at the same time as a very particular community with a unique history. In the case of All Saints, from its very beginning the parish had clear institutional structures—geographical boundaries, a priest pastor, an annual census of parishioners reported to the diocese, a set of consistent administrative records dating from 1860 that still rest in a safe in the parish office. As I discussed in chapter 1, however, the parish of All Saints actually turned out to be many different parishes through its history—small-town county-seat parish for German and Irish parishioners, devotional center for a Catholic minority, the social center of a growing Catholic community, suburbanized site for Vatican II reforms, and large shared parish with both an immigrant community and a Euro-American community.

This kind of tension between uniformity and particularity has had a paradoxical effect on Catholics' general understanding of the parish. Jerome Baggett locates this paradox in the nature of religious tradition itself: "Stated simply, religious traditions are paradoxical in that they both conserve and change. They preserve a particular conception of the sacred across time and space, but, in doing so, they ultimately alter that conception."[10] Baggett goes on to illustrate that American Catholics both accept central ideas from the tradition and appropriate them for themselves in their own context. In the same way, centralized ideas about the parish appear to predominate in the minds of U.S. Catholics, but many of these ideas—as well as their presumed interpretation—are actually a product of the particular environment of Catholics, or at least that of their theologians and leaders.

For example, the first centralized compendium of Roman Catholic church law, the 1917 Code of Canon Law, describes the parish as an internal division of the diocese (c. 216), the responsibility of a pastor (c.

451), and a "benefice," that is, a rightful source of income for the pastor (c. 451, 1409–1488). The idea of the latter, a benefice, is a vestige from the participation of the Church in the feudal culture of medieval Europe. That feudal vestige, as well as the focus on the rights and responsibilities of the pastor, emerges from the nineteenth-century Catholic hierarchy's rejection of modernity. The hierarchy used medieval nostalgia to argue against modern democratic traditions. The faithful were divided into the invisible and passive laity and the ruling clergy, both interacting within a static *societas perfecta* ("perfect society") that was the Church. To accomplish this, theologians lionized conceptions of a medieval Catholic synthesis.[11]

In a similar way, Euro-American parishioners at All Saints conceived of their parish as corresponding to a uniform Catholic ideal. Like any other parish, it had a church building with pews and an altar; it had a priest pastor who reported to the bishop; it had groups and activities to which one could belong if one chose. But these seemingly uniform characteristics were, in reality, the result of particular historical circumstances. The Second Vatican Council pushed the altar forward and made it the focus of worship; in the United States, this was often taken as license to make churches more "Protestant" by minimizing side altars, statues, and images. Pews were a late medieval invention in Europe that mushroomed as a result of the Reformation's emphasis on the Word and congregational worship, and the current uniform pew setup in Catholic churches came about as a rejection of the social inequalities of a "pew rent" system.[12] Moreover, having a resident priest pastor in a large, rural diocese like Port Jefferson meant the parish had a certain importance for the diocese. Finally, the profile of groups and activities manifested voluntarism, the very American idea that, for a nation of joiners, church participation is always a personal choice. Voluntarism is a significant part of de facto congregationalism, the institutional profile contemporary sociologists of religion associate with local faith communities in the United States.

Shared Parish Life and De Facto Congregationalism

Not infrequently in conversation and interviews, parishioners at All Saints spoke about their parish as a unique faith community. Some of them expressed this in terms of their choice of the parish. A middle-aged man told me he had chosen the parish on account of its cultural diversity. A young couple spoke of visiting numerous other parishes in the area; in the end, they chose All Saints because it catered to people with diverse socioeconomic backgrounds. Others chose the parish on account of the priests. A thirty-something woman said she liked the new pastor and his more relaxed style. The daughter of a longtime parishioner told the story of how her husband's desire to marry in the Church led them to befriend a priest that attracted them to the parish. Several people in the Latino community noted that All Saints had a uniquely strong sense of structure or organization, largely the fruit of Father Ignacio's labors. A few Euro-American parishioners referred to a certain friendliness or hospitable quality they had experienced from other parishioners. A mother of two said she felt "more comfortable" at All Saints, even though she did not live nearby. Parishioner Peggy O'Brien, a veterinarian in her forties, described arriving in the parish in the mid-1990s: "When we came here, we knew no one, and it was like the first day we came to church here we had six or seven people come to talk to us. . . . 'We've never seen you before. Have you moved here? Are you visiting?'" Of the thirty-seven formal interviews we conducted at All Saints, twenty-seven included some sort of claim about the uniqueness of the parish. Only four people said that all Catholic parishes were essentially the same.

Against stereotypes of Catholic uniformity—the Church as a multinational religious conglomerate headquartered in Rome but with local offices or branches—these interviews and conversations suggest a pervasive sense among All Saints parishioners of the parish as a congregation, that is, as a faith community chosen by its members and possessing a unique and emotionally significant esprit, or personality. Sociologists describe this very American approach to the local faith community as "de facto congregationalism":

De facto congregationalism [is] an institutionalized bias of American religious life toward affectively significant associations under local and lay control. . . . De facto congregationalism implies that the local religious community is in fact constituted by those who assemble together.[13]

Congregationalism in this sense has historical significance in the Reformation churches. William Tyndale first used the word "congregation" in his 1525 English translation of the New Testament. He used the word to render the Greek *ekklesia,* following Martin Luther's translation of *ekkelsia* not as *Kirche* ("church") but as *Gemeinde* ("community").[14] In American church governance parlance, "congregationalism" refers to Protestant church communities whose members themselves decide about the clergy leadership, financing, ministries, direction, and even—at times—the beliefs or creed, such as those in the Congregationalist or Baptist traditions of Christianity.

Sociologists identify this ecclesial tendency toward local decision making as an organizational form. According to thinking spawned by the "new institutionalism" movement in organizational sociology, the organizational form of the congregation serves as an example of institutional isomorphism, a tendency toward a single organizational form.[15] This single organizational form is widely available in the United States as a cultural resource for religious groups shaped by the presence of some institutions (for example, laws treating churches as nonprofit voluntary associations) and the absence of others (for example, government funding for Catholic parochial schools or a society-wide network of Buddhist monasteries). Local faith communities with different historical backgrounds access this common cultural resource in order to accommodate the larger institutional life of the United States.

The general characteristics of the congregation as an institutional form include: (1) a commitment to voluntarism in membership and participation; (2) achieved identity by choosing to join rather than by living in a territory; (3) lay leadership; (4) regular fund raising and nonprofit status; (5) professionally employed clergy; (6) cultural homogeneity of a greater or lesser sort; (7) multiple functions and activities; and (8) worship on Sunday.[16] According to several American sociologists of religion, even Christian groups with episcopal or presbyteral polities, such as Roman Catholics or Presbyterians, tend toward the congregational form in the United States. Paul Numrich and others have observed that non-Christian immigrant groups—such as Buddhists, Jews, and Muslims—do as well.[17]

The congregation as an institutional form arose as a result of the disestablishment of religion in the antebellum United States. The gradual withering away of established state religion during the Revolutionary era created a free space for an explosion of religion during the Second Great Awakening. A series of revivals and a general atmosphere of religious creativity diversified the religious makeup of the country. Religion turned into an achieved or chosen identity rather than an ascribed or given one. Immigration furthered that process. Religion became "a refuge for cultural particularity" for immigrants who struggled with their identity in a new land.[18] Over the long run, voluntary religiosity increased even as geographic mobility positioned people far from their original communities.[19] Disestablishment privileged flexible religious structures like the congregation to aid the development of religion in a society in rapid flux. It became "a tried-and-true way of concentrating religious energies in a society that approves of religion in general but doesn't provide it as a public service."[20]

This idea of American faith communities exhibiting a de facto congregationalism developed as part of a new approach to the sociology of religion in the 1980s and 1990s. This "new paradigm" came about as a reaction to early twentieth century sociological theories of religion, especially the sect–church continuum and secularization theory. The church–sect theory, as articulated by Max Weber and his student Ernst Troeltsch, placed faith communities on a continuum between the sect, charismatic and countercultural, and the church, compromised by the demands of institutional perpetuation and expansion.[21] Secularization theory, whose high-water mark was the publication of Peter Berger's *The Sacred Canopy* in 1969, posited that modernity's disenchantment of the world would gradually make traditional religious practice and belief irrelevant.[22] These theories framed an understanding of religion itself and local faith communities in particular as moribund bastions of a vanishing age.

Yet, especially in the United States, religion did not wither away. By the 1980s, sociologists of religion began questioning secularization theory and looked for new theoretical ways of framing the sociology of religion. For example, some began to use the cultural theories of Clifford Geertz to make sense of local faith communities, treating them as distinct cultural groups not unlike Geertz's Indonesian or Moroccan villages.[23] Others used rational choice perspectives to conceive of the American environment as a "religious marketplace" where

different groups could compete for membership.[24] De facto congregationalism itself emerged when sociologists tried to make sense of the
organizational complexity of local faith communities. They recognized
that faith communities functioned as open, indeterminate systems
with multiple purposes.[25] At the same time, these indeterminate systems tended toward the more-or-less standard institutional form, the
congregation.

Not all sociologists of religion agree with this assessment of American religion, that all groups eventually adopt some form of de facto
congregationalism. Of course, a full evaluation of de facto congregationalism as a hypothesis goes beyond the scope of this book.[26] Nevertheless, we need to understand to what extent the concept can be used
to understand Catholic parishes in the United States. Are they really
congregationalist at heart? Many scholars, including Catholics, think
so. R. Stephen Warner, perhaps the leading theorist of de facto congregationalism, certainly asserts its influence in American Catholicism.
So does the best-known contemporary historian of Catholic parishes,
Jay Dolan. Dolan has especially noted the importance of lay leadership in the period between the American Revolution and the Civil War,
though he also notes its strong presence in immigrant parishes of the
nineteenth century.[27] But sociologist Wendy Cadge cautions us about
congregational isomorphism. She contends that many assert de facto
congregationalism without placing it in a specific organizational field.
In her view, all the local faith communities of all religions in the United
States cannot constitute an organizational field; this is too large and
hodgepodge a collection of communities. Yet U.S. Catholic parishes
could constitute such a field: they are aware of each other, share information, conceive of one another as involved in a common task, have
leaders who share a common institutional language.[28]

There has been some general discussion of de facto congregationalism as applied to Catholic parishes. James Davidson and Suzanne
Fournier reviewed congregational/parish surveys that included both
Catholic and Protestant local faith communities, identifying both the
differences and similarities. Their critique of these surveys is that in the
large-scale comparative studies, several things occur: (1) congregational
isomorphism is assumed rather than assessed; (2) a degree of congregational autonomy and voluntarism is asserted that does not fit Catholic

circumstances; (3) the Protestant terminology of "congregation" and "denomination" is maintained despite its unfamiliarity to Catholics; and (4) Catholic parishes are so demographically underrepresented as to make conclusions tentative at best.[29] Manuel Vasquez, within a larger discussion of what the field of migration studies has to offer the study of American religion, finds de facto congregationalism wanting, especially vis-à-vis Catholic and other immigrant faith communities. From his perspective, its valorization of Protestant congregationalist polity amounts to "organizational Americanization" applied to immigrant religions, a crypto-normativism that ignores practical considerations as well as whatever cultural resources migrants bring from their own homelands. The result subtly enshrines American exceptionalism.[30] Sociologists Wendy Cadge, Peggy Levitt, and David Smilde also warn about the Protestant Christian "templates" implicitly guiding religious research. "They narrow the range of scholarly focus and filter the analysis through American narratives and frames."[31] They argue for "provincializing the United States," that is, rejecting the normativity of American Protestant models and making the United States into just one more geography alongside others.

David Maines and Michael McCallion undertook a specific investigation of de facto congregationalism in Catholic parishes in the Detroit Archdiocese. Their conclusions were less critical. They acknowledge contemporary evidence regarding voluntarism among Catholics—parish shopping and the decoupling of parish and neighborhood—but they also stop to explain intrachurch historical factors. A new, Vatican II emphasis on parish as community in the 1983 revision of church law replaced the exclusive focus on territory in the 1917 Code of Canon Law. Thus, they suggest that, in effect, we should not consider the congregationalism among Catholics as purely de facto but that it is also de jure, since church law itself has loosened its definition of where people must go to church. Furthermore, they regard lay leadership as encouraged by church law and leadership since Vatican II. The conciliar reforms indicated a "top down" rather than grassroots approach; they permitted and inspired greater lay leadership rather than simply justifying what already existed. Maines and McCallion also point to the way in which such reforms, for better or worse, coincided with an increasing focus on individualism and personal rights in American society.[32]

As I noted at the beginning of this chapter, my own research at All Saints confirms one way in which contemporary Catholics tend toward congregationalism. R. Stephen Warner sees Catholics' increasing sense of "ownership" of their parishes as a sign of congregationalism. This has historical roots in both trusteeism and the ethnic/national parishes of old, which were often specifically requested or even established by lay people who then financially and culturally sustained them for decades. Warner also believes that contemporary geographic mobility increases people's ability to choose their parishes, that is, to parish shop.[33] Paradoxically, residential stability may also contribute to voluntarism. When a certain percentage of parishioners have committed time and resources to the parish over the years and undergone multiple family rites of passage there—baptism, first communion, confirmation, marriage, funerals, and so forth—they really feel a sense of ownership over the parish. Two different elderly men at All Saints, for example, each with a long history at the parish, insisted that All Saints belonged to them regardless of what any pastor might do. One of them told the story of how he had confronted a beloved pastor twice for obstructionism, once for not consulting the people before forming a renovation plan, another time for refusing to accept Vatican II liturgical reforms mandated by the bishop. In another county not far from Havenville, a lay leader told me how older parishioners in his parish complained that they who "built the parish" were being "pushed out" by a rapid influx of Latinos.

Just because Catholics feel more "ownership" over their parishes, however, does not mean they actually own them. Legally, the U.S. Catholic parishes in most U.S. states are owned by the diocesan bishop as a "corporation sole." "The theory of the corporation sole is that a single person, by virtue of holding a particular title, can become a corporation."[34] Catholics as well as Episcopalians and Mormons make use of this legal form. It protects the authority of a single hierarch; most legal corporations—whether for-profit or nonprofit—vest proprietary authority in a corporate board of some sort. While corporation sole, like all legal structures, always exists in tandem with the informal power arrangements of any complex organization, it reminds us that any understanding of congregationalism in Catholic circles has to contend with the persistence of a centralized power structure.[35]

That centralized power structure privileges the authority of the priest pastor. The 1983 Code of Canon Law affirms that by virtue of church law the priest pastor has sole final authority in the parish, what we might call a "canonical monopoly." The pastor ordinarily functions as a solitary leader (canons 515 and 519) with full responsibility for decision making within the parish, especially administrative decision making (c. 532). He is charged with oversight of parish records (c. 535). Though church law encourages the advice of a pastoral council, it does not require it (c. 536). The only legal (canonical) requirement is that the pastor have a council of laypeople to advise him on financial matters, advice that remains consultative rather than deliberative (c. 537). Practically speaking, of course, many U.S. parishes have more shared authority than the law suggests. Professional staff—lay and clergy—share in decision-making authority. Nevertheless, while many European dioceses directly hire the professional laypeople who serve as music directors, pastoral associates, and religious educators at parishes, in the United States the priest-pastor almost always has sole discretion. Put simply, all lay employees serve at the pleasure of the pastor, who may dismiss them at any time for any reason the civil law permits. This is certainly not very congregational, and it has been shown to inhibit a greater collaborative spirit among priests and lay employees.[36]

Another indication of the limits of congregationalism (and associated voluntarism) in Catholic parishes may be the fact that they are more culturally diverse, a point of particular importance in considering the shared parish. Most Protestant congregations display what sociologists call cultural homophily; that is, their voluntarism has a "homogenizing" effect on their demographics. In the face of a complex and demanding world, people choose other people like themselves with whom to worship.[37] Now many Catholic parishes exhibit this tendency as much as their Protestant brothers and sisters do. After all, residential segregation reinforces cultural homogeneity in neighborhoods and communities, and Catholic parishes more often reflect their local geography than those Protestant congregations gathered exclusively by personal choice. But the recent Catholic custom of parish shopping may also (again paradoxically) prove to be a homogenizing force as people choose a parish with people like them. Parishioners establish the ecclesial equivalent of what the authors of *Habits of the Heart* call "lifestyle enclaves."[38]

Nevertheless, at least some research suggests that Catholic parishes tend to have more culturally or racially diverse congregations than most other denominational groupings.[39] With the higher percentage of Roman Catholics among immigrants, this should not come as a surprise. But clearly ecclesial structure and leadership matter, too. As occurred at All Saints, bishops and pastors (and the professional bureaucracies who work with them) can establish shared parishes even when parishioners would generally resist them in favor of homophily.[40] As most literature on multiracial and multicultural congregations indicates, given congregational choice, only a very small number of local faith communities would take on the challenge of building such a community and only under very limited conditions.[41] Thus, in a sense, it is precisely noncongregationalist elements—a centralized power structure and geographical ties—that permit the establishment of shared parishes as a substantial and growing element of Catholic parish life in the United States.

Finally, we need to consider in greater depth this central issue of choice in de facto congregationalism. Are Catholic parishes really voluntary gatherings of people? Certainly the data presented by Maines and McCallion on "parish shopping" in the greater Detroit area offers convincing evidence of Catholics choosing their parishes. Sociologist Jerome Baggett, who interviewed more than three hundred parishioners at six distinct parishes in the San Francisco Bay area, finds significant evidence that Catholics choose their parishes there. "They chose their current parishes and would conceivably choose other ones if their individual needs should ever change."[42] Even in Havenville, a city with one parish, located within a mostly self-contained county with only three other parishes, people described the experience of temporarily attending other churches, usually because of a priest they could not stomach.[43]

Behind this apparently simple question of whether people choose their specific faith community lie deeper cultural questions about the nature of choice in social groups. American sociologist Talcott Parsons spoke of social groupings as "achieved" or "ascribed." One enters by choice or by being born into them. Like most sociologists of his era, he saw a tension between these two social values. He imagined industrialized society inching toward larger associations valuing achievement and dispensing with the emotionally rich, ascribed group identities of the past.[44] "New paradigm" sociologists, however, see congregations as social groupings one enters by choice, but the resulting bonds remain affectively rich and oriented to face-to-face contact. Here American individualism complicates the picture. The individualist ethos conceives of all groups (even, in marked contrast to Parsons, the family) as voluntary. As a result, Americans almost always underestimate the degree to which some of the groups to which we belong have an ascribed quality. We are not sure we could belong to communities of people without having autonomously chosen them. But Bellah and his *Habits of the Hearts* coauthors note that local communities of faith often function in exactly that way: "The community exists before the individual is born and will continue after his or her death. The relationship of the individual to God is ultimately personal, but it is mediated by the whole pattern of community life. There is a givenness about the community and the tradition. They are not normally a matter of individual choice."[45]

For Roman Catholics living in a traditionally Protestant society, belonging to a parish seems inevitably to function as a choice about membership. Indeed, different parishioners at All Saints thought about it as such. They carefully described why their parish was unique and why they had chosen it. This was as true in the Latino community as in the Euro-American community. In the Latino community, the *evangelizar* narrative articulated by many parishioners celebrated a person's adult choice to be involved at All Saints and to educate himself or herself in the Catholic faith. That same narrative viewed those who had not made such a choice as "pew warmers" with a shallow understanding of their own faith life. But autonomous individualism can convey the impression that an isolated subject chooses amidst an open field of options. Yet most people chose All Saints because it was a Catholic parish, and they saw themselves as Catholic. Most Euro-American parishioners at All Saints had grown up Catholic. Choosing the parish confirmed an identity that they had not chosen but received as children. Many Mexican parishioners articulated their choice of All Saints as a means of deepening their participation in a Catholic community and identity they associated with their families and home culture.

Parishioners chose All Saints among the limited pool of Catholic parishes available to them. Many perceived the choice not as coincidental or even geographical but intentional for particular reasons. As Jerome Baggett puts it, "[Parishes] are institutional carriers of the religious meanings embedded in the symbolic repertoire that is the Catholic tradition, but not every parish does this the same way. Each one customizes this repertoire to better reflect the lived reality of its members."[46] Catholic identity, Baggett implies, is not a fixed thing, and parishes adjust accordingly. They offer the opportunity not only to be part of a Catholic community but part of a particular kind of Catholic community. We saw this at work in the small number of Euro-American parishioners who chose All Saints precisely because of its diversity or in the Mexican parishioners who approved of the organizational style. All of them wanted to associate themselves with a certain kind of Catholicism.

This fits well with discussion of the concept of identity in sociology and ethnic studies today. Identity comes not as the achievement of choosing a group to belong to or the ascription of having been born into one, but as "negotiated" in a world of limited choices. Stephen Warner emphasizes how migrants renegotiate their religious and cultural identities upon arrival in the United States in response to the particular cultural and institutional environment they encounter. Yet Manuel Vásquez reminds us that this was already true back in their home countries.[47] Identity is rarely entirely given or determined; people must negotiate their identities, both accepting the concrete circumstances they live in and making choices about them.[48] Negotiated identity emerges from the way a person manages his or her participation in the groups and communities presented to him or her. Identity includes both ascribed and achieved participation in groups.

What does all this mean for our understanding of Catholic parishes in the United States? At root, we must accept that de facto congregationalism does indeed describe something of the unique form and function of U.S. Catholic parishes. Because of a complex series of institutional factors in U.S. society—separation of church and state, individual rights, suburbanization, postindustrial capitalism, and the legal organization of religious groups as nonprofit organizations—Catholic faith communities in this country tend toward congregationalism. The elements of congregationalism—voluntarism, a personal sense of ownership, lay leadership, the importance of groups and activities—exist in most American parishes, perhaps more so than in Catholic parishes in other lands. At the same time, congregationalism does not adequately explain certain elements of parish life. U.S. Catholic parishes bring greater cultural heterogeneity. Power and decision making remain mostly centralized. And Roman Catholic identity has a translocal quality. Parish participation connects a person to a worldwide communion and its multiple shared symbols, even as particular parishes resource and manage that connection in unique ways. Moreover, the Catholic hierarchy of pope and bishops remains relevant to that resourcing and management of global Catholic identity. At least some of their teaching provides an agenda for Catholics framing their own identity, whether local parishioners' response to that teaching be conscientious observance, selective appropriation, or even thorough rejection.

In the end, if by "parish" we mean strictly a local ecclesial unit defined by firm geographical boundaries and uniform activities and authority structures, then U.S. Catholic churches are not really parishes. Too many people attend church outside their parish boundaries, and most Catholics see their local faith communities as unique rather than as interchangeably uniform. In that sense, the U.S. Catholic parish functions more like a congregation, a community defined by those who choose to belong to it. On the other hand, if a congregation is defined largely by its local presence and vests its final authority in a lay board, then U.S. Catholic parishes are not congregations. Local Catholic faith communities in the United States are both, and they are neither. Perhaps the seemingly contradictory term that historian Jay Dolan used to describe American Catholic parishes still works best—"congregational parish."[49]

The Shared Parish and American Catholic Narratives

"Congregational parish" may serve as the best approximation of the structure of U.S. Catholic parishes today, but we should take care in adopting the terminology uncritically. Dolan's notion of the congregational parish emerges almost exclusively from the Anglo-American

Catholic context after the American Revolution. The democratic impulses of the era had in part touched the Church of that time, which seemed to value lay participation more than in later years. Dolan's focus on voluntary lay participation in the congregational parish comes to us as a revisionist response made for the post–Vatican II American Catholic context. The postconciliar context did away with a view of Catholic uniformity as the last defense against the encroachment of the modern world. This allowed for a retrieval and rediscovery of uniquely American aspects of U.S. Catholicism, including democratic impulses during the Revolutionary era and subsequent reactions against them. Dolan and historians like him also wanted to challenge an exclusive focus on the actions of bishops and priests in previous American Catholic historiography. Finally, Dolan wrote in part for an American Catholic audience exulting in perhaps a peculiarly American reaction to the Vatican Council's recognition of the importance of the laity—seeing church as an experience of voluntary participation.

The contemporary Catholic parish—including the shared parish—shares in that uniquely American heritage, but too much focus on that heritage in understanding the congregational parish may inadvertently reproduce a conventional narrative of American Catholic history that minimizes the importance of immigrants and cultural diversity. Yet immigrants and their immediate descendants will soon become the dominant group in U.S. Catholicism.[50] This conventional narrative sees American Catholic history as a narrative about the Americanized descendants of European immigrant Catholics.[51] The narrative still sounds something like the following:

> But if the first generation of these [Catholic] ethnic groups clung to their respective ghettos, their children were much less content to do so, and their grandchildren broke entirely with the Old World framework and sought—with striking success—to enter the mainstream of American life. One of the clearest indications of this success is the swelling number of Catholic families whose income has enabled them to become full-fledged members of the affluent society of the late twentieth century. And with the new affluence these families, like their Protestant, Jewish, and non-religious counterparts, have long since quit the scene of their

grandparents' original settlement, indeed, even that of their parents, and are among the inhabitants of suburbia.[52]

While this articulation of the "migrant to mainstream" narrative comes from before the present era of immigration, many writers and scholars continue to make use of it. They supplement it with mention of the election of John F. Kennedy as president, some with the ecumenical and secular rapprochement encouraged by Vatican II, and still others with reference to the disappearance of distinctions between Catholics and other (Protestant) Americans in terms of attitudes and positions in society. The gist of the narrative, however, remains the same: Catholics join the Anglo-American Protestant mainstream.[53]

This narrative presents serious historical problems. It overlooks crucial pieces of American Catholic history—principally, the Spanish and Mexican Catholic heritage of the Southwest, the French Catholic heritage of Louisiana, and the African American Catholic experience in the southern states as well as several northern cities. But maintaining such a narrative today presents ever-graver problems. Given the demographic data—not only projections for the future but also contemporary surveys reporting that over a third of Catholics are Latino or Hispanic and over half of Catholics under thirty are not white[54]—maintaining the old narrative requires that we either (1) ignore the magnitude of the current wave of Catholic immigrants, (2) marginalize that wave as not part of the main story of U.S. Catholicism, or (3) consider their arrival a new development or break in the story (for example, speaking of the "new immigrant church"). While many Euro-American Catholics may inadvertently do the first, and some authors have done the second,[55] both stem from ethnocentric views of American Catholicism. Catholics simply cannot deny the scale of demographic change today, and they minimize its importance at their own risk.

The third option, considering today's immigration as a break in the historic pattern of immigration, requires positing a strong distinction between the nineteenth-century immigrant experience and that of immigrants today. Such a distinction between the two experiences of migration is generally predicated on the idea that earlier European migrants quickly assimilated into the dominant culture of the United

States while contemporary immigrants do not.[56] Yet this is not fully supported by historical data—on either side. Nineteenth-century Catholics remained divided on the issue of the pace of adaptation to Anglo-American culture; many German immigrants actively resisted it. Alejandro Portés and Rubén Rumbaut have similarly shown how both assimilation and resistance to Anglo-American culture form a part of contemporary Latino families' strategies of adaptation.[57] In reality, there exist both continuities and discontinuities between previous and current waves of Catholic immigration. Rather than posit a radical disconnect between the two experiences, it makes more sense to see Catholic parishes as consistently impacted by cultural diversity, with a relative respite of a few decades where immigration restriction and a strong emphasis on Americanization held particular sway. Or as historian James Fisher summarizes, "America is a nation of immigrants and the story of Catholics in America is largely the story of an immigrant church."[58]

*   *   *

Focusing on American Catholicism as a religious group consistently impacted by diverse cultural groups from different places may ask us to reimagine our cultural geography a little bit. American historical narratives almost always begin on the Eastern Seaboard with European colonists and then move west. This turns the U.S. Catholic parish into an East Coast institution transplanted to the Midwest and Sunbelt. Yet if we take seriously the Latin American and Asian presence in American Catholicism, we may want to supplement that cultural geography with one that wanders north from Latin America and east from across the Pacific Ocean. Especially in examining shared parishes like All Saints, we have to consider the ways in which parish life in the United States has roots in Mexico and other parts of Latin America.

Hoping to gain a greater sense of the influence of such roots on the parish at All Saints, I made a research trip in the spring of 2008 to two major cities and two small towns in central Mexico, places from which All Saints parishioners had originated. I met with and interviewed family members of Havenville immigrants as well as their neighbors and parish priests. I attended mass and parish events at several different parishes.[59] Speaking with people, I discovered that many Mexican churches (*templos* in Mexican Spanish) do not actually possess the juridical title of "parish" (*parochia*). They are called "chapels" or "chaplaincies" (*capilla, capilleta, or capellanía*), though they often function like parishes. Second, while rural parishioners saw themselves as "belonging" to their local church in the manner of the congregational parishes of the United States, they saw this not as a question of voluntary membership in a faith community but as an outgrowth of belonging to the social unity of a neighborhood, town, or village. Being Catholic remained a culturally ascribed identity rather than a chosen one. In urban environments, the dynamics of "parish shopping" did occur, but people also felt free to attend different churches at different times, almost as if the churches were all interchangeable.

Parish statistics from across Latin America complicate this qualitative portrait, mainly on account of the powerful trends in urbanization. In Latin America since the 1960s, economic changes have resulted in large-scale migration to large metropolises. One ecclesial outcome has been dramatic increases in the average size of city parishes—with as many as fifty thousand per parish in some large cities.[60] It becomes difficult to imagine such enormous parishes as communities of voluntary participation. Parish churches operate with masses at every hour on the hour, many with multiple chapels spread across the city or countryside. Priests move exhaustedly from one sacrament and celebration to another (one Mexican priest in the United States compared parishes to factories). Perhaps the smaller faith communities run by catechists in many of these parishes could be described as communities of choice. But the smaller communities could not, at the same time, be described as Eucharistic communities; mass is celebrated only sparingly.

Moreover, for Mexicans the parish does not usually function as the most significant local ecclesial referent, as it does in the United States. Popular religious practices like the *posada* in Mexico occur in the neighborhoods, not parishes. Religious formation is more the outcome of intergenerational relationships and home practice than of religious education or parochial programming. Sacraments and ceremonies may take place at popular shrines rather than in the neighborhood parish.

In summary, an entirely different conception of the parish obtains for Mexico. Sacramental life (not only mass but also the *ceremonias* of marriage, baptism, and the quinceañera) is administered from the parish (or chapel or shrine), but the formation of Catholic identity and popular religious practices are largely inculcated at home and in the neighborhood.[61]

Some of these trends clearly influenced the development of the Latino framing of parish life at All Saints. While Euro-American parishioners consistently used "All Saints" to describe the parish, Latinos spoke of *la parroquia de Havenville* (the Havenville parish) or *la parroquia de Brookton*, accenting the parish's emergence from the Latino community of a town or city. As in Mexico, a lot of social life got organized around the godparent networks created through sacramental celebrations like baptism, first communion, and marriage. Father Ignacio organized his voluminous educational efforts around these sacramental celebrations (baptism, first communion, confirmation, marriage) as well as around similar ceremonies such as the quinceañera coming-of-age ritual for girls. The Latino community raised money less through the Sunday collection in the Euro-American manner and more through the donations and fees that accompanied these celebrations and the classes that prepared for them. The community also made use of the Mexican custom of raising money through the selling of food after mass. Finally, most Latino parishioners marked off the religious calendar using the biggest popular religion celebrations—the Virgin of Guadalupe and the Good Friday Way of the Cross (Via Crucis)—rather than via Sunday worship or the official church calendar.

Perhaps even more salient than the transfer of these trends, however, were the ways in which Mexican parish customs were reshaped or repurposed for life in the United States. For example, Father Nacho did not want All Saints to simply reproduce the properties of a Mexican parish. Parish life in a new nation provided him the opportunity to reorganize certain elements of parish life to correct what he saw as deficiencies back home. Even as he retained the traditional Mexican focus on sacraments, celebrations, and popular religion, he could use each as an opportunity to deepen people's education in the Catholic faith (an agenda he brought from his education and experience in central

Mexico). He understood that the communities taken for granted back home—small town, neighborhood, and intergenerational extended family—had not developed to the same extent in the fluid environment of immigration to a new country. He worried that, in their loneliness, people would turn to dissolute living or, even worse, would turn on one another within their marriages and budding families. In essence, he thought that people needed parish life more in the United States. He encouraged the creation of more activities and groups, more leadership training, more opportunities to socialize. Younger people spent a lot of time at church, perhaps as much time as did the older women who dominated lay leadership back home.

Whether one agrees with Father Ignacio's vision for the parish or not, his approach had a strong effect. We have seen how relationships formed around parish activities and groups took the place of extended family and neighborhood in providing support and networking. We have also seen how the popular Catholicism of home and neighborhood in Mexico got moved to the parish. Finally, at All Saints, the parish life of voluntary participation in groups, ministries, and activities became a canvas on which people painted their conversion narratives, stories of alienation, loneliness, and temptation transformed into involvement and a deeper Catholic faith. It was not so much that the Latino community at All Saints set up a parallel parish modeled on a Mexican parish but that they came with their knowledge of parish life back home and fashioned a new hybrid to fit their particular needs. The new approach incorporated Mexican cultural resources around parish life, but it also built on existing parish structures and customs in the United States.

The Shared Parish and the Organizational Niche

Much of the research on local faith communities has theorized them through the theoretical lens of de facto congregationalism. As we have seen, there are many advantages to using that lens. In particular, it draws attention to the reasons and ways parishioners choose to participate in their parish. It highlights the role of lay leadership. In classifying shared parishes as parallel congregations, it helps us focus on the distinctness of each cultural community operating on its own.

Still, the approach has weaknesses. It does not easily account for the communities' relationship to one another or to the larger social environment. Other theoretical tools might prove to be of service as well.

Organizational ecology, a sociological approach that applies insights from population ecology to the sociology of organizations, speaks of the organizational niche that organizations occupy. The organizational niche is that social space where an organization interacts with its larger social environment and pulls its resources. That space can be broad or narrow, a measure usually described as "niche width."[62] Organizations that pull resources from across a broad expanse of their social environment are called "generalist" while organizations that focus in on a specific field of resources are called "specialist." Ethnic organizations—such as newspapers—are often described as specialist since they interact and pull resources from a specific cultural group as opposed to the broader social environment of a whole city.[63]

Organizational sociologists have barely begun to apply the insights of organizational ecology to religious organizations.[64] What might they make of a shared parish like All Saints? At first glance, All Saints looks like a textbook generalist organization, drawing on Catholics from across the Havenville area. In fact, many large territorial parishes across the United States function in this way, though many also cater to specific populations such as ethnic groups or progressive or traditionalist Catholics.[65] A Protestant pastor in the area described All Saints as the equivalent of ten churches in his denomination, each catering to a different subgroup. Indeed, as postwar Havenville grew and expanded geographically, All Saints developed multiple groups and ministries that catered to different communities and interest groups among Havenville Catholics. An older group of more progressive Catholics had their faith-sharing group. The RCIA group (an initiation group for new Catholics) was dominated by more traditionalist Catholics. School parents constituted another group, and there were countless more. As with the case of the Hebron Baptist megachurch in Nancy Eiseland's study of the religious ecology of a Georgia exurb, the different groups at All Saints found ways to include both longtime residents and recent arrivals. As at Hebron, All Saints parishioners seemed to appreciate large-scale events, from the well-attended midmorning mass in English to the Lenten fish fries to the school fund-raisers.[66]

On the other hand, this generalist profile really applied more to the parish attended by Euro-American Catholics. The Latino community at All Saints seemed to occupy what organizational sociologists call a specialist niche. Indeed, Ashley Palmer-Boyes has described Latino Catholic parishes in general as occupying a specialist niche—appealing to Catholics with an immigrant background and Latin American cultural origins.[67] These parishes are cultural specialists in that they provide a more charismatic and emotionally expressive style of worship that seems to appeal to many Latinos. They are immigrant specialists in terms of having a younger demographic profile and a tendency toward social services specifically for immigrant parishioners.[68] This sounds much like the Latino community at All Saints. It hosted a mainly young demographic, and its social services focused on poor Latino immigrants. While specific charismatic prayer practices were rare at All Saints, worship did have a more emotive style. While Euro-American research team members evaluated Holy Week worship as positive or negative, Latino research team members spoke of its emotional impact. Padre Nacho preached passionately and at length. Latino parishioners saw mass in Spanish as a unique form of worship permitted for their distinct social space.

Understanding the cultural communities of a shared parish like All Saints as part of a larger social ecology creates a nuanced portrait of the way demographic change shapes Catholic parishes. It has helped me frame this unfolding reality in greater depth, just as it did for Nancy Eiesland in her Georgia study: "Organizational ecology perspectives drew my attention to how change happens less through adaptation and more by organizational replacement. Some organizations cannot respond to the requirements of altered environments. They become obsolete and new organizations with a better 'fit' come in to fill their place."[69] For the Havenville of the post–Vatican II era, All Saints had served as a generalist niche organization among many other Protestant churches occupying specialist niches. Demographic change, however, restructured the social ecology of Havenville, making it into a bifurcated city. The generalist parish could not accommodate the special needs or marshal the right resources to minister to the new immigrant community. Something else would have to take its place.

Initially, this translated to the creation of a new outreach ministry for immigrants managed by a diocesan priest and a team of couples, some Latino, some mixed Latino and Euro-American. A deacon arrived from Texas, and the parish hired a Spanish-speaking Euro-American woman to help coordinate religious education for Latino children. The religious education coordinator went on to coordinate all Hispanic ministry for a while following the deacon's departure. These efforts forged the burgeoning outreach ministry into a specialist niche organization that served immigrant and Latino populations yet operated under the auspices of the generalist organization that was All Saints Parish. In general, these two communities did not compete for the same resources. They had different sets of donors, different hours of worship, and different customs for taking care of the church and its environs. They were there for distinct sets of people with different languages and different cultural expectations.

But Father Ignacio's arrival and parish-building work grew the Latino community until its specialist niche organization rivaled the previous parish in size and complexity. Their niches began to overlap more. The numerical parity meant that two sizable groups shared the same physical space, the same parking lot, and the same clergy. A small number of bilingual persons began to go back and forth between the services in English and Spanish. Parents transferred their children from the Spanish to the English religious education programs, infuriating Padre Nacho. Some put their children in parochial school, which increased their participation in social networks involving Euro-Americans. The overlapping social spaces—parish rooms, parking lots, school gatherings, the church building itself—became sites for more and more frequent intercultural negotiations. As we have already noted, however, these negotiations took place within a larger social ecology characterized by asymmetrical power relations.

Though it remains too soon to tell, I would venture to guess that ongoing demographic change will eventually turn the Euro-American community at All Saints into a specialist organization as well. The

Latino part of the parish constituted a specialist niche on account of its appeal to a distinct culture in contradistinction to the mainstream Euro-American culture and for the special needs of marginalized immigrants. If the idea of a specialist niche reflects the need of a social or cultural group for specific resources within a larger social environment, it would seem that the group of Euro-American Catholics at All Saints did not demonstrate such a need. They still had significant access to the resources of the larger social environment, such as government, businesses, and media. They found little need among themselves for the parish's social services. With some exceptions, most parishioners either had sufficient resources or were practiced in accessing those of the larger social safety net.

But the social ecology in Havenville was changing. The bifurcation of the community had created, in effect, the need for Euro-American Catholics to think of themselves as a coherent cultural group in contradistinction to the Latinos, instead of just as the mainstream. With people speaking Spanish and engaging in new and unfamiliar Catholic customs, Euro-American Catholics found that they did need a narrowed social space expressly for the English language and Euro-American Catholic customs. They could find in that social space a simpler and more emotionally restrained style of worship familiar to them. They could expect mass in English aimed at a more settled and comparatively older demographic. I would argue that, during my time in Havenville, the generalist parish of All Saints was turning into a confederation of two specialist organizations. Further research can determine if this pattern is characteristic of the development of the thousands of parishes shared by Latinos and Euro-Americans in the United States.

Finally, we should note that occupying a specialist niche did not seem to move All Saints parishioners away from de facto congregationalism. It appears to redouble the tendency toward the voluntarism associated with de facto congregationalism, especially within the specialist niche of the Latino community. Latino parishioners reported choosing All Saints because of its cultural and immigrant specialist dynamics. They saw those dynamics as part of its unique personality, a unique personality that also consisted in a higher level of organization and training than other parishes they had attended. Some traveled from a distance to choose this culturally Mexican specialist organization, bypassing a more pan-Latino parish in a nearby city. Most significantly, the conversion narrative of *evangelizar* (as described in chapter 2) articulated how many parishioners experienced themselves as personally transformed by access to cultural/immigrant specialist resources like religious education and ministry training. They articulated a personal conversion—possibly influenced by evangelical and Pentecostal tropes as well—that included a deepening of faith allied with the individual choice to participate more fully at this unique parish. In short, the shared parish of All Saints continued to function as a congregational parish even as its two parallel communities moved toward occupying interconnected specialist niches.

Beyond a Sample of One

All Saints constitutes a sample of one. This makes it difficult to conclude if the theoretical approaches here apply across the country. Do shared parishes everywhere possess a parish structure with de facto congregationalist elements, hierarchical authority structures, and specialist niche dynamics? Some research appears to confirm that they do. Ebaugh and Chafetz, for example, found a pattern of congregationalist structure in a shared parish in Houston, but again, their data comes from a sample of one.[70] Part of the challenge here is that social scientists have expended much of their recent efforts studying non-Christian congregations, despite their smaller numbers as a percentage of the population. This is, in part, to make up for a previous Christian Protestant bias already noted. Nevertheless, we need more comparative studies of shared parishes as well as statistical analyses on a larger scale. Such research, for example, might unearth patterns in shared parishes or even a kind of classification system we have not yet imagined. Perhaps shared parishes could be distinguished by the number of languages they use or the number or types of cultural groups.

Further research might also shed light on the impact that shared parish life has on the Catholics who inhabit them, especially their experience of cultural diversity. As cultural diversity continues to increase in the United States, shared parishes constitute that rare social space where different cultural groups actually do interact, though often in a limited way. It might provide us with some crucial lessons on how to address cultural diversity fruitfully. In the chapter that follows, I pose crucial questions about that experience of cultural diversity among contemporary American Catholics who worship in shared parishes.

5

Challenging Cultural Encapsulation in the Shared Parish

In November of my parish year at All Saints, I attended a civic event sponsored by the city government of Havenville. This "community dialogue" gathered several dozen people from the different cultural groups in town. They came together one evening at the local college campus, everyone seated in plastic chairs facing a lectern. The event began with a short speech by a white-bearded city councilman wearing an oxygen tube. On behalf of the mayor and city council, he greeted us and offered a brief history and appreciation of the city's cultural diversity. The dialogue then began in earnest. The chairperson, a middle-aged white woman, separated us into cultural groups—European American, Mexican, Central American and Caribbean, South American, and Russian/ Ukrainian. We discussed in these groups what we liked about Havenville, what helped us feel comfortable, and what difficulties we had encountered in feeling welcome there. Then we returned to share with the larger group what had happened in our small groups. During that large group conversation, the fault lines of intercultural life in Havenville became visible. While the European American group told pleasant stories about life in Havenville, the other groups brought forward tales of discrimination, alienation, and difficulty finding work.

The community dialogue meeting constituted one of the few events I attended in Havenville where people from different cultural groups congregated and shared their diverging stories. On the one hand, it provided an opportunity for a civic leader to publicly offer an inclusive vision of multiculturalism, what I will call in this chapter a "folk paradigm" for addressing cultural diversity. On the other hand, the reporting of tensions drew everyone's attention to their mutual cultural encapsulation. It turned out that people knew little about one another's worlds.

Cultural encapsulation is a concept from counseling psychology first defined in the 1960s as a way of recognizing the potential for cultural misunderstanding in the therapeutic relationship. "Cultural encapsulation is the lack of understanding, or ignorance, of another's cultural background and the influence this background has on one's current view of the world. The purpose of this encapsulation, or 'cocoon,' is to allow people to protect themselves from the rapid global changes occurring in technology, families, economy, education, and social health."[1] This is to say that encapsulation has the positive aspect of insulating groups from one another as they gradually adjust to the dramatic changes that increasing cultural diversity creates in a community. At the same time, cultural encapsulation perpetuates mutual ignorance of other groups' perspectives. In turn, that increases tensions by keeping groups unaware of the ways in which their actions might be interpreted in a negative light by another group. It also allows the dominant group to maintain the status quo that favors them, even as they continue to believe that cultural diversity has only introduced minor ruptures in life as they know it.

The meeting provided a rare social space for exploring the consequences of this cultural encapsulation and for beginning to break it down. Participants were confronted with the truth about the different lives they led. Shared parishes, I believe, could offer the same necessary (though often unwelcome) service. This becomes more and more important as cultural diversity—and the cultural encapsulation that accompanies it at first—grows to a level not seen since the turn of the twentieth century. The U.S. Census Bureau reports that, according to the 2010 Census, Latinos now constitute 16.3 percent of the national population; they are the largest of any group aside from the white majority. Racial diversity breaks down in this manner: Asians and Pacific Islanders are 5 percent of U.S. residents, and blacks constitute 12.6 percent. Non-Hispanic whites are now 63.7 percent of the U.S. population.

This diversity will only grow since the birthrate among immigrants and their children outpaces that of the resident population. It exists

despite the fact that the percentage of the U.S. population born outside
the country is less than it was a century ago. According to decennial
census figures, the foreign-born population of the United States peaked
in 1890 and 1910 with 14.8 percent and 14.7 percent of the population
respectively. According to the 2010 American Community Survey
(ACS), the current foreign-born population of the United States is 12.9
percent. But contemporary immigration patterns indicate a broader
cultural and racial diversity than ever before. In 1910, 87.2 percent of the
foreign-born were from Europe and most of the rest (9 percent) from
Canada. According to the 2010 ACS, 12.1 percent of today's immigrants
come from Europe, 28.2 percent from Asia, 4.0 percent from Africa, 0.5
percent from Oceania, and 53.1 percent from Latin America.

*   *   *

At the community dialogue meeting back in Havenville, I had listened to the city councilman acknowledge his own family's immigrant
heritage and the tenacity with which they had held to their culture
of origin. He reported that they had spoken German for six generations at home. He then made reference to contemporary immigrants
in Havenville, mentioning the Latino, Russian, and Japanese communities.[2] He concluded his welcome by reminding everyone that this
influx of newcomers was part of the tremendous growth of the city in
recent years, implicitly asking people for patience as everyone adjusted
to the changes. After he finished painting this portrait of multiculturalism in Havenville, I joined the European American group as they
met apart from the other cultural groups. The tone of the discussion
within that group remained very positive throughout. Members of the
group become quite animated talking about the positive and welcoming spirit of the town. They highlighted the willingness of Havenvillers to volunteer, and people noted how the college and the city had
really come together over the last few years. Though the instructions
for the dialogue had asked us to talk about people's experience of welcome or the lack thereof upon moving to Havenville, the facilitator of
the group allowed the focus to shift to general city problems. People
spoke of traffic and crowded schools. Finally, one woman in her sixties,
a parishioner at All Saints, got up and bluntly noted that "there is hatred

in Havenville." People began to murmur, and it took a few moments for the group to settle down again.

Before the group could fully process this comment, the other cultural groups returned from their separate discussions. Each presented a report on their group conversations to the whole assembly. Immediately it became clear that the other groups had a very different kind of conversation than the European American group. Each of them emphasized the difficulties in becoming part of the Havenville community. The Central American and Caribbean group talked about skin color and racism, how people looked at you funny. When the facilitator reiterated the question, "What helped you feel part of the community?" several people in that group responded, "Which community?" They knew what made them part of the Latino community, but they did not feel a part of the Anglo community at all. The Mexican group then discussed immigration problems, including people not having papers and struggling with the English language. They believed that if you spoke English, Anglos would happily accept you; that was the price of acceptance here. Some members of the South American group mentioned that they were once professionals in their country but here they worked in factories.

As this went on, the chair made sure everyone saw the differences in the responses between minority and majority groups. Then the Russian and Ukrainian group spoke through their interpreter, arguing that the town needed more Russian translation, just as things were available in Spanish. But mostly, the interpreter said, her group needed jobs. By way of example, she described a woman who lost her husband in a factory accident. Because she had no experience in this country working, she had been unable to find work. The interpreter then highlighted some of the skills people in her community had. The group brought forth a sampling of arts and crafts (such as domestic tablecloths) that they had made to demonstrate their sewing skills. The assembly applauded.

I have already noted how rare such an explicit and public discussion about different cultural perspectives was in Havenville. While this self-selecting group was not entirely representative of those perspectives— the cultural groups had roughly equal membership at the meeting, even though Mexicans and Euro-Americans far outnumbered the other groups in the city population—the gathering poignantly illustrated the dilemmas of a culturally diverse environment with asymmetrical power dynamics. The structure of the evening—a combination of conversation in distinct cultural groups along with large group conversation based on the group reports—lent itself to a safe expression of the tensions in the city. People spoke of racism, unemployment, linguistic discrimination, and a lack of legal papers. The Russian and Ukrainian group unhappily compared themselves to the Latinos with their greater access to resources in Spanish. All of these concerns came as a surprise to the Euro-American group, who had an overwhelmingly positive experience of living in Havenville. They had little idea of the conflicts and tensions other groups experienced as a matter of course.

I also argued that this kind of experience of cultural encapsulation has both positive and negative effects. It establishes a safety zone between cultures, on the one hand, but it reinforces naïveté about the dysfunctional status quo on the other hand. The latter effect demonstrates the usefulness of social spaces like the community dialogue. These spaces provide for limited, safe interaction between cultural groups under the banner of an inclusive multiculturalism. All those who attended the community dialogues walked away with a slightly different perspective on life in Havenville. People from the newcomer cultural groups developed new social networks with people from different groups, what social scientists call bridging social capital. The Russian group members showed their interest in bridging social capital as they attempted to demonstrate their skills and inquired about social connections that would increase employment opportunities.

But it was the European American group that potentially benefited most from the experience, though they may not have articulated it that way. The stark reality of different experiences of city life took most members of that group by surprise. In the preceding chapter, I noted that the social isolation of a dominant group can insulate its members from awareness of the asymmetrical power relationships that afford them social advantages—what racial theorists call privilege. Here they heard stories of how immigrants had to adjust to the rules and customs they—the dominant group—have long established and assumed to be benevolent and fair. Over a longer period of time, the newcomer groups may accumulate more influence and feel strong enough to express their dissatisfactions with the existing power structure more frequently and more publicly. But until this happens, the dominant group will have blessed few opportunities like this to be challenged in their culturally encapsulated perspective. They will continue to know little about the life of the newcomer groups.

If the community dialogues provided a unique site to challenge the negative effects of cultural encapsulation, shared parishes like All Saints have the potential for functioning similarly. After all, at All Saints, at least some parishioners earnestly desired such an outcome. They hoped that shared Catholic faith might afford them an opportunity to learn about the other community, even as the language, culture, and power differences seemed insurmountable. If, as it appears, shared parishes are growing across the United States, then perhaps a local experience of cultural diversity may have a significant impact on parishioners' overall understanding of and attitudes toward cultural diversity. Yet, as we have seen, intercultural encounters at the shared parish are complex and do not always end in greater mutual understanding. Many people learn from the experience that the best solution is to avoid other groups as much as possible. Does the frustration of intercultural experience at the shared parish sour Catholics on diversity? Does it increase the desire for cultural encapsulation among Latinos? Does it spark or increase anti-immigrant feeling among Euro-American Catholics? Does coexistence provoke gentler, more irenic approaches to intercultural interaction and negotiation? And what does the shared parish experience suggest about how parishioners consider and live cultural diversity?

Cultural Encapsulation at Catholic Parishes

Because Roman Catholicism constitutes the largest of the more culturally diverse religious groups within the U.S. population, its institutions often stand at the cultural crossroads. While this includes many different institutions—social service agencies, advocacy groups, hospitals, schools and universities—the previous chapter illustrated how the parish plays a central institutional role in Catholic life. Shared parishes like All Saints become a privileged Catholic site for cultural diversity and therefore for cultural encapsulation in twenty-first-century American life.

Euro-American Roman Catholics often seem taken by surprise by the scale of cultural diversity in this country and by the transformations it

has engendered. My own undergraduates at a West Coast Jesuit university, majority white and majority Roman Catholic in background, routinely underestimate the cultural and racial diversity in Southern California where we all live. This probably indicates a broader experience of
cultural encapsulation engendered by cultural and racial segregation.
Evidence suggests that cultural diversity within Roman Catholicism is
concentrated in certain types of parishes. According to researchers at
the Center for Applied Research in the Apostolate (CARA) at Georgetown University, 38 percent of U.S. parishes qualify as "multicultural,"
meaning they have masses not in English, are less than 40 percent non-
Hispanic white, or show a high probability that two randomly sampled
parishioners would be of different cultural or racial groups. While, on
average, 78 percent of parishioners within Catholic parishes are white,
only about half of those in the average multicultural parish are white.[3]
In other words, a smaller number of Euro-American Catholics worship
in parishes that cater to multiple groups; the majority of churchgoing
white Catholics attend homogeneous parishes isolated from the cultural diversity of the larger Church and society. Nearly three-quarters of
U.S. parishes have mass only in English, and 88.2 percent of the parishioners in "English only" parishes are white.[4]

We can surmise that, at the very least, shared parishes better prepare
Euro-American people for a culturally diverse world simply by more
realistically representing the demographic facts on the ground. Yet
greater awareness of these facts does not necessarily guarantee a positive adjustment or attitude toward them. In the past, some political scientists theorized that mere exposure to cultural differences would lead
to a greater appreciation of other cultures and their different mindsets.
They called this "contact theory," but little evidence has accumulated
in its favor over the years.[5] In contrast, intercultural communication
theorists have concluded that people must *seek* and *be taught* cultural
sensitivity and intercultural expertise.[6] Unfortunately, parishes have a
poor track record when it comes to encouraging their parishioners to
positively engage any difficult social issue, especially social issues that
emerge around relations and power dynamics between different cultural and racial groups.

Sociologist and priest Joseph Fichter first observed in 1949—based
on his own study of a southern urban parish—that Catholic beliefs had

much less hold on parishioners than secular beliefs, especially those having to do with racism and interracial contact. He contrasted official Catholic teaching opposing racism and supporting integration with the segregationist culture of southern Catholic parishes in the Jim Crow era.[7] In contemporary parishes in Northern California, Jerome Baggett recently documented a widespread disregard of church teachings on social morality and justice. He cites scholarship on institutional factors in U.S. Catholicism that distance Catholics from their Church's teachings on social issues. Because of the size of parishes, Catholicism provides fewer opportunities for participation, networking, and involvement in church life. The impressive presence of different Catholic social institutions—for example, hospitals, social service agencies, and schools—leaves the impression that professionals do the "heavy lifting" when it comes to justice and social service. Finally, an emphasis on the position and status of the clergy has historically discouraged initiative on the part of the laity.[8]

Baggett did not specifically address attitudes toward migration or cultural diversity in his study of parishes. In fact, only a small amount of specific data exists on these attitudes.[9] In the absence of comprehensive data, however, some scholars have looked at limited ethnographic studies and found some hope for the positive impact of shared parishes and other local faith communities that encompass cultural diversity. The religious studies scholar Kathleen Garces-Foley initially conducted research in this vein on multiethnic Evangelical churches. But she then turned to Catholic shared parishes. She argues that multiethnic churches—Evangelical or Catholic—constitute a niche in the marketplace of churches. They attract people who value diversity. They also present an opportunity to learn intercultural communication skills for those who wish.[10] "Multiethnic churches are training grounds for boundary crossers, but they can only teach those willing to learn."[11] She acknowledges that Catholic shared parishes, given the "parallel congregation" structure they assume, sometimes struggle to provide these skills. Yet she believes that they do provide them, though more incrementally through the intermittent intercultural contact that fiestas, "union" or "bridge" masses, and joint committees provide.[12] Most of all, Garces-Foley sees the value and impact of bridge people (intermediaries), not only within the parish but for the larger community.

Other scholars look specifically at the positive impact of shared parishes on immigrant parishioners in a culturally diverse society, measuring it through the concept of "social capital." The political scientist Robert Putnam describes social capital as "social networks and the associated norms of reciprocity and trustworthiness."[13] Sociologists Michael Foley and Dean Hoge studied immigrant faith communities in Washington, DC, as part of the Pew Gateway Cities Project. They describe how social networking there has offered immigrants advantages both in terms of rich supportive bonds with one another and connections to outside resources. In describing this positive impact, Foley and Hoge make the customary distinction between bonding social capital (social networking with people like them) and bridging social capital (social networking with those not like them). The latter could cross class, profession, or culture. Larger faith communities—such as Catholic parishes—are seen to be better at bridging social capital, since they tend to offer people more access to information about the larger society. Larger faith communities serve as gateways to addiction groups, social services, and community development projects. They offer more ties to larger organizational networks. However, they often fail to do so with everyone. In a large community, many people never develop close enough ties (bonding social capital) to enjoy those services and resources.[14] In the memorable but somewhat pejorative phrase of Padre Nacho, in Catholic churches many people merely "warm the pew" (*calientan la banca*).

My own study at All Saints did not attempt to account for the impact of the shared parish environment on parishioners' cultural encapsulation. I had no previous baseline with which to compare the situation in 2007–2008, and we did not specifically ask about or attempt to measure intercultural sensitivities. Nevertheless, I make a few observations. All Saints, like almost any Catholic church, had many people who attended mass but did not get involved. They had little knowledge of parishioners from their own cultural communities let alone any cross-cultural acquaintances. In sociological terms, they experienced little bonding social capital and less bridging social capital. Many people did depend on the priests to address the complex bifurcated cultural world of Havenville; they would never have dreamed of getting involved in trying to bridge it themselves. Furthermore, the bifurcated environment itself encouraged more building of social capital within the Latino community than it did bridging social capital for either community across cultural boundaries. We must, of course, acknowledge exceptions, such as a bilingual children's publishing venture between a Euro-American artist and a Latino writer, both within the parish.

The previous ethnographic chapters discussed how, for Euro-Americans, sharing the parish created a desire for unity but did not necessarily create equivalent skills for unity or even intercultural relationships that might facilitate it. The language barrier and cultural misunderstandings continued to loom large. Only a small number of people crossed back and forth between the two communities. Mere contact between cultural groups did not build cross-cultural bonds. In fact, some of the contact between parishioners occurred in such a vacuum of understanding that it decayed cross-cultural goodwill. Overall, most parishioners remained—in Jerome Baggett's turn of phrase—"heterognostic" rather than "heteroglossic" when it came to the other culture. They knew about it without having any real in-depth conversational familiarity with it.[15] At the same time, those few parishioners from both sides who purposefully sought out cross-cultural contact and intercultural communication skills were rewarded with success. A handful had even come to All Saints because of its cultural diversity. Others committed themselves to intercultural contact and skill building because they felt called to it as a "sign of the times" given the local situation. Naturally, struggle ensued when people worked at this, but those who sought it out generally expected this and withheld judgment in the difficult moments of intercultural negotiation.

As recounted in the previous chapter, my research at All Saints did uncover the different ways people framed cultural diversity. In the Euro-American community, a small number of people framed it in terms of assimilation, another group used "love and relationships" language, but most simply acknowledged the diversity that now characterized their parish without having any blueprint to make sense of it. In the Latino community, most people accepted that cultural diversity inevitably brought divergent perspectives, but many focused their attention on the internal success and unity of the Latino community. They had little trust in the success of any larger integrative intercultural project. A few younger men with more experience working with Euro-Americans had greater interest in learning about Euro-American ways.

In the pages to come, I argue that two larger folk paradigms at work in American society—assimilation and multiculturalism—have a significant impact on the way Catholics at All Saints and nationally frame the experience of cultural diversity. Although both of these folk paradigms exist as formal theoretical models for immigrant adaptation and coexistence in a multicultural society, I am more interested here in the way these approaches have entered into the popular imagination and how they help ordinary Catholics make sense of cultural diversity. I argue that they function less as coherent theories and more as loose cultural schemas or narratives that people access as cultural resources in their everyday attempts to understand the diversity around them. In a similar way, the American political theorist Nancy Fraser distinguishes between two formal philosophical theories of justice—redistribution and recognition—and the folk paradigms that emerge from them. In a parallel way, these folk paradigms of justice help people frame how social justice should work in society.[16] Here I consider the folk paradigms of assimilation and multiculturalism in turn and evaluate their usefulness in helping Catholics in the United States break through cultural encapsulation, especially in the context of a shared parish like All Saints.

Framing Cultural Diversity in America: Assimilation

Many American Catholics believe that assimilation (known sociologically as forceful assimilation or historically as Americanization) provides the best approach to incorporating different cultures into the United States. As a folk paradigm, assimilation imagines American history as a continual process of immigrants discarding the language and culture of their homeland and adopting the English language and Euro-American customs. Although some scholars on the left view this kind of assimilation more as a means of eradicating cultures than incorporating them, assimilation has enduring influence in American history and contemporary society.[17] Benjamin Franklin famously complained about German settlers in Pennsylvania failing to accept English customs. National survey results indicate that significant numbers of Catholics still find assimilation an adequate approach to cultural diversity in the Church and society. In a March 2006 survey by the Pew Center for Religion and Public Life, 41 percent of Roman Catholics felt that immigrant newcomers threatened American customs and values.[18]

In a May 2008 survey of mass goers at All Saints, 15.5 percent of Euro-Americans thought having church with both cultural communities would work only if people spoke English and learned American customs. A Latino Protestant pastor told me he believed many Euro-Americans in Havenville supported the rights of different groups to their own cultures only under the assumption that they would all fade away when families eventually assimilated into American culture. This assumption also surfaced in controversies over religious education at All Saints. Father Nacho wanted Latino parishioners to follow the structured religious education program in Spanish he had gradually created, but Joanne Joyner, the English director of religious education, saw no reason why students should not be permitted to move laterally to the English program, since the presumed goal was their assimilation into Euro-American culture.

The power of assimilation as a folk paradigm comes not only from its historical importance but also from the way it continues to be institutionalized in American life. Especially in post-1990 gateway communities like Havenville, English remains the sole language of most commerce and many government services. Public schooling is conducted entirely in English. Citizenship tests require extensive understanding of American history and civic institutions. Most voluntary organizations run procedurally using Robert's Rules of Order. Assimilation also asserts influence as an ideological discourse—that is, as "an interpretive framework that can be described in terms of framing rules and feeling rules."[19] Framing rules give us ways of ascribing meaning to situations. Assimilation frames cultural diversity as a temporary in-between state as immigrants gradually release themselves from their culture of origin in order to take on Euro-American culture as their own. It frames culture as an either-or rather than a both-and proposition. This offers a more definite shape to the otherwise complex and somewhat amorphous process of adaptation to a new cultural context. The fluid and confusing transnational tug-of-war of immigrant acculturation is rendered a simple linear progression from one mutually exclusive cultural world to another.

Perhaps even more persuasive and influential in American life are the "feeling rules" associated with assimilation. Feeling rules are "the social guidelines that direct how we want to try to feel . . . a set of socially shared, albeit often latent (not thought about unless probed at), rules."[20] Such rules tell us what we have the right and duty to feel and not feel, the extent to which we may feel it, and the appropriate duration of such feelings. They offer us parameters within which we negotiate our way between how we want to feel and how we sense we ought to feel.[21] Part of the emotional power of assimilation resides in the range of feelings it promotes as appropriate in response to cultural diversity. Feeling rules inspire comfort with Euro-American folkways but cautious discomfort around those of other cultures, especially when they appear in stereotypically American situations (recall the discomfort one parishioner had at seeing Spanish signs on Havenville's downtown shopping district). Indeed, for many Euro-Americans, cultural diversity "feels right"—induces feelings of comfort and security—only when accompanied by some momentum toward uniformity. Unity "feels right" when framed as uniform belief and practice.

*　　*　　*

Underneath the folk paradigm of assimilation lies a theoretical model for immigrant adaptation and for handling cultural diversity in American society. It first emerged in the nineteenth century. In fact, two distinct conceptions of assimilation existed during the nineteenth century and into the early twentieth: (1) Anglo conformity, a process of relatively quick adaptation to the dominant Anglo-American culture; and (2) the "melting pot" theory, a melding together of different cultures.[22] Anglo conformity insisted in a straightforward way that newcomers should shed the culture they arrive with and take on the original Anglo-American culture of founders of the United States. A resolutely ethnocentric model, it found little value in the home cultures of immigrants, often seeing them as a threat to a perceived American cultural consensus. Anglo conformity has a static and essentialist notion of culture, and it sees culture as perfectly coterminous with the modern nation-state. This position persists, for example, in the writings of the late political theorist Samuel Huntington, who worried that the Anglo-American

Protestant culture of the United States (which he saw as relatively fixed) was threatened by the presence of so many Latin American immigrants who would not embrace it.[23]

The melting pot approach has a more complex history. The metaphor refers not to food but to a crucible where different metal alloys are heated and merge into one. Its explicit appearance in American popular consciousness coincided with the production of a 1908 play called *The Melting Pot* by the British writer Israel Zangwill. The play's protagonist, a Russian Jewish immigrant, leaves his Christian fiancée when he finds she is the daughter of the man who killed his family back in Russia. Yet by the play's end, he reunites with her, and together they describe the United States as a crucible of races and cultures. The play captured an emerging position on immigration that clashed with the overt anti-immigrant prejudice of the era. Its image of newcomers blended into one ideal culture intentionally left the details vague, though it implied a letting go of Old World customs and values. Similarly, the melting pot position on assimilation sounds like an equitable union of diverse peoples, but its omission of the role of home country customs or values in the process suggests that the future inevitably forms around a modern Anglo-American culture shorn of the influence of immigrant cultures.[24]

Whatever the historical content of assimilation as a theory, for much of the nineteenth century it functioned more as a tool of debate than a consistent process of incorporation. Immigrants concentrated geographically, frequently forming ethnic enclaves.[25] Many insisted on preserving their native language and culture through institutions like newspapers and churches. Many German children, for example, attended bilingual or German-language schools. In the northern half of one midwestern state in 1900, only 12 percent of the Catholic churches were English-speaking.[26] Continuing waves of newcomers to ethnic neighborhoods kept cultural elements from the home country practical and useful. Assimilation—especially envisioned as Anglo conformity—did occur, but it was far from a universal grassroots fact of life. Nevertheless, many intellectuals vociferously argued for it. In 1912, the socialist writer Percy Stickney Grant invoked it to combat restrictionism. Even before that, Catholic bishops like John Ireland of St. Paul (Minnesota) and James Gibbons of Baltimore argued for greater Americanization of immigrant Catholics while their colleagues in New York City and Rochester (New York) resisted.[27]

A number of factors turned earlier theories and images of assimilation into the more concrete program of Americanization that occurred between 1900 and the World War II. A major influence was World War I. Frances Kellor wrote in 1919, "There is in America a national impulse called Americanization, which was understood as a war necessity before it had developed in time of peace."[28] Part of this impulse was directed at Germans, the largest cultural group in the United States up to that time. War with Germany made the perpetuation of German culture and institutions suspect. Many institutions chose to go silent, stop using the German language, or simply disband.[29] At the same time, the grand purpose of war seemed to demand greater cultural unity. Even before the war, social reformers and politicians allied with the Progressive movement had discussed the merits of a campaign of Americanization conducted through the public school system, the settlement houses, large companies, and other institutions that routinely dealt with immigrants. World War I brought their debate into furious, nationwide action.[30]

At the same time, the simmering debate over immigration restriction—propelled in part by scientific racism, anti-Semitism, and anti-Catholicism—boiled over. By the 1920s, immigration from countries in southern and eastern Europe from which most immigrants were coming was legally restricted out of existence. Just as efforts toward Americanization were ramping up and capturing the popular imagination, immigrants from southern and eastern Europe stopped arriving en masse. Without new immigrants to reinvigorate the home country culture within ethnic enclaves, Americanization proceeded apace. Finally, World War II brought more interethnic bonding among whites on the battlefield. This increased appreciation of the "melting pot" notion of assimilation in the popular imagination.

During this period of less immigration and greater Americanization, Robert Park and others at the University of Chicago began to develop a coherent sociological theory of assimilation. Their approach aimed, in part, to oppose coercive Americanization programs. They saw assimilation as the inevitable endpoint of a "race-relations cycle" that moved from intercultural contact to competition among groups to an ethnically divided accommodation period and then finally assimilation. It should proceed at its own speed. By the 1960s, a scholarly consensus on assimilation built up around Milton Gordon's multidimensional approach. Gordon saw assimilation as a one-way process with a trajectory into the middle-class, Anglo-American Protestant culture—what he termed the "core culture" of the United States. Herbert Gans and Neil Sandbert supplemented this model with their notion of "straight-line" assimilation, which shared Gordon's trajectory but simplified the content and proceeded in generational steps.[31]

By the 1970s, legal segregation had declined, racist attitudes were somewhat attenuated, and ethnic nationalist movements pushed back against the dominance of Anglo-American "core culture." Today's scholars of immigrant adaptation still speak of assimilation, but now many distinguish between forceful assimilation and "segmented assimilation," a process by which at different rates and according to a myriad of factors including personal agency, race, and social-economic status, persons and their families adapt to a segment of American society. Such scholars acknowledge that the dominant culture of the United States has a strong impact on migrants, but they also note that ethnic enclaves persist and that people retain and adapt elements of their home country cultures over the long haul.[32] Nevertheless, the folk paradigm of assimilation retains a more traditional approach to assimilation reminiscent of Anglo conformity or the melting pot. And it remains a powerful symbol in public speech and the popular imagination.

*   *   *

Despite the continuing salience of assimilation as a folk paradigm, the leadership of the Roman Catholic Church in the United States has largely rejected it as an acceptable approach to cultural diversity.[33] One of the first explicit rejections of assimilation came in the bishops' 1987 pastoral plan for Hispanic ministry: "Integration is not to be confused with assimilation. Through the policy of assimilation, new immigrants are forced to give up their language, culture, values, and traditions and adopt a form of life and worship foreign to them in order to be accepted as parish members. This attitude alienates new Catholic immigrants from the Church."[34] Clearly this opposition to assimilation came from the experience of ministry with and advocacy for Latino Catholics. Yet it is also consonant with post–Vatican II Catholic theologies of culture that emphasize cultures as "this particular way in which persons and peoples cultivate their relationship with nature and their brothers and sisters, with themselves and with God, so as to attain a fully human existence."[35] Vitally intertwined with human beings' interactions with their social and physical environment, culture runs deep. "It is the whole of human activity, human intelligence and emotions, the human quest for meaning, human customs and ethics. Culture is so natural to man [sic] that human nature can only be revealed through culture."[36] It is not so easily exchanged, one for another.

If assimilation underestimates the hold that culture has on immigrants, it also fails to challenge the negative effects of cultural encapsulation for Euro-Americans. While there can be no doubt that the dominant culture of a society exerts strong pressure on immigrants to adapt—recall how Milton Gordon spoke of multiple dimensions of assimilation, from language to work cultures to intermarriage—assimilation as a folk paradigm de-emphasizes the role of home country cultures in the process of adaptation. Yet immigrant cultures persist in their influence, even as they are altered not only by the dominant culture but also by the influence of other groups in a multicultural society.[37] Immigrant cultures have also enriched and altered both the mainstream Euro-American culture of the United States and African American culture, as any examination of food, language, or customs will demonstrate.[38] But these facts are rendered invisible by the folk paradigm of assimilation. The "Old World" simply disappears into the mist. This reinforces the notion that Euro-Americans need not learn about or adapt to the cultures of newcomers. Why learn about something that will inevitably disappear anyway?

Folk Paradigms for Cultural Diversity: Multiculturalism

If assimilation does not adequate challenge the negative effects of cultural encapsulation, what about other folk paradigms? At the beginning of this chapter, I described the folk paradigm of multiculturalism in action at the community dialogue meeting in Havenville. The city councilman explicitly acknowledged the coexistence of multiple cultural groups as being good for Havenville. He accepted as a matter of course the long-term presence of distinct cultural identities and the persistence of home country languages. Multiculturalism as a folk paradigm—often adopted by educational institutions and left-leaning organizations and civic leaders—makes space for the reassertion of the cultural values and customs of non-majority groups in the context of a shared democratic vision of public life. Nancy Fraser describes "mainstream multiculturalism" thus: "This approach proposes to redress disrespect by revaluing unjustly devalued group identities, while leaving intact both the contents of those identities and the group differentiations that underlie them."[39] In other words, multiculturalism allows historically marginalized groups to assert cultural identity without asking any questions about the cultural resources they use to do so or about the cultural impact of asymmetrical power relationships in the larger society.

Parishioners at All Saints felt the influence of multiculturalism as a folk paradigm in different ways. Some brought assumptions into the parish shaped by the salience of multiculturalism as a folk paradigm at other sites. One young couple with small children, the Potts, said they had explicitly chosen All Saints because of its diversity; they compared its cultural diverse social environment to that of the school district where they both worked. Emphasizing the importance of encountering and celebrating the cultural expressions of other groups, Jami Potts said, "I don't really see it happening outside, other than the education system." Several members of a progressively minded small faith community spoke approvingly of local Protestant churches' embrace of multiculturalism, and one of them worked with the community relations committee of the city and helped to staff its Diversity Day. A few Latino parishioners had encountered multiculturalism through social service agencies, some of them influenced by local Protestants. At a first communion party at the house of a Mexican family, I met a local Euro-American Protestant man who spoke Spanish fluently. He was introduced to me as the founder of a local housing nonprofit. He lamented how unfair life in Havenville had been for Latinos, and he shared his own participation in trying to change that.

Some Catholics may also embrace multiculturalism as a folk paradigm as a result of its use by their leadership. Multiculturalism shows up in the teaching of Catholic bishops and is embedded in various Catholic organizations and institutions. During the 1960s and 1970s, the U.S. Catholic bishops moved from overtly promoting Americanization (as they had done before Vatican II) to recognizing the importance of cultural pluralism and then later focusing more attention on unity across cultures under the rubric of "multiculturalism."[40] They have consistently used multiculturalism in recent documents on migration and cultural diversity. All of the bishops permit and most encourage the use of immigrant languages and home country customs in worship and ministry. In many dioceses, regional masses and other celebrations almost always involve multiple languages and music from various cultural backgrounds. Papal visits involve similar explicit displays of different cultural expressions of Catholicism. Influential ecclesial organizations, such as the National Association for Pastoral Musicians and the National Federation for Catholic Youth Ministry, promote the appreciation of distinct cultural celebrations and expressions.

*   *   *

As with assimilation, behind the folk paradigm of multiculturalism lies a complex political theory. In this case, it has divergent developments in different Western countries. The philosopher Charles Taylor describes its origins in what he calls the "politics of recognition." In the modern West, identity has gradually shifted away from status and honor to the equal dignity of all individuals. This gives rise to the value of authenticity and the project of the self: "We might speak of an *individualized* identity, one that is particular to me, and that I discover in myself."[41] Yet because we remain social creatures in reality—a favorite point of Taylor's—authenticity requires recognition. Unrecognized identity amounts to a loss of dignity. Yet subject peoples not only go unrecognized in their differences, they also have the dominant culture's identity thrust upon them, especially in former settler colonies like the United States, Canada, Australia, and New Zealand. Taylor identifies an inherent inhospitality to differences in certain strands of Western individualism, an inhospitality that makes it difficult for non-mainstream cultures to survive.[42] The British political theorist Bhikhu C. Parekh argues that this forcing of a dominant culture on a minority culture (assimilation) proves destructive, undermining that people's self respect and willingness to participate in a multicultural society as well as undermining the dominant culture's own ethics—its respect for others.[43] A reversal of that process is seen to restore dignity and end second class citizenship.[44]

Taylor and Parekh have powerfully captured some of the chief ideas of multiculturalism—identity, respect, and the potential damage done from a lack of both. Yet their arguments—especially Taylor's—can seem to abstract multiculturalism from the specific historical and cultural circumstances that have given rise to it. In almost all the Western nations that entertain some form of multiculturalism, increases in immigration and a history of racial or ethnic discrimination play in the background. Scholars generally see Canada as the first country to formally adopt a policy of multiculturalism in 1971; the Canadian policy originated with the restive assertions of French Canadians of their rights to their own language and culture. Australian multiculturalism traces its origins to a reversal of the "white Australia" policy that institutionalized discrimination against Aboriginal peoples.[45] British multiculturalism has its roots in the gradual nineteenth-century emancipation of Catholic and Jewish religious minorities and in national laws from the 1960s and 1970s forbidding racial discrimination against postwar immigrants from Commonwealth countries in the Caribbean, Africa, and South Asia.[46] In the United States, multiculturalism arose largely in the universities in response to ethnic consciousness movements that followed the civil rights movement.[47]

Multiculturalism as a political theory has its critics. Some find it insufficiently appreciative of the way cultures constantly shift and change as a result of their interaction with one another. They are dynamic and relational realities. Accordingly, Latino theologian Peter Casarella argues that multiculturalism shortchanges the internal diversity of the Latino community in the United States: "The multicultural ideal thus tended to promote assumptions about Latino identity as monolithic and self-enclosed."[48] A broader critique of multiculturalism has formed around its lack of attention to economic injustice: "Multiculturalism's focus on social based differences can be at odds with theories that emphasize the economic basis for alienation and oppression."[49] Nancy Fraser, however, sees multiculturalists' concern with "recognition" as a means for analyzing and redressing social injustice as entirely compatible with more traditional economic concerns over the unequal distribution of resources. She argues for a "two-dimensional conception of justice" based on what she calls "parity of participation": "Justice requires social arrangements that permit all (adult) members of society to interact with one another as peers."[50] Historical experiences of gender and racial discrimination clearly demonstrate how both unequal distribution of resources (for example, men's higher salaries) and a lack of cultural respect (for example, stereotyped portrayals of black men as criminals) prevent equal participation in society, often in tandem.[51] Justice then requires both a fair distribution of material goods (redistribution) and equal respect for all cultural groups in social institutions (recognition).[52]

*   *   *

Despite the endorsement of the U.S. Catholics bishops, multiculturalism—both the theoretical construct and the folk paradigm—has its critics among Catholic intellectuals. Conservative-minded Catholic intellectuals sometimes caricature multicultural celebrations and liturgies in public discourse.[53] Some argue that multiculturalism's defense of the cultural rights of various groups amounts to a relativistic unwillingness to make moral judgments. They also worry that Catholics will abandon the cultural heritage of the West.[54] Even more progressive Catholic intellectuals have their issues with multiculturalism. The theologian Roberto Goizueta finds multiculturalism suspicious because of its dependence on postmodern intellectual frameworks. These frameworks lionize particularity and eschew shared truth or norms, settling instead for an intersubjectively and rationally inaccessible meaning. This occurs, he notes, at precisely the moment when communities of color possess the personnel and competencies to contribute to a search for shared truth on a more level playing field:

> If all experiences and all values are equally valid, equally irrational, then our experiences and values as U.S. Hispanics are valid for us and, as such, ought to be respected and listened to—but they can make no claims on non-Hispanics, e.g., the dominant groups. Moreover, if all experiences and values are arbitrary and irrational, then there is, literally, no reason

why the dominant groups should see themselves implicated in what we have to say. Those groups become effectively immune to criticism; after all, they have as much right to their positions as we to ours.[55]

In other words, if no one's experience can compare with anyone else's, marginalized groups cannot dialogue with dominant groups or attempt to hold them accountable for their relative privileges.[56] Cultural encapsulation stands unchallenged.

Popularly, this may translate to the common phenomenon of cultural diversity construed as something for ethnic groups only, as a concern irrelevant to the mainstream. Whites do not have to pay attention, and so they remain racially and cultural encapsulated. Faustino Cruz, a pastoral theologian, pastor, and former official with the U.S. Conference of Catholic Bishops (USCCB), describes the concrete situation in many Catholic dioceses:

> In some dioceses, an office of ethnic ministry or migration functions as a microdiocese. *De facto*, ethnic ministry is segregated from the mainline functions and resources of other diocesan offices, such as family life, religious education, worship, or lay ministry. Consequently, ethnic and language-specific issues, challenges, and exigencies are relegated to a desk or department that must comprehensively attend to the catechetical, liturgical, educational, and other pastoral care needs of newcomers, mostly with limited staff and funding. While advancing unity and inclusion—at least in principle—such structure could inadvertently advance a culture of "separate and unequal."[57]

Simply put, the Church's Euro-American mainstream (and perhaps that of the society as well) remains uncertain that cultural diversity pertains to it at all. Minority groups trying to avoid entanglement with the dominant culture may inadvertently contribute to this perception.

I suspect that part of the problem lies in the way American institutions only sparingly incorporate multiculturalism. Civic institutions in particular operate under the aegis of individualist universalism. Cultural rights are not written into state or federal constitutions. Even as the U.S. Catholic bishops have promoted multiculturalism as teaching, they have rarely thoroughly shaped parishes and dioceses to reflect that teaching. Multiculturalism functions mostly as what one might call an ethical option. People may choose it, but they often do not. Thus, a few people may wish to broaden and transform their perspectives with exposure to a different group, but most people at least begin from a resolutely ethnocentric position.[58] Who can blame them? The kind of intercultural engagement that expands horizons is unsettling. As noted in the previous two chapters, people generally avoid intercultural contact if they can get away with it.[59] Sociological research on local faith communities demonstrates a general orientation toward homophily—staying with those like us.[60]

The result is that cultural groups may be given the institutional means to preserve and express their cultural identity (as in the Catholic Church and many universities), but people from the dominant group do not have to respect or engage that identity. This reproduces a situation where the mainstream need not concern themselves with "diversity." At All Saints, many Latinos, stung by discrimination and a lack of trust, seek not engagement and negotiation with the dominant culture (even from the safety of an enclave) but rather a protective shield to ensure minimal contact and interference. In the end, multiculturalism becomes something much less than the kind of democratic commonwealth that Charles Taylor envisioned, where cultural groups have rights of expression and where critical judgments about that expression are made through expanded and transformed perspectives. Instead it becomes more like what I described at All Saints in terms of intercultural negotiations—an intentional and customary practice of tense avoidance.

In the end, multiculturalism does not challenge the negative effects of cultural encapsulation. Instead, we often end up with a kind of minimalist "museum" form of multiculturalism:

> Another common way of dealing with intercultural understanding revolves around what I call the museum approach. We stage East-West Philosophers' Conferences. We organize symposia in which the participants describe patterns of family, death customs, religion, rites of passage, relationships between the generations in a variety of societies. We have libraries that can boast of hundreds of thousands of books and papers on and from the non-Western world.[61]

Some Catholic pastoral workers describe this as "showcase multiculturalism."[62] Parishes and other institutions hold celebrations with many kinds of ethnic foods, dress, and perhaps even music and dancing, but people do not discuss clashing cultural expectations about emotional expressiveness in worship or the way in which financial giving styles clash. Such clashes, absent real dialogue, lead to mutual stereotyping— that Anglos are "cold," or Hispanics "lively party people." An unhealthy romanticism may enter in. In an odd reversal of assimilation, people regard minority cultures as requiring protection in order to remain in their "natural state" (whatever that is), unperturbed by influence from the dominant culture.[63] This is an understandable reaction to the history of imperialism and cultural eradication by dominant cultures, but it misses the point. Inevitably and unalterably, we live in an intercultural world. Cultures impact one another, and the cultural identity of both persons and cultural groups will be shaped by other cultures.

Building a New Folk Paradigm: Communion

If neither assimilation nor multiculturalism effectively challenges cultural encapsulation, then perhaps the shared parish might be a site for exploration of a different approach, the development of a new folk paradigm. I recommend beginning with a body of theologies of the Church that has begun to take on the status of a kind of folk paradigm within mainline Protestant and Catholic circles. That body of theologies is known as "communion ecclesiology."[64] As it is generally understood across Christian denominations, communion ecclesiology offers a vision of church where human beings are invited into a personal encounter with God in the midst of and through their encounter with other believers, both those who are nearby and like them and those who are far off and quite different. Many Christians believe that a "communion," or social bond, results, uniting believers together in their communities of faith across time and space, drawing people together despite considerable human differences in geography, economy, lifestyle, and culture.[65]

Rather than a simple image of the Church, communion ecclesiology has the quality of a multifaceted, multidenominational, and international theological language. Dennis Doyle describes it thus:

Amid the various versions of communion ecclesiology, four elements remain fairly constant. First, communion ecclesiology involves a retrieval of the Church presupposed by Christians of the first millennium, prior to the divisions among Eastern Orthodox and Roman Catholic and Protestant manifestations of Christianity. Second, communion ecclesiology emphasizes the element of spiritual fellowship or communion between human beings and God in contrast to juridical approaches that over-emphasize the institutional and legal aspects of the Church. Third, communion ecclesiology places a high value on the need for visible unity as symbolically realized through shared participation in the Eucharist. Fourth, communion ecclesiology promotes a dynamic and healthy interplay between unity and diversity in the Church, between the Church universal and the local churches.[66]

Most formal articulations of communion ecclesiology have emphasized its roots in the Christian doctrine of the Trinity—three distinct persons (Greek *hypostases*) in one divine substance or being (Greek *ousia*). Almost all Christian theologies of communion see the global Church as a communion or social bond in the second person of the Trinity, Christ the Son of God, and created by the action of the third person in the Trinity, the Holy Spirit. Protestant theologians have tended to focus on the spiritual fellowship of believers, while Catholic and Orthodox theologians emphasize that fellowship as effectively symbolized in the sacraments (especially baptism and the Eucharist) and in the bishops and clergy as living symbols of unity. All these traditions accept that the dynamic interplay of unity and diversity remains crucial to being Church.

Communion as a theology of Church largely developed in the early centuries of Christianity as a means of bridging together communities of faith (Greek *ekklesiae*, gatherings) as the geographical and cultural distance between them increased. These local faith communities, sometimes isolated, were the islands in the larger archipelago of the Universal Church. "Communion" was the name given to the spiritual bond among these communities of believers symbolized by exchanges of letters, visitors, and the Eucharistic bread. Nevertheless, "communion" has also come to describe the bonds within a local community among the believers there. From that perspective, communion could serve parishes and congregations struggling with cultural diversity. It provides a vision of church unity that does not require cultural uniformity, but it also demands more of Christians than simply a vague and distant tolerance.

The French Canadian Catholic theologian Jean-Marie Tillard sees communion (or *koinonia*, as it is described in the New Testament) as the establishment of a new set of relationships among human beings and with God, a remaking of humankind within the Church: "Briefly, *koinonia* in the New Testament context designates, in its most profound sense, the entrance of every baptized person and of each community of believers into the sphere of reconciliation opened up by Christ on the Cross and which the Spirit makes apparent through the break on Pentecost."[67] Tillard uses early Christian interpretations of the Pentecost event (Acts 2:1–41) as a reference point; according to these interpretations, the coming of the Holy Spirit upon a crowd of Jesus's followers at Pentecost reverses the cultural divisions initiated by the confusion of human languages at the Tower of Babel (Genesis 11:1–9).[68] Christians of diverse cultures across time and space become united in communion while they are at the same time bonded with "divine realities" rooted in the Trinity.[69] The Greek Orthodox theologian and bishop John Zizioulas adds to this understanding by taking a deeply philosophical view of such a communion of persons. Working with Patristic era sources and Trinitarian theology, he argues that any *person* is a relational being. He roots this analysis in the Trinity, where the three persons are at once absolutely *other* and yet in relationship, in communion. "As a result, finally, otherness is inconceivable without *relationship*. Father, Son, and Spirit are all names indicating relationship. No person can be different unless he [sic] is related."[70] Zizioulas sees the Trinitarian experience as so relational that he does not even concede that human beings can experience mystical communion with God as an individual experience.[71]

From the point of view of these two theologians, Christianity exists in part to move humankind beyond individualism and egocentrism. "To be oneself is to be oneself in communion, in relation. This is God's way of being, and the Church is like a school in which Christians learn how to *be* relationally in the way that God is."[72] For Zizioulas, fear of the other has made us identify difference with division. The folk paradigm of assimilation may be a case in point; it expects newcomers to become like longtime residents. If not, residents see them as a threat or a burden. According to the theology of communion, human beings cannot solve the problem of misidentifying difference with division by a simple ethical imperative to do so; people need to be shaped to it. For these theologians, this happens through participation in the Christian Church.[73] Tillard argues that communion within the Church combats cultural tensions. He notes that communion manifests itself in the New Testament in times of tension, crisis, and even conflict between communities. Historically, divisions occur and then are healed in communion. More personally, Christ himself demands of Christians a commitment to conversion.[74]

The African American Catholic theologian Jamie Phelps focuses her attention on this demand to conversion. Arguing from the U.S. context, she sees theological continuities between the theology of communion and Martin Luther King Jr.'s metaphor of the "beloved community." The beloved community is an inclusive vision of community characterized by reconciling Christian love. Phelps argues, with the Black liberation theologian James Cone, that the dehumanization of racism and other oppressive political and economic systems prevent the Church from becoming that community, which is its true nature: "We are seeking *liberation from* oppressive divisions in the human community and *liberation for* a new or beloved community that embraces all into one communion under God."[75] In the U.S. context, this specifically means acknowledging complicity in sinful systems in church and society, seeking forgiveness from victims, and working together toward a different kind of community rooted in the bonds of communion, one with more inclusive relationships, participation, and decision-making.[76]

I would argue that the theologies of communion reviewed thus far offer a vision of the Christian Church relevant to the situation at shared parishes. They assert that unity accommodates cultural differences as long as (paradoxically) those differences are respected and not minimized. In fact, this accommodation of the cultural differences between Christian Jews and Christian Greeks was part of the earliest struggles of the Church as it spread across the Roman Empire. Thus, a Christian writer using the apostle Paul's name wrote to a Greek community in the late first century: "So [Christ] came and proclaimed peace to you who were far off [Greeks] and peace to those who were near [Jews]; for through him both of us have access in one Spirit to the Father. So then you are no longer strangers and aliens, but you are citizens with the saints and also members of the household of God" (Ephesians 2:17–19; NRSV). According to the theologies of communion, difference does not mean division. In fact, as Zizioulas argues, relationality and difference belong together.

Thus, against the vision of unity as cultural uniformity in the folk paradigm of assimilation, this vision of unity reminds shared parishes that cultural differences must be respected and yet they can be drawn together in unity by the social bonds of communion. For Catholics, these bonds are symbolized and made visible in the sacraments, especially baptism and the Eucharist. In fact, Christians are said to express their cultural differences united in communion each time they celebrate these sacraments.[77] Assimilation, at least theologically, is what happens when believers give up on the Holy Spirit as a means of bonding them together and depend instead on cultural uniformity. Without a doubt, a communion approach proves risky and complicated. As Jamie Phelps pointed out, the bonds of communion demand that believers turn away from racism and other oppressive systems that disrupt our bonds to one another. They have to submit to preaching and teaching about racism and prejudice as sin, and they must share power among the different cultural groups. Latino parishioners at All Saints agreed; more than one out of every three adult Latino parishioners thought Euro-American racism was a great obstacle to their communion at All Saints.[78]

All this sounds good in theory, but it remains the theological vision of elites. Can communion really serve as a folk paradigm for addressing cultural diversity? Could such a vision shape communities like the shared parish in the real world? How might it combat the isolation and ethnocentrism that cultural encapsulation perpetuates?

Building a Folk Paradigm in the Shared Parish

At minimum, a folk paradigm built around the theology of communion would require recognition within shared parishes that all parishioners rightfully belong to it by virtue of their common baptism, regardless of their cultural background. It might also emphasize commonly held symbols and symbolic action—the church building itself with its statues and images, the celebration of mass, the priests and other leaders as persons who belong to the combined community. It would also require a real acceptance of cultural difference not as a problem or temporary distraction but as part of the very experience of church. Such a folk paradigm would have institutionalized means for cultivating bonds among the faithful from different backgrounds, in part by forming bridge people who move back and forth across communities. Finally, it would have to find some means for addressing the asymmetrical power relationships that prop up an unjust order of things. Is all this really possible? Must communion remain nothing more than a sectarian theological vision of human connectedness? Can it really serve as a blueprint for shared parishes and other institutions struggling with cultural diversity?

In many ways, my parish year at All Saints indicated that it can. One afternoon I sat at lunch with an older couple from the parish at the Veterans of Foreign Wars club in town. I had recently performed a bilingual baptism ceremony at the behest of a Euro-American grandfather they knew. His son had married a Mexican woman, and the baptism itself was a mix of languages and cultural customs. The elderly veteran answered, "It wouldn't have bothered me one bit whether my grandkid got baptized whichever way it was as long as they were baptized." This attitude was typical. No one disputed the right of people from both groups to receive baptism and belong to the parish. And people from both groups made reference to the symbols they shared. Euro-Americans could be found praying at the Virgin of Guadalupe statue and Mexicans at the Immaculate Conception statue. Parishioners from both sides often made respectful comments about the two priests as leaders shared by the communities.

But parishioners also knew how challenging it could be to share a parish. They knew that negotiating the shared space often led to cultural misunderstanding, tensions, hurt feelings on both sides. Many people felt that the leadership of the two priests was what held the communities together. Some felt that more leadership was needed in this area. Parish council member Mary Kruk commented to me on the reported advice of the bishop to Father David to "unify the two communities":

> But the most important thing that happens at the parish now, I think, is resolving the feelings in both communities. I think the most important

thing now, for me, is to have an explanation of what "unify the communities means." It sounds good, it's a nice phrase, but what does it
mean and what are the perceptions on both sides? And I don't know that
either side of us has been clearly directed. And maybe there isn't a way to
direct it. By not having a little clearer definition of what it is and what is
expected and how/what are the goals. Are the goals to have nothing but
bilingual masses? What are we talking about here? I think that would
remove on both sides a lot of things that get blown out of proportion
or fall under great misconception. And as I say, I don't know if Father
Nacho or Father David either one have been directed by the bishop, or
[had it] explained to them. But that's where I'm putting the blame.

She clearly felt that the burden for framing a vision of how the communion could live together in some semblance of communion fell heavily
on the bishop and the two priests.

Congregational studies scholars like Jackson Carroll would agree.
Using social scientific theory and research, they theorize how leadership can and should work so that people feel a part of a community
with a purposeful trajectory. According to Carroll, reframing parish life
to adjust to a transformed social environment—like that of All Saints or
any shared parish—is crucially the work of parish leadership. Carroll
describes leadership as an activity of cultural production:

> As producers of congregational culture, clergy give shape to a congrega-
> tion's particular way of being a congregation—that is, to beliefs and prac-
> tices characteristic of a particular community's life and ministry. Strange
> though the image may seem, it offers a helpful way of describing a pas-
> tor's core work, which obviously is undertaken in interaction with con-
> gregational participants and in a particular time and place. Through the
> core work of the pastoral office—preaching, leading worship, teaching,
> providing pastoral care, and giving leadership in congregational life—
> a pastor helps to "produce" or at least decisively shape a congregation's
> culture.[79]

Catholics might be tempted to understand this role of cultural production exclusively in terms of the exercise of power of a centralized
authority, but the laity are not simply faithful soldiers waiting to be told

what to do. They have their own interpretations and opinions about the situation, and they may hold on to many of these interpretations even as congregational leadership moves in a different direction. For example, many Euro-American parishioners at All Saints operated under the assumption that "illegal equals immoral"—that a lack of legal papers demonstrated a blatant disregard for the law. This seemingly self-evident belief would not easily subside even should the priests decide to publicly contest it.

Nevertheless, as Mary Kruk's comment indicates, people do desire from their leaders a meaningful vision or direction for the faith community to pursue together, one that speaks to the challenges in their particular context. Pastoral leaders, especially but not exclusively priests in Roman Catholic tradition, constitute an authoritative source from which people draw cultural resources to make sense of their world. But parishioners may remain skeptical of a pastor's vision; they will ask questions and want dialogue. The leaders have to sell their vision for the parish.

The process by which leaders sell their vision can be seen as a form of cultural production. It happens less through orders or statements than through everyday pastoral activities. A pastor relies on resources from Christian tradition and on the social capital built up via reciprocal bonds of trust to make his or her case for the direction the parish should take. Leadership becomes less a matter of administration of goods and services and more "direction setting: helping a congregation to gain a suitable vision and direction for its ongoing drama or story and then to develop programs and practices to embody their vision."[80] To explain how this works in practice, Jackson Carroll draws upon sociologist Wendy Griswold's image of cultural production as a diamond.

Griswold observes that human beings conceive of culture in two different ways—either as ideas and artistic expressions, "the best that has been thought and known" in poet Matthew Arnold's memorable phrase, or as that "complex whole" of beliefs, customs, values, habits, and practices that constitute a community's way of life.[81] Griswold ties the two perspectives together by defining culture as "the expressive side of human life—in other words, to behavior, objects, and ideas that appear to express, or to stand for, something else."[82] She argues that it functions as an interactive relationship between those who create cultural expressions and those who receive them. The relationship is further complicated by the facts (1) that "producers" and "receivers" interact within a specific social ecology, and (2) cultural products themselves are not inert messages; they have a life of their own once created. Thus, Griswold envisions cultural production as an interactive "cultural diamond." Each of the four corners represents a different active element in the relationship: the cultural producer, cultural products, receivers, and the social ecology in which production occurs.[83]

In church, Carroll sees pastors and pastoral leaders as the cultural producers; local interpretations of Christian narratives, worship, and religious practices as cultural products; the congregation as receivers; and the local sociocultural and ecclesial context as the social ecology in which production occurs. He urges pastors to proactively shape congregational culture, levying their formal authority and social capital in the congregation to respond to congregational inertia in the face of changes in the social ecology. They must provide theological narratives—pastoral visions or articulations of congregational mission—that explain the need for new or continuing programs and practices. Finally, those programs and practices must be seen to put the articulated vision into practice.[84]

Does such leadership conceived as a strategy for shaping parish culture actually work? Public policy scholar Katherine DiSalvo, in her study of a predominantly Latino parish in New York City, demonstrates that it can. She noted how parish leaders there redirected parish practice, beliefs, and feeling toward a more shared and participative style of church. Employing a theological narrative of baptismal empowerment, they cultivated practices of shared leadership, promoted volunteer recruitment practices, and operated with a loose rather than rigid sense of control. The parish staff visibly put their trust in the variety of trained leaders. Their success in shaping the parish culture contrasts with a larger Catholic deficit in congregational and civic participation, a backdrop thought to be engendered by larger numbers, lower rates of integration into volunteer networks, and a more hierarchical structure.[85] Shaping the culture turned out to be even more effective than Catholic social structures seemed to allow.

Theologies of communion could provide a general theological narrative to shape the congregational cultures of a shared parish. As a cultural product adapted from church tradition, it enjoys ecclesial legitimacy. A pastor or leader can use that legitimacy to propose it to the "receivers," that is, the parishioners, noting how it responds to their particular dilemmas and context. For example, in a world of multiple and often mutually unintelligible cultural expressions of Catholicism, communion theologies preach not the minimal tolerance of multiculturalism but the virtues of accepting bonds of unity within an atmosphere of diversity. They allow that people need not celebrate mass in the same language or minister in the same way in order to experience unity. A folk paradigm rooted in communion theologies could frame unity instead (1) in terms of common symbols (for example, church building and art, Catholic sacramental rites, parish mission statement) and (2) through intermittent, structured means for parishioners to interact socially and liturgically (for example, union or bridge masses, parish picnics, multicultural food festivals).

Even a very persuasive framing of these bonds of unity, however, will not prove sufficient to replace older ideologies like assimilation with both their framing and feeling rules. "One can defy an ideological stance not simply by maintaining an alternative frame on a situation but by maintaining an alternative set of feeling rights and obligations."[86] Discomfort with a lack of uniformity has to be edged out by an emphasis on curiosity about differences and pleasure in demonstrations of unity across cultures. Relying on both formal authority and social capital within each cultural group, parish leaders need to propose and model the new emotional register while they articulate the alternative framing of unity.

Leaders also have to link this alternative narrative of unity with concrete practices. English-American theologian Nicholas Healy, in his reflections on theological method in ecclesiology, argues that concrete practices often get left out of theology. And Healy includes communion theologies among what he calls "blueprint ecclesiologies," grand statements about the Church that gloss over the concrete realities of ecclesial life. The Catholic orientation toward the visible Church probably makes this worse, since Catholic theology tends to make more specific connections between these grand statements and visible ecclesial structures.[87] In a similar Protestant proposal, Christian Batalden Scharen responds to what he believes is an overidealized theology of the Church in Protestant theologian John Milbank's theology, known as radical orthodoxy. Milbank assumes that the Christian narrative in itself creates an alternative vision that captures the imagination of believers. Scharen argues that it might if pastors can make connections between that narrative and everyday Christian practices. He suggests that ethnographic accounts of church life (like this one) provide "judicious narratives" that fill out a portrait of the Church in real life and help us understand how theology actually works in practice. Milbank admitted such narratives were often lacking in his own accounts of the Church.[88]

To understand the relationship between a folk paradigm of communion and concrete practices in a shared parish, we might look again at intercultural negotiations as an informative detail. Given the continued widespread availability of assimilation ideology as a cultural resource in the United States and its emotional power, Euro-Americans often imagine intercultural negotiations as taxing, extraordinary means for maintaining tolerant coexistence (as required by multiculturalism) until distinct cultural groups wither away on the road to their total assimilation into Anglo-American cultures. They turn into ordeals for the interim, a necessary evil. Framed in the light of communion, they instead become ordinary, daily means of cementing the bonds of unity that already exist on account of baptism. This is closer to the reality of everyday practice. After all, wherever different groups coexist and desire interconnectedness, they must engage in intercultural negotiations. Thus, we could reimagine intercultural negotiations not as tension-filled ordeals but rather as the ordinary work of the Church. This is communion enacted on an everyday basis in a complex, culturally diverse parish context.

In cultural anthropology and the sociology of culture, scholars describe various repeated patterns of human action as "cultural work," since these practices make, alter, and especially reproduce the culture from day to day. Ann Swidler gives us the ordinary example of the way courtship is structured and the institution of marriage reinforced by middle-class Americans' cultivation of the emotions and actions involved in seeking a unique other as mate and "falling in love" with that person.[89] Reframing intercultural negotiations in terms of communion makes those negotiations into a species of cultural work. The reframing can normalize the cultivation of certain emotions (such as patience and curiosity about cultural differences) and actions (use of short phrases in a different language for greeting, pantomiming messages, waiting for a translation) as part of the process of making, altering, and reproducing the local culture of the shared parish. In other words, reframing the challenging intercultural encounters according to a shared vision shaped by a folk paradigm of communion is possible. But it requires intentional leadership and effort. The theologian Nicholas Healy agrees: "The identity of the concrete church is not simply given; it is constructed and ever reconstructed by the grace-enabled activities of its members as they embody the Church's practices, beliefs, and valuations."[90]

Cultural Encapsulation and Power

Even if pastoral leaders successfully create a working folk paradigm that recognizes both cultural differences and social bonds between groups, they cannot succeed unless they address asymmetries of power within the church. Unequal power relationships perpetuate a status quo that favors the dominant group. Tensions simmer over time. Less powerful cultural and racial groups develop powerful resentments when the situation appears unalterable.[91] As the anecdote at the beginning of this chapter indicated, cultural encapsulation cloaks this unequal distribution of power, especially for the dominant group. At All Saints, many Euro-American Catholics had little awareness of the asymmetrical operations of power in the parish. Isolated in their own community, few considered that they might possess social advantages not afforded to most Latinos and that Latinos might covet these advantages. Thus, it simply did not occur to them that they might need to share their power. Some even felt powerless, seeing changing demographics as inevitably sidelining them. Others assumed their own community's possession of power was natural and fitting. After all, before the arrival of Latino immigrants, *their* world had effectively been *the* world.

Part of the problem occurs because modern people tend to identify power with coercion or force, as with Max Weber's famous definition of the state as that institution with a monopoly on violence.[92] But more recent theoretical approaches to power tend to stress the operation of power without explicit coercion or force. They examine more invisible aspects of power dynamics, such as the hegemonic assumptions that no one thinks to question or the way individuals discipline themselves in order to comply with the requirements of authorities.[93] In the culturally homogenous Havenville of the 1940s and 1950s, for example, no one had to compel the handful of Mexican families in town not to speak Spanish. One of the few Mexican Americans who grew up in Havenville commented as follows:

> One of the things that I recall, and it kind of bothered me, speaking English so much that you forget your Spanish. And it wasn't until we had our Hispanic ministry here, and I was one of the members when it first started, that when I started working here, I had to have more communication with Hispanic families, having to learn again all of the different things I had forgotten.

The unquestioned cultural dominance of English and Euro-American culture in that era left Mexican residents with no alternatives but to speak English. Mexican children disciplined themselves, unaware that they were losing the language of their families (often their first language at home) without any recourse.

By 2007, however, the era of English and Euro-American hegemony had ended in Havenville. Some Euro-Americans held to their position of linguistic and cultural privilege using ideological discourse to justify it, especially what cultural anthropologist Leo Chavez calls the "Latino Threat Narrative." In select local media and in certain public conversations, Latinos were stereotyped as invaders and freeloaders who would not integrate into American society. They were not immigrants trying to navigate a foreign culture in a new homeland; they were obstinate operators taking advantage of the system. Latino community members heard these rumblings, which reinforced a belief that the position of Latinos in Havenville remained unjustly inferior. By and large, however, Latinos did not complain openly to Euro-Americans, not wanting to disturb an already precarious situation. Unfortunately, this protected Euro-American Catholics' cultural encapsulation. Instead complaints emerged in the "hidden transcript," political scientist James Scott's zone of hidden conversation, performances, and jokes.[94] Offered a ride home one afternoon, I was sarcastically asked (in Spanish) to point to one direction or the other to indicate whether I lived among the Anglos and the affluent or on the poorer Hispanic side of town. A man told me that he and his family could only vote in a local election at their dining room table.

Without intervention and especially when unnoticed by the more powerful group, asymmetrical power dynamics obstinately persist. As a result, the leadership of any shared parish has the unenviable task of drawing attention to the differences in power and privilege. They have to find a way to ensure that people see the need to share power and then actually do share it. The combination of a resolutely hierarchical power structure coupled with the rising importance and role of lay leadership complicates this task. On the one hand, theoretically, bishops and pastors could simply insist that cultural groups in a parish share power. At different times at All Saints, people from both cultural communities came to joint meetings to negotiate just because one of the priests required them to come. On the other hand, because voluntarism and lay leadership have become such a part of Catholic parish life, people often feel free to not comply or to do so minimally. So is Roman Catholic centralization of power a good thing or a bad thing for sharing power in the shared parish?

Psychologist Mark B. Borg has argued that the centralized power structure of the Roman Catholic Church can dovetail with local cultural and economic power arrangements to calcify asymmetrical power arrangements in a parish. Borg studied a parish shared by English-speaking American Chinese, wealthier Cantonese-speaking immigrants, and poor and often undocumented Mandarin-speaking immigrants. He found that pastor-centered leadership, hierarchical Confucian respect for elders, and local and exploitive economic relationships conspired to perpetuate the asymmetrical power of Cantonese and American Chinese over the mainland immigrants who worked for almost nothing in the businesses they owned. Moreover, as at All Saints, identifying the asymmetry provoked shock and resentment in the group in power.[95]

Nevertheless, Borg acknowledges that not everyone in the powerful group resisted identification of the power dynamics and some movement toward power sharing: "We noticed that some Cantonese speakers *did* reach out to the newcomers, often at great personal sacrifice."[96] Similarly at All Saints, several Euro-American parishioners had long realized the need for some form of power sharing and took responsibility in different ways. One moved into significant immigration activism. The Euro-American pastor symbolized power sharing by washing the feet of his Mexican associate pastor (along with eleven other Mexican and Euro-American parishioners) at the annual Holy Thursday bilingual mass. Others awakened to the asymmetry in a jolt of consciousness. Walking through the empty church after a parish council meeting, I encountered one of the Euro-American parish council members at prayer. He whispered for me to come over to where he was kneeling. Pointing out the beautiful Christmas décor, he noted that Euro-American community members do all the decorating, effectively excluding the other half of the parish from that ministry. He did not think this was right, even though they did such a beautiful job.

Still, power sharing remained a difficult practice to embrace at All Saints. Euro-Americans families had long preceded the Latinos. They had expanded and paid for the parish facilities Latinos now shared. Euro-American parishioners understood how to negotiate the dominant culture and access the organs of government and commerce. Euro-American children were socialized into that world of presumed access to businesses, government, and other institutions. Even as hegemony subsided and people realized they were sharing a city and a church with a different cultural group, Euro-Americans found it difficult to imagine sharing the relative power they had. Research shows that people conceive of power as an innate competition between interests, what game theorists call a "zero-sum game." People believe they have to lose power for others to gain it. At All Saints, Euro-Americans worried that pastoral attention to the Latino community automatically amounted to a withdrawal of pastoral attention to the Euro-American community. But even in game theory, a zero-sum situation only occurs in a closed system, where few external factors have an impact. Parishes and congregations are generally open systems in constant relationship with the larger social environment.[97] Nevertheless, people may perceive power as a mutually exclusive competition of interests, making power sharing more difficult.

The Road Not Chosen

At an ecumenical gathering during my year in Havenville, I spoke with a group of Protestant pastors about shared parishes like All Saints. Trying to make sense of the arrangement I described to them, one of them asked if All Saints might be better off split in two, each as its own parish. I answered that perhaps it would, but the Catholic diocese had neither the resources nor the priests to make that happen. As often happens when persons with a different perspective ask an unexpected question, however, this one made me reflect further. The pastor was operating from a congregationalist set of assumptions, that a local faith community was by nature a group of people who *choose* to come together. Yet one of the fundamental challenges of life in a shared parish is exactly that people did not really choose to come together. A newcomer group arrives, and some sort of outreach to that group begins, usually in an ad hoc way. There is seldom a master plan. Parishioners already in residence rarely express an explicit desire to become a multicultural (or multiracial) parish. The situation simply develops. In this case, Mexican immigrants arrived, a few at first and then in great numbers. A priest saw the increasing need, and he gathered a small group of parishioners—either Latinos or mixed couples—to figure out how to address that need. In a way, the shared parish of All Saints was the largely unforeseen consequence of that initial outreach. The Latino and Euro-American communities did not really choose to be yoked together as a parish. It just happened.

Later, parishioners developed strategies for making sense of what had happened. I explored some of those strategies in chapters 2 and 3—notions of the social order, approaches to worship, a narrative of conversion seen as evangelization, and various constructions for framing parish unity. In this chapter, I examined two folk paradigms for addressing cultural diversity in the larger society that had an impact specifically at All Saints but also influence U.S. Catholicism at large. I wondered if, in the hands of pastors and pastoral leaders, another folk paradigm formed by a Christian theology of communion might prove more effective in an organization devoted to both respecting cultural differences and establishing some sort of social bond across cultures.

Scholars of culturally diverse faith communities suggest that what happened at All Saints—wandering into cultural diversity and then trying to make sense of it—is often the least successful way to form a multicultural or multiracial congregation; the best outcomes occur when a community adopts as its identity the mission of creating a diverse community, or at least takes on that project in service of some other greater mission.[98] That mission becomes the "niche identity" of the local faith community.[99] It often attracts young, cosmopolitan urbanites with a strong interest in diversity ("boundary crossers"), who provide important resources for taking on that mission: "In addition to the value they place on the multicultural experience of church, however, boundary crossers bring skills for negotiating the ambiguity and discomfort that arise in the multicultural setting."[100] Some shared parishes may find their way to articulating such a mission or at least to motivating themselves for it by reference to another deeply felt sense of mission.[101]

For shared parishes like All Saints, however, the involuntary, nearly accidental process of the sharing of a parish by different cultural communities does not lend itself to this mission-driven approach. Rather than consciously serving a niche identity as multicultural or multiracial, they function more as a larger hub loosely linking together distinct communities who themselves may serve a particular niche. All Saints had only a handful of the kind of diversity-embracing young adults described above, though these few did seem to have an impact in both cultural communities. But most parishioners did not feel they had chosen the shared parish arrangement; it had been thrust upon them, and so they felt only a little responsibility toward it. A language barrier and cultural misunderstanding made interaction across cultures costly. Avoidance usually seemed like a safer strategy. Cultural encapsulation was difficult to challenge.

This involuntary sharing of the parish also made it difficult to alter asymmetries of power and privilege in the parish. Longtime residents had not set out to share the resources and facilities they had so painstakingly built up over the decades, and many felt a strong sense of ownership over those resources and facilities. This made it difficult for them to conceive of a larger group of newcomers as equal partners. For their part, Latino parishioners never lost sight of the inequalities they perceived in the larger social ecology of Havenville. The gratitude of many to the Euro-American community for "allowing" them to worship at All Saints betrays the way they still felt like guests. Others explicitly articulated how they would be better off left on their own as much as possible.

Although challenging, this state of affairs mirrors the way the larger society—in Havenville and elsewhere—struggles with diversity. Because Americans think of religious communities as voluntary gatherings of people—the basic principle of de facto congregationalism—we naturally look upon communities brought together by fiat or circumstance as less than ideal, and with good reason. But in the larger society, newcomer groups come to a neighborhood or city in an ad hoc manner. The resident community may extend small gestures of hospitality, but ordinarily they come to terms with the changes initiated by demographic transformation only because they do have any choice. Havenville, like All Saints, did not form its civic mission around becoming a multicultural city. Instead it became one and then tried to make sense of it. Ideal or not, the way the cultural communities found themselves thrown together at All Saints more accurately mirrors the real experience of diversity in American society. Shared parishes are a microcosm of the larger society.

As such, they participate by fits and starts in a gradual movement beyond cultural encapsulation. After all, the involuntary paring of the cultural communities at All Saints did create previously unavailable opportunities for intercultural contact. Some who would never have *sought* much intercultural contact on their own found they could scarcely avoid it due to their participation in parish ministry or leadership. Some parishioners welcomed opportunities for contact, even if they only took advantage of them in small ways. They smiled at one another on the way in or out of church. They attended schoolchildren's birthday parties dominated by the other group. They sheepishly tried to offer a handshake of peace across cultural lines at bilingual masses. They were moved by the powerful religious symbolism of a Euro-American priest washing the feet of a Mexican priest. Euro-American parish council members cooed over the new baby of Latino parish council members. A few parishioners formed lasting friendships or even married someone from the other group. Even those who experienced anxiety-producing confrontational encounters sometimes learned something about the perspectives of people from the other group. In summary, the shared parish as an institution provided limited but badly needed opportunities for people to make sense of the reality of their coexistence in a multicultural society. Even if the majority of such opportunities do not break down cultural encapsulation, some will.

Conclusion

Whither the Shared Parish?

The experience of the shared parish recounted here mirrors the ways in which U.S. society and American Christianity in particular have been inexorably altered by the waves of immigration that began in the second half of the twentieth century. Some writers, social scientists, and theologians speak of this demographic transformation as the "browning of America" or the "de-Europeanizing" of American Christianity.[1] It appears even more dramatically in Roman Catholicism, since so many of the sending countries of today's immigrants have a disproportionately Roman Catholic religious makeup. According to the 2010 census, of the top nine nations sending migrants to the United States, five are majority Roman Catholic countries (all are Latin American nations except the Philippines). This includes Mexico, which is overwhelmingly Catholic (85 percent).[2] Mexico provides almost 30 percent of all immigrants to the United States.[3] Though most Asian countries besides the Philippines have a tiny Roman Catholic population at home, in the United States, the Vietnamese, Indian, and Chinese communities include surprising numbers of Roman Catholics.[4]

Statistics can measure the breadth of these demographic changes, but they cannot tell us much about the transformation of daily life in light of them. We need testimonies like those that appear within the pages of this book. They are the "the window in the wall" church historian Jay Dolan described; they help us to peer through to the fabric of everyday life in changed times.[5] Although Dolan used the phrase to describe how study of the Catholic parish can capture a sense of people's everyday lives in an ever-changing social environment, in truth parishes provide only one such window. One could examine any number of other institutions that reflect the transformation of U.S. society—towns and neighborhoods, businesses, sports leagues, schools and universities. What Catholic shared parishes have provided in these pages is a view of both the distinct cultural worlds that make up U.S. society today and the often-incipient character of the interaction between these cultural worlds.

To that end, in this book I have attempted to capture the complex life of the shared parish as manifested at All Saints in Havenville. Despite the widespread local use of the shared parish structure by the Roman Catholic Church to respond to demographic changes from immigration, this volume is in fact the first to highlight the shared parish form per se. Previous studies have generally examined several parishes as case studies in the larger exploration of immigration in an urban area, or have taken a single (often national) parish as an exemplar for good ministry among immigrants or other people of color.[6] Here we have looked at All Saints as a way of discovering how the daily life of a local faith community continues in a social and ecclesial context demographically transformed by immigration.

In the process of spending ten months at All Saints observing parish life, interviewing parishioners, and studying historical documents and artifacts from the parish, I unearthed some of the principal strategies that parishioners developed in order to adapt to a demographically transformed world. Some of these strategies are recognizable from earlier research on parishes and congregations, including: the connection between worship and identity,[7] the role of conversion narratives,[8] the influence of the Roman Catholic program of "new evangelization,"[9] and the role of popular religion adapted to a different context.[10] In these pages, however, I have described how the shared parish environment put a slightly different stamp on these strategies and created a fertile opportunity for new theorizing about cultural and religious identity in a culturally diverse local faith community. Other strategies uncovered in that parish year at All Saints—such as differing views of the social order—place in bold relief the radically different perspectives of two different cultural communities that were nevertheless influenced by sharing the parish with one another.

Chapter 3 offered up an "ethnography of unity" in order to discover what discourses of unity meant to different groups in the parish and why. More research is needed on these conceptions of unity, and we need to explore more deeply why people insist on it without being particularly articulate about what it looks like or how to get there. "Unity" has appeared as a thematic concern in previous research on "parallel congregations" or "multiethnic congregations," but this book has tried to move away from imagining unity as an either-or phenomenon (stepping away from Euro-American cultural biases that tend to theorize unity in terms of uniform belief and practice) in order to understand how distinct perspectives on unity emerge from the shared parish context and what these perspectives say about the struggles of each cultural community to adapt to the sharing of the parish. Chapter 3 ended with an exploration of intercultural negotiations as part of an unwelcome but necessary struggle in the shared parish. The perceptive reader will note that these reflections almost always focused on the perspectives of either Euro-Americans or immigrants. I have said little about the children of immigrants born in Havenville. Because most families had immigrated relatively recently, most of those in this group remained fairly young. But much more needs to be said about their experience of life in the shared parish.

Chapter 4 looked at influential concepts of the parish and congregation in social science (especially through the lens of the "new paradigm" of the sociology of religion) and sorted through those to theorize the Catholic parish in the United States today, especially its contemporary manifestation as the shared parish. In the process, I qualified the notion of de facto congregationalism for the life of today's "congregational parish," evoking both the advantages and limitations of de facto congregationalism for a church that exhibits voluntarism and lay ownership but also a centralized authority structure and an institutional tilt toward the larger Church. It concluded with an introductory examination of the social ecology of organizations (and especially the concept of "niche") as a theoretical approach to understanding the shared parish. This was but the tip of the iceberg, and I suspect much more could be done to develop social ecology as a theoretical approach to congregational research in the United States.

Chapter 5 explored two contemporary folk paradigms for imagining and understanding cultural diversity in U.S. faith communities—assimilation and multiculturalism—and argued that both assimilation and multiculturalism have served as loose social imaginaries by which Catholics frame the experience of cultural diversity. As such, they have also shaped the response of church leadership to changing times. The first, while still influential among many Euro-American Catholics, has been abandoned by Catholic leadership en route to a greater appreciation of the Catholic identity of different cultural groups (and, it is hoped, in search of more equitable power relationships). Multiculturalism, however, is often reduced to a caricature of itself, a showcase for superficial tolerance of diversity that never addresses the reality of dynamic cultures in relationship to one another or the asymmetrical power relationships that often exist between concrete communities. In the U.S. context, multiculturalism also suffers from being less structurally embedded in social institutions and so functions more as an ethical option. Many people do not think of it as one pertaining to them.

Looking for a new folk paradigm to employ, one that effectively imagines the tension between cultural difference and limited intercultural interaction so characteristic of the shared parish, I turned to a Christian theological vision, that of communion as a theology of Church. Communion provides a powerful vision of multicultural community that preserves the tension between cultural differences and the sharing of church across cultures. But could it really become a folk paradigm? I looked to social scientific theories about leadership as cultural production and everyday cultural work as reproducing culture to see if there were ways of imagining this vision embodied in a concrete local community of faith.

Communion may not strike a chord for many social scientists or religious studies scholars given its explicit emergence from Christian theological tradition. In part I find it congenial because I am a believing Christian. Perhaps it might serve us better to reimagine that vision of unity in diversity without the theological trappings. Even without its focus on the Christian doctrine of the Trinity or an explicit commitment to sacraments and Christian symbols, this approach to cultural diversity still accepts cultural differences as important even as distinct cultures impact one another and become intertwined over the generations and attends to the shared symbols and everyday intercultural negotiations that link distinct groups in a shared social environment. There might be other nontheological ways to name this approach—perhaps "interlinked distinctiveness" or "confederationism." This study of the shared parish might also serve as a springboard for exploration of other institutions that embed both distinction and sharing. I can imagine comparative study of labor unions with culturally accented local organizations or research into multicultural public and private schools. Some multinational corporations and nongovernmental organizations also demonstrate the way in which cultural distinctiveness can persist in institutions that are shared by multiple cultural groups. Whether or not such study really turns out to be analogous and whether or not such a construction proves theoretically sound to sociologists and religious studies scholars, I leave to others to judge.

＊　　　＊　　　＊

Religious studies scholar Ian Linden has written about the difficult process of trying to understand global Roman Catholicism in a world of stunning diversity. "Seeking a truthful presentation of the Roman Catholic Church as a coherent historical entity," he writes, "entails a process not unlike tuning into a long conversation in which four people talk at once."[11] Certainly studying the shared parish had that quality at times. Yet it is worth noting that, in the world of music, multiple and simultaneous voices often suggest harmony and beauty rather than discord and division. Perhaps musical or artistic representation can lead us to more congenial means of imagining the power and beauty of diversity held together in unity.

In the Roman Catholic Cathedral of the Blessed Sacrament in Sacramento, California, the Chapel of the Martyrs contains a mural depicting the resurrected Christ above a large freestanding crucifix affixed to the ground before the mural. Around Christ stand a selection of martyrs from the early Church, men on the right, women on the left. But underneath the arches painted below them stand martyrs of later centuries, conspicuously representing the different cultural communities of the Sacramento diocese, from St. Andrew Duc Lac of Vietnam to St. Maximilian Kolbe of Poland. Each martyr is identified in large lettering.[12] The effect is to connect Catholic life in Sacramento today across boundaries of time, space, and especially culture—communion across diversity. The same effect occurs in the gigantic Communion of Saints tapestries by artist John Nava at the Roman Catholic Cathedral of Our Lady of the Angels in Los Angeles. These tapestries depict 136 people, including 124 famous people canonized (as saints) or beatified (as "blessed") by the Church as well as 12 anonymous contemporary people from different cultural backgrounds, most young and some of them children.[13]

With these works of art, these two cathedrals present an image of Church tailored to the developing social context of two California dioceses. Both invite visitors to imagine a world where a common Christian faith can hold together groups with significant cultural differences. Like newer and culturally specific images of Christ, the Virgin Mary, and the saints now decorating churches across the world, these images self-consciously replace older Eurocentric images of the communion of saints that dominated the Roman Catholic Church for centuries. They suggest that we do not have to imagine faith communities ethnocentrically and that we can embrace both differences and unity. They "normalize" the juxtaposition of cultural difference and shared faith. Perhaps like the shared parish itself, they ask us to consider the possibility of living in the tension between cultural difference and human interconnectedness.

Life in the midst of that tension is not easy. The shared parish can easily become a kind of permanent crucible of grief where resentments and frustrations dominate the scene over time. It can be turned into a kind of waiting room that permits immigrant groups to manage their own cultural expressions of religiosity but only until such a time as they can be pragmatically coerced into adapting Euro-American religious customs. But over time parishioners in shared parish just might find new ways of institutionalizing the creative tension between cultural difference and sharing a common life and faith. When a fire destroyed the church of a shared parish in Holland, Michigan, for example, parishioners from three distinct communities (Latino, white, and Vietnamese) came together in a joint process of planning a new church building that honored all three communities equally. Pastor Stephen J. Dudek writes, "The new [church] home rises as a prophetic voice against a culture of standardization. Designed specifically for a culturally diverse context, it promotes unity without uniformity. Both ambiguity and clarity are held up as values within and beyond its walls as it speaks of the mystery of God in whose image all have been fashioned."[14]

A shared parish faces many challenges, but it can become an icon of a human unity that embraces the sharing of power and a mutual respect for cultural differences. The writer Marilynne Robinson believes that, in a sense, this joining together in equality of those who are strangers to one another is the function of all human communities. She writes, "I would say, for the moment, that community, at least community larger than the immediate family, consists very largely of imaginative love for people we do not know or whom we know very slightly."[15] With cultural diversity ever increasing, even in formerly homogenous communities like Havenville, this kind of "imaginative love" is sorely needed. Shared parishes, when they find ways of imaginatively grappling with the seeming contradiction of cultural distinctiveness and human unity, may provide us with valuable tools for living together well in a complex, multicultural society.

APPENDIX: RESEARCH METHODOLOGY

The exploration of All Saints Parish—seen through the lens of its transformation in response to changing demographics—forms the heart of this study of the shared parish. It is rooted in ten months of ethnographic fieldwork from late August 2007 to early July 2008 at All Saints. I chose All Saints for numerous reasons. One, it had undergone and continued to undergo the demographic transitions associated with shared parishes across the United States. Two, located in a midwestern manufacturing town far from the border states, it had few layers of history regarding immigration or cultural diversity—this was a relatively new phenomenon here. Three, the leadership of the parish remained open to the project and interested in hearing observations rooted in research.

Concretely, I engaged in fieldwork over the course of what I call a "parish year." The August-to-July parish year roughly maps onto the parochial school year. To a lesser extent, it follows the contours of the Catholic liturgical calendar, which begins in late autumn with Advent and then Christmas, continues through Lent in the winter and early spring, and then peaks with the high holy days of Holy Week and Easter. Near the beginning of that parish year, I spent a great deal of time observing Sunday masses, networking with parishioners, and visiting various parish groups and events. I was able to enlist different parishioners from each cultural community to take me on tours of both the parish facilities and the city of Havenville. After Christmas, as I described in chapter 1, I organized a meeting of older parishioners to talk about the history of the parish as they remembered it and to share artifacts and photos from generations past. During January and February of 2008, I trained a team of ten parishioner co-researchers. During my remaining months in Havenville, they cooperated with me both in conducting research and helping to interpret the results of research procedures already completed.

Priest and Researcher

During this parish year at All Saints, I was an ordained Roman Catholic priest and a member of a religious order, the Paulist Fathers (I have since taken leave of that community and the active priesthood). Catholics do not see the priesthood as a function or a temporary role; they believe it confers a lasting ministerial identity. It embeds a person in a set of relationships both locally and globally within the Church.[1] Parishioners I served in New York City, Chicago, or Northern California referred to me as their priest and wherever I travelled in the world Catholics called me "Father" and "Padre." Thus, there was no question about how I would present myself at All Saints. Nor did I misunderstand that the priesthood afforded me connections and access I might have had to fight for otherwise. I found Allw Saints through successive recommendations from other priests, one a professor at a Catholic university, the other a pastor in his same religious community. When I first called the pastor of All Saints, Father David, and asked if I might come to research the parish, I disclosed that I was a priest and where I had served. To a certain extent, Father David saw my identity as a priest as engendering trust, though cautiously so. He later contacted my superior and checked my status in official directories. When I came to visit All Saints in the spring of 2007, I again presented myself as a priest to Father David, Father Ignacio, and other members of the parish staff. I carefully explained the project and asked them for permission to conduct research there. Some remained a bit skeptical, but they also agreed.

When I arrived to begin research in August of 2007, I emphasized in my encounters with parishioners that I was both a priest and a researcher. No doubt the former role remained more familiar than the latter. But I believe that any efforts to deemphasize the former would have been seen as disingenuous and possibly as a hurtful deception. Given the recent context of the priest sex abuse scandal, they might have worried that I had downplayed my priesthood in order to hide some offense that precluded me from publicly presenting myself as a priest; when I told Father David that some scholars might argue that I should not act as a priest while doing this research, he suggested that parishioners would have assumed that my official permission to preach and preside at mass (canonical faculties) had been rescinded (they had not). In any case, at Father David's specific request, I donned my clerical collar on my first weekend in Havenville and introduced myself from the pulpit as both a priest and a researcher. I explained over and over again in personal encounters. During my early days in Havenville, I distributed cards in English and Spanish that noted that I was both priest and researcher and that people could refuse to speak with me. Occasionally they did.

There is actually a long historical tradition of priest-ethnographers. The sixteenth-century priests and friars Bernardino de Sahagún and Diego Durán ministered to Nahuatl-speaking indigenous people in colonial Mexico, but they also systematically observed and reported on their culture and way of life.[2] The French Canadian anthropologist Jean Michaud has compared the ethnographic work of French missionary priests in sixteenth-century North America and early-twentieth-century Vietnam.[3] There are contemporary examples as well.[4] Theorists generally regard practitioners who also perform research with the designation "outsider/insider researcher." In this context, outsiders are those "particularly concerned with knowledge seeking for its own sake, although there may be an action orientation as well," and insiders as "those individuals whose personally relevant social world is under study."[5] One can function as both at the same time. In fact, the categories operate both absolutely and relatively. There may exist clear insiders and outsiders in a setting, but people will also be relative insiders and outsiders in comparison to one another.[6] Thus, at All Saints, I was an outsider in the sense that I did not come from Havenville or live for many years in the parish. The role of researcher itself made me an outsider in a mostly working-class parish where only a handful of people had advanced degrees. I functioned as an outsider relative to the pastor, who grew up in the diocese, but as an insider relative to local Protestants or to researchers at the local college.

In fact, for ethnographers and other qualitative researchers, the boundaries of outsider and insider rarely remain clear. Differences of education, class, and experience often divide them from the people they study even within their own countries. Long-term fieldwork of non-native anthropologists certainly leads to a level of personal involvement and ties that challenges any conventional notion of "outsider."[7] In fact, all of us possess multiplex identities, of which different parts come to the fore in different contexts. We and others accentuate and form our identities as we interact. Research itself alters the relationships when these interactions take place.[8] Rather than a disruption, this is part of the research process.[9] "Outsider" and "insider" are not fixed identities but roles we perform that depend on context. The outsider practices detachment, the refusal to align oneself with any side, and that becomes particularly useful at times when fixed boundaries matter less. The insider practices engagement when boundaries and commitment remain crucial. The same scholar may appropriate both approaches at different times.[10]

At All Saints, I practiced both the detachment of an outsider and the engagement of an insider in my work with parishioners. At the request of the priests and staff, I performed basic ministerial tasks at the parish. I presided and preached at periodic masses, and more sparingly heard confessions and performed baptisms. Although I initially resisted doing any of this, over time I came to see it as a means of repaying the community for its hospitality to me. As in most rural dioceses in the United States, the priest shortage was acute in Port Jefferson Diocese. I occasionally helped out in neighboring parishes as well. At the same time, I spent far more time systematically observing masses from the perspective of the congregation than I did presiding at them. I attended ministry meetings and parish events, listening and observing. I was seen as often out of my clerical collar as I was in it. I jotted notes down at parish events and then expanded them into full-fledged field notes. I conducted oral histories and open-ended ethnographic interviews, carefully obtaining informed consent and then recording and then later transcribing these interviews. I listened carefully and bracketed my own pastoral perspectives even as I took in a parish life somewhat familiar to me. As much as I could, I delayed drawing conclusions until I had gathered narratives from multiple sources and in multiple settings. Some parishioners seemed to understand and appreciate my commitment to a degree of detachment as a researcher. Knowing that my project focused on the interplay between the different cultural communities, they asked me detailed questions about the relationships between cultural groups in their particular community and in the Catholic

Church in general. Latino parishioners asked me to explain Euro-American customs, and Euro-American parishioners asked me to comment on Mexican Catholic customs.

Nevertheless, just because the people of All Saints understood my status as both insider priest and outsider researcher does not mean that the role of priest-researcher presented no challenges or complications. Although people at All Saints rarely came to me for pastoral counseling or spiritual direction, when they did I had to erect a mental wall between whatever information I gleaned from these one-on-one ministerial encounters and the rest of my research work. In fact, most qualitative researchers have to make judgments about withholding information obtained in privileged personal exchanges. Still, the priesthood brings the possibility of assigning a sacred aura to such exchanges. Theologian Donald Cozzens speaks of a "mystique" people attribute to the priesthood, which he associates with celibacy. Priests are seen as somehow set apart from other people.[11] As a result, laity and clergy often relate to one another according to power dynamics that tend to reify the clerical state and its privileges. The priest-researcher with a blurred outsider/insider identity—one foot in each world—may miss this entirely and unwittingly help to reproduce these very dynamics.[12] I tried to attend to signs of deference shown to me and constantly emphasized that people did not have to speak to me if they did not wish to. At the same time, I respected the agency of the parishioners with whom I worked. Often they appeared as if they had been waiting for someone to listen to their stories. They offered questions, skepticism, and alternative interpretations to my own. Perhaps because members of the Euro-American community saw me as Spanish-speaking and an advocate for the Latino community, and members of the Latino community identified me as Euro-American, everyone seemed to question my interpretations as potentially biased by my allegiance to the other group.

All that being said, a particular advantage accrues to someone who combines outsider and insider perspectives. Both the outsider and the insider have a privileged epistemological perspective—the outsider on account of formal training, a discipline of detachment, and the desire for generalizable results, the insider on account of membership in the studied community and concern with particular results and their practical application.[13] Put another way, we might say that one privileges experience-distant concepts and the other experience-near concepts.[14] Combining these perspectives creates a new and marginal perspective with all its attendant creative tensions. New questions and answers surface previously unimagined by outsider or insider alone.[15] At All Saints, my outsider-insider perspective allowed me to experience and participate as a Catholic and priest (to be "engaged") as well as to apply theoretical perspectives and evaluate and interpret the data as an academic researcher (to be "detached").

Framing Insider-Outsider Research

This mixed status meant I needed to frame my parish year of fieldwork at All Saints in a way that made sense both ecclesially and social-scientifically. I framed it as an interdisciplinary process of collaborative investigation and reporting I called "participatory witness." The metaphor of "witness" is juridical, but it has theological resonance.[16] I trusted that the people of All Saints had something to say—both through their words and actions—about their social and ecclesial context and how they were responding to it as a parish. I saw formal ethnographic procedures as conduits for a process of bearing witness to their ideas and practices. But I also assumed that these ideas and practices had religious as well as social and cultural significance. Still, my approach remained rigorous by traditional standards of ethnographic research. I gained institutional review board approval, planned out triangulating research procedures, took detailed field notes, obtained written consent in English and Spanish for oral histories and interviews, and I (or my team) recorded and transcribed interviews unless persons objected.

   I did all this carefully and purposefully, but I also understood that detached observation—an epistemological approach sometimes referred to as "separate knowing" and associated with Western modernity—does not automatically confer objectivity and has epistemological limitations.[17] Any pretense of an untainted neutral perspective in research actually occludes (1) observer bias—the way a researcher selects data and frames information according to his/her own perspectives, (2) observer-incomprehension—the way a researcher will "miss the point" on account of lacunae in his/her knowledge of the studied community's world, and (3) observer-effect—the impact of the researcher on the data by his/her own presence and behavior.[18]

This suspicion of neutrality has emerged alongside a great deal of qualitative research theory about the involved researcher with a personal commitment to the community being studied. Feminist research traditions speak of connected knowing, where knowledge is collected via empathy and patient consideration of others' points of view.[19] Anthropologist Stephen Tyler describes a postmodern ethnographic epistemology in similar terms:

> Because post-modern ethnography privileges "discourse" over "text," it foregrounds dialogue as opposed to monologue, and emphasizes the cooperative and collaborative nature of the ethnographic situation in contrast to the ideology of the transcendental observer. In fact, it rejects the ideology of the "observer-observed," there being nothing observed and no one who is observer. There is instead the mutual dialogical production of a discourse, of a story of sorts.[20]

I saw my own work as following in these traditions of research, especially with an appreciation for polyvocality—a diversity of accounts. This seemed especially appropriate for a culturally diverse Catholic parish with distinct communities.

The Parishioner Research Team

In order to facilitate this polyvocality, I recruited ten trusted members of the All Saints community—five from the Latino community and five from the Euro-American community—to join me in conducting research through the second half of the year. The team met regularly in subsequent months, and they all conducted ethnographic interviews with parishioners (a few also did some participant observation of parish events). Plans for the recruitment, training, and activities of the team came from community-based research traditions such as participatory action research (PAR). Community-based researchers operationalize the combination of insider and outsider perspectives not in one person but through team research. "The parties, in

a colloquial sense, keep each other honest—or at least more conscious than a single party working alone may easily achieve."[21] Professional researchers recruit local community members to serve as co-
researchers. They train and work together, and together they attempt
to keep the good of the community center stage through a mutually
critical correlation of perspectives. "As each [participant] engages
with the relative foreigner who is her partner in the venture, that party's own world is made to some extent more foreign in her own eyes.
The native's usually tacit knowledge is thus made accessible through
questions reflected in the outsider's questioning looks."[22] Chroniclers
of participatory action research (PAR) and other forms of community-based research describe research as a creative fusion of the perspectives of scientific experts and practitioners in the service of social
transformation.[23]

At All Saints, I chose persons from varied backgrounds, socioeconomic status, and positions in the parish power structure. Among the
Latinos I chose one stay-at-home mother, three factory workers, and
a full-time student; among the Euro-Americans there were a retired
professor, a retired man of blue-collar background, an emergency
room nurse, a full-time student, and a part-time illustrator/artist. All
had completed high school (or *secondaria* in Mexico), but only two
had completed college (the nurse and the professor). The group skewed
slightly young and female. There were two Latino men in their twenties, a Latina in her twenties, two Latina women in their early thirties,
a Euro-American woman in her twenties, a Euro-American woman in
her forties, a Euro-American man in his late fifties or early sixties, and
two Euro-American women in their late sixties or early seventies. All
possessed some openness or skill at bridging cultural and class differences. The insider and lay status of these team members allowed for a
different type of access to parish communities, eliciting different information, and shaping different interpretations of data than my own status as a priest provided for. Internal diversity on the team further mul-
tiplied perspectives.

I recruited team members during November and December
through the recommendations of the two priests and other parish
leaders and based on my own networking within the parish as well.
I wanted the team membership to balance the two major cultural

groups and represent at least some of the major ministerial and interest groups within the parish. Members would have to have a basic interest in getting to know parish members beyond their own cultural group. I recruited two fully bilingual members as well as others who could provide access to more marginal members of the parish, lest those voices be lost.[24] Once I had recruited a team member, I asked him or her to read a one-sheet explanation of the team member's role and sign a consent form.

In January 2008, I held two lengthy training and orientation meetings with the new team, all conducted in English and Spanish with me interpreting back and forth. In the first session, I had each team member tell his or her own story of faith in the context of the parish. Several of the Euro-American team members expressed wonder at the difficult migration journeys that had brought the Latino team members to the parish. At that same meeting, I introduced them to the research project. I specifically had the group read and discuss bilingual materials explaining the research methodology, aims, and parish context. That reading and discussion continued in the second meeting, during which we went over research procedures (participant observation and ethnographic interviewing) and role-played them. In subsequent regular meetings, we group tested interview schedules and discussed challenges that arose in interviewing, especially the way in which undocumented parishioners agonized over whether or not to participate. As the year came to a close, we had structured conversations about the interview data itself and what it might mean. The group met one last time on a return visit to Havenville where we debriefed the research experience, and they all spoke about their subsequent involvement in parish activities.

Aside from recruiting, training, and working with the research team, I sought the feedback and participation of other parishioners in the research process. I offered in-person oral reports on the research to parish leaders and to the parish council. At Christmas and at the year's end, I distributed a two-page report to the entire parish via the church bulletin. I carefully recorded responses and feedback on these occasions. I returned to Havenville twice more after I had finished the research year, updating team members and the priests on what I had discovered, again soliciting their feedback through informal conversations and structured meetings. These techniques also came from community-based action research traditions and were designed to ensure that as much of the data as possible found its way back into the hands of parishioners and parish leaders for local use.

Data Collection and Analysis

I largely relied on common ethnographic procedures during my year in Havenville. Both team members and I engaged in participant observation and semistructured interviews. For the latter, we used an interview schedule of eleven questions derived from testing both within the research team and on a few other parishioners. I used additional procedures adapted from the literature on congregational studies, including (1) the congregational timeline—long-time community members creating a descriptive timeline of the cultural memory of the parish—and (2) the area tour—knowledgeable community members from each community offering geographical and cultural commentary on Havenville and its environs.[25] To augment the historical context created by the timeline exercise, I went through materials on the history of the parish found in both the parish and the diocesan archives. I also conducted a number of open-ended oral history interviews with longtime parishioners, each lasting approximately an hour and tracing their life history as it pertained to the parish and local area.

In the tradition of community-based research, I asked the team for advice in tailoring research procedures to their specific context. As a result, we created an abbreviated interview schedule and "back of the vestibule" ad hoc interview process to engage parishioners who attended mass but had no involvement in ministries. Team members also recommended focus groups for older children in the religious education program. Finally, I conducted a written survey of basic information and attitudes at each mass over the course of two Sundays in May 2008.[26] All these different methods with their different epistemological orientations provided triangulation and checks upon one another in the interpretation of data.

During the first half of my parish year, I focused attention on participant observation, oral history interviews, and archival research.

I conducted twelve oral history interviews lasting an hour or more, including four Latino and ten Euro-American parishioners as well as the former pastor; some interviews were with couples. The youngest interviewee was in her late thirties, the oldest in his nineties. I coordinated a community timeline exercise in January with seventeen parishioners, most over the age of seventy. When we exhibited information and artifacts from that exercise in the parish hall in February, I stood near the exhibit and asked visitors for their feedback (on which I took notes). I also positioned response forms near the exhibit in the parish hall and next to posted summaries of the exhibit in the church entrances. A handful of people filled them out.

During the second half of my parish year, team members and I conducted thirty-nine semistructured ethnographic interviews of parishioners using the interview schedule already mentioned. This included eighteen interviews of twenty-nine people in English (two men and five women by themselves and eleven married couples) and twenty interviews of twenty-three people in Spanish (seven women and ten men by themselves and three married couples). We also interviewed one bicultural couple in a combination of English and Spanish. Interviewees ranged in age from twenty-two to eighty years old. Only two of the Latinos interviewed were fifty years of age or older.

I had trained team members in interviewing over the course of several team meetings within a two-week period. They learned the "grand tour" style of open-ended interviewing, rather than the more tightly structured style used to produce statistically comparable quantitative data.[27] Their interviewing experiences naturally varied. A few of the Latino interviewers would not record their interviews (and some of the interviewees would not consent to be recorded). They took extensive notes, but as a result some of the Spanish interviews do not compare in detail or length to the English interviews. Especially in Spanish, interviewees seemed freer and less formal speaking with team members than they did speaking to me. Indeed, research suggests that leaders (such as a priest) doing interviewing may inhibit responses among the rank and file.[28] However, research also suggests that the practice of interviewing itself communicates in an in-depth way that a project takes community members' points of view seriously, and we found people appreciative that their thoughts and feelings were solicited at All Saints.[29]

The initial list of interviewees was rooted in early attempts to map out the "stakeholder groups" in the parish and the networks of leaders and active parishioners around them. Since we aimed to discover parishioners' thoughts and practices regarding parish life, I proposed to the group that—at least initially—influential persons at the parish would yield the best results. We broadened my initial list in several informal ways: (1) by brainstorming names of persons well regarded by many parishioners, (2) by asking the priests, and (3) via the "snowball" technique of obtaining names from those we talked to informally or in interviews. Ultimately we found we had a lopsided account that focused too much attention on highly involved parishioners. To compensate, we made an effort to conduct condensed interviews with less-involved people in the back of the church over a series of Sundays. We simply stood in the back of the church before or after mass and approached those who had been sitting or standing near the back. All of us made an effort to interview only those people we did not recognize. In this manner, we interviewed four Euro-American women, six Latina women, and two Latino men. The Euro-American subjects were all middle-aged or older, and the Latino subjects were all under fifty. Since all the interviews were with adult parishioners, I also conducted open-ended focus group interviews with three different youth groups (one Euro-American and two Latino) and four religious education classes for teenagers.

Because parishes, like all cultural worlds, are interconnected with the larger political and economic systems, I found it necessary to research and treat elements of the larger economic or political scene as background material to this process of ethnographic observation.[30] I met with an economist, studied statistics about the local economy, kept up on the state and local controversies around immigration, and asked local factory workers about their wages and potential discrimination across racial and cultural lines. Sociologist Michael Burawoy recommends approaching the wider social and economic interconnections with the local context in the manner of an extended case study, following the threads of microprocesses across time and space to the external forces involved.[31] In the case of All Saints, this necessitated a research trip to two cities and three villages in two of the three states in Mexico in which the vast majority of Havenville's Mexican people had originated. Visiting with families of All Saints parishioners, I took extensive notes. I talked to family members, priests, and neighbors. This included three semistructured ethnographic interviews with family members, one with a neighbor, and three with parish priests.

NOTES

AUTHOR'S NOTE ABOUT TERMINOLOGY AND
THE IDENTITY OF PERSONS AND PLACES

1. See, for example, Anthony M. Arroyo-Stevens, "The Emergence of a Social Identity Among Latino Catholics: An Appraisal," in *Hispanic Culture in the United States: Issues and Concerns,* ed. Jay P. Dolan and Allan Figueroa Deck, Notre Dame History of Hispanic Catholics in the U.S., vol. 3 (Notre Dame, IN: University of Notre Dame Press, 1994), 77–130.

INTRODUCTION

1. Gino Black [pseud.], *History of the Port Jefferson Diocese* (Port Jefferson: PJ Catholic Press [pseud.], 2006), 97; Fr. John Nowak [pseud.] and the Sesquicentennial Committee, *The History of All Saints Catholic Church, 1840–1990* (Havenville: All Saints Parish, 1990), 8–9.

2. Russell E. Richey, Kenneth E. Rowe, and Jeanne Miller Schmidt, *American Methodism: A Compact History* (Nashville,TN: Abingdon Press, 2010), 191.

3. Other Reformation churches occasionally use the term "parish," though "congregation" is really the term of choice for American Protestants. The traditions mentioned have exceptions to the rule of one church per local area.

4. Charles M. Whelan to papal nuncio at Paris, New York, 28 January 1785, quoted in James Hennessey, *American Catholics: A History of the Roman Catholic Community in the United States* (New York: Oxford University Press, 1981), 75.

5. See Stephen J. Shaw, *The Catholic Parish as Way-Station of Ethnicity and Americanization: Chicago's Germans and Italians, 1903–1939,* Chicago Studies in the History of American Religion (Brooklyn, NY: Carlson Publishing, 1991); and Kathleen Neils Conzen, *Making Their Own America: Assimilation Theory and the German Peasant Pioneer* (New York: Berg Publishers, 1990).

6. Aristide R. Zolberg, *A Nation by Design: Immigration Policy in the Fashioning of America* (New York: Russell Sage Foundation, 2006), 205.

7. Timothy L. Smith, "New Approaches to the History of Immigration in Twentieth-Century America," *American Historical Review* 71, no. 4 (July 1966), 1267–1269.

8. Philip Gleason, *The Conservative Reformers: German-American Catholics and the Social Order* (Notre Dame, IN: University of Notre Dame Press, 1968), 172–203; Stephen Cornell and Douglas Hartmann, *Ethnicity and Race: Making Identities*

in a Changing World, 2nd ed. (Thousand Oaks, CA: Pine Forge Press, 2007), 133–135; Conzen, *Making Their Own America*, 29.

9. Shaw, *Way-Station*, 20–28.

10. Philip Gleason, "In Search of Unity: American Catholic Thought, 1920–1960," *Catholic Historical Review* 65, no. 2 (April 1979): 185–205.

11. Zolberg, *A Nation by Design*, 199–293. See also Peter Schrag, *Not Fit for Our Society: Immigration and Nativism in America* (Berkeley: University of California Press, 2010), 41–76.

12. Richard Alba and Victor Nee, *Remaking the American Mainstream: Assimilation and Contemporary Immigration* (Cambridge, MA: Harvard University Press, 2003), 127.

13. Edward R. Kantowicz, "Cardinal Mundelein of Chicago and the Shaping of Twentieth-Century American Catholicism," *Journal of American History* 68, no. 1 (Jun. 1981): 63–68.

14. This is Stephen J. Shaw's term.

15. Peter R. D'Agostino, *Rome in America: Transnational Catholic Ideology from the Risorgimento to Fascism* (Chapel Hill: University of North Carolina Press, 2004), 1–96.

16. Kantowicz, "Cardinal Mundelein," 60–63.

17. Mark S. Massa, *Catholics and American Culture: Fulton Sheen, Dorothy Day, and the Notre Dame Football Team* (New York: Crossroad, 1999), 1–4.

18. Gleason, "In Search of Unity," 185–205. See also Matthew Pehl, "The Remaking of the Catholic Working Class: Detroit, 1919–1945," *Religion and American Culture: A Journal of Interpretation* 19, no. 1 (Dec. 2009): 36–67.

19. Massa, *Catholics and American Culture*, 1–10.

20. One of the clearest articulations of this narrative occurs in John Tracy Ellis, *American Catholicism*, 2nd ed. (Chicago: University of Chicago Press, 1969), 166–168. More contemporary are these accounts: Massa, *Catholics and American Culture*; and Peter Steinfels, *A People Adrift: The Crisis of the Roman Catholic Church in America* (New York: Simon & Schuster, 2004), 3–7.

21. Conzen, *Making Their Own America*, 1–7; and Cyprian Davis, *The History of Black Catholics in the United States* (New York: Crossroad, 1990), 238–259. See also Kathleen Neils Conzen, "Foundation of a Rural German-Catholic Culture: Farm and Family in St. Martin, Minn., 1857–1915," Working Paper Series, American Catholic Studies Seminar, no. 2 (Spring 1977).

22. Kitty Calavita, *Inside the State: The Bracero Program, Immigration, and the I.N.S.* (New York: Routledge, 1992), 31–43, 46–61, 74–85, 141–159. See also George J. Borgas and Lawrence F. Katz, "The Evolution of the Mexican Born Workforce in the United States," in *Mexican Immigration to the U.S.*, ed. George J. Borgas (Chicago: University of Chicago Press, 2007), 13–17; and Stuart Anderson, *Immigration* (Santa Barbara, CA: Greenwood, 2010), 92–97.

23. Gina Marie Pitti, "'A Ghastly International Racket': The Catholic Church and the *Bracero* Program in California, 1942–1964," Working Paper Series, Cushwa Center for the Study of American Catholicism, series 33, no. 2 (Fall 2001): 1–21; and Gina Marie Pitti, "To 'Hear About God in Spanish': Ethnicity, Church, and Community Activism in the San Francisco Archdiocese Mexican-American *Colonias*, 1943–1965" (Ph.D. diss., Stanford University, 2003).

24. See Ana María Díaz-Stevens, *Oxcart Catholicism on Fifth Avenue: The Impact of the Puerto Rican Migration upon the Archdiocese of New York* (Notre Dame, IN: University of Notre Dame Press, 1993).

25. Kathleen Garces-Foley, "From the Melting Pot to the Multicultural Table: Filipino Catholics in Los Angeles," *American Catholic Studies* 120, no. 1 (2009): 27–53. See also Kathleen Garces-Foley, "Comparing Catholic and Evangelical Integration Efforts," *Journal for the Scientific Study of Religion* 47, no. 1 (2008): 17–22. And see U.S. Conference of Catholic Bishops, "Welcoming the Stranger among Us: Unity in Diversity," *Origins* 30, no. 26 (7 December 2000): 421n5.

26. In the wake of the civil rights movement, national parishes could be seen to resemble a form of segregation. Also, Latin American immigrants did not have clergy or many influential church leaders to advocate for such a solution. Allan Figueroa Deck, *The Second Wave: Hispanic Ministry and the Evangelization of Cultures* (New York: Paulist, 1989), 58–61.

27. Ebaugh and Chafetz, following Paul Numrich, use the term "parallel congregations." Helen Rose Ebaugh and Janet Saltzman Chafetz, *Religion and the New Immigrants: Continuities and Adaptations in Immigrant Congregations*, abridged student ed. (Lanham, MD: Altamira Press, 2000).

28. Jay P. Dolan, *The American Catholic Experience: A History from Colonial Times to the Present* (Notre Dame, IN: University of Notre Dame Press, 1992), 159.

29. According to the 2010 American Community Survey of the U.S. Census, 12.7 percent of the population is foreign born. This is the highest percentage since the 1920 decennial census showed 13.2 percent. The highest ever was in 1890 and 1910 when it approached 15 percent (14.8 percent and 14.7 percent respectively). Diane Schmidley, "Profile of the Foreign-Born Population of the United States: 2000" (Washington, DC: U.S. Census Bureau, 2001), 9.

30. According to the Pew Forum on Religion and Public Life, 46 percent of all immigrants are Roman Catholic, far and away the largest religious group (all Protestant groups together compose 24 percent). Luis Lugo et al., "U.S. Religious Landscape Survey" (Washington, DC: Pew Research Center, 2008), 47. According to a study by the Pew Hispanic Center, 74 percent of foreign-born Latinos—the largest group among immigrants—are Catholics. Roberto Suro et al., "Changing Faiths: Latinos and the Transformation of American Religion" (Washington, DC: Pew Research Center, 2007), 12.

31. Lugo et al., "U.S. Religious Landscape Survey," 23–26; William V. D'Antonio et al., eds., *American Catholics Today: New Realities of Their Faith and Their Church* (Lanham, MD: Rowman and Littlefield, 2007), 21; and Center for Applied Research in the Apostolate, "Special Report: Young Adult Catholics" (Washington, DC: Georgetown University/CARA, 2002), 4–5.

32. Campbell Gibson and Kay Jung, "Historical Census Statistics on Population Totals By Race, 1790 to 1990, and by Hispanic Origin, 1970 to 1990, for The United States, Regions, Divisions, and States," Working Paper Series no. 56, Population Division (Washington, DC: U.S. Census Bureau, 2002), table 1.

33. According to the 2010 American Community Survey, 4.0 percent of immigrants come from Africa, 28.2 percent from Asia, 12.1 percent from Europe, .6 percent from Oceania, and 53.1 percent from Latin America. According to the 1910 census, 87.2 percent of the foreign born were from Europe and most of the rest (9 percent) from Canada.

34. Richard Rodriguez, *Brown: The Last Discovery of America* (New York: Viking, 2002), xi–xv.

35. According to the 2010 Census of the Population of the United States, U.S. Census Bureau.

36. Joyce A. Martin et al., "Births: Final Data for 2006," National Vital Statistics Report 57, no. 7 (Hyattsville, MD: National Center for Health Statistics, 2009), 52.

37. R. Stephen Warner, "Immigration and Religious Communities in the United States," in *Gatherings in Diaspora: Religious Communities and the New Immigration,* ed. R. Stephen Warner and Judith G. Wittner (Philadelphia: Temple University Press, 1998), 4.

38. Lugo et al., "The U.S. Religious Landscape Survey," 44.

39. Ibid., 44, 53; Suro et al., "Changing Faiths," 14; and Matthew Bunson, ed., *Catholic Almanac 2008* (Huntington, IN: Our Sunday Visitor, 2007), 426. On methodology questions regarding ascertaining the number of Hispanic Catholics, see Suro et al., "Changing Faiths," 10; and Paul Perl, Jennifer Z. Greely, and Mark M. Gray, "How Many Hispanics Are Catholic?" Center for Applied Research in the Apostolate (Washington, DC: Georgetown University/CARA, 2005), 1–35.

40. Barry A. Kosmin, "Research Report: The National Survey of Religious Identification, 1989–90" (New York: Graduate Center of the City University of New York, 1991), 7; and Barry Kosmin, Egon Mayer, and Ariela Keysar, "American Religious Identification Survey, 2001" (New York: Graduate Center of the City University of New York, 2001), 35. Both reports are available at http://commons.trincoll.edu/aris/publications/. Suro et al., "Changing Faiths," 14–16.

41. "Hi, how are you?" "Where is the bathroom?" "Another beer, please."

42. The pastor noted to me that, since the 2002 sex abuse priest sex abuse revelations, it would be a fatal mistake to refrain from priestly ministry in the parish. Such nonparticipation would have aroused unfounded and disturbing suspicions.

43. For a more comprehensive sense of the methodology, see the appendix.

44. Contemporary national parishes or ethnic missions do get established (or maintained) when a group has sufficient financial resources and influence to both fund and lobby for them, as in the case of Vietnamese Catholics in California or Texas, or when priests or other church leaders lobby for a marginalized group, such as occurred with Haitian Catholics in Miami. Terry Rey and Alex Stepick, "Refugee Catholicism in Little Haiti: Miami's Notre Dame d'Haiti Catholic Church," in *Churches and Charity in the Immigrant City: Religion, Immigration, and Civic Engagement in Miami,* ed. Alex Stepick, Terry Rey, and Sarah J. Mahler (New Brunswick, NJ: Rutgers University Press, 2009), 72–76.

45. Since the Council of Trent in the sixteenth century, Roman Catholic parishes have had geographical boundaries. By church law, leadership at the parish consider themselves responsible for all (especially all Catholics) within these boundaries.

46. See Anselm Kyongsuk Min, "Korean American Catholic Communities: A Pastoral Reflection," *Religion and Spirituality in Korean America*, ed. David Yoo and Ruth H. Chung (Champaign: University of Illinois Press, 2008), 28–32.

47. Anthony M. Stevens-Arroyo, "The PARAL Study: The National Survey of Leadership for Latino Parishes and Congregations," part 1 (Brooklyn, NY: Religion in Society and Culture, 2002), 3.

48. Only 2 percent of parishes in the other three dioceses had "trilingual" parishes. Ken Johnson-Mondragón, "Ministry in Multicultural and National/Ethnic Parishes: Evaluating the Findings of the Emerging Models of Pastoral Leadership Project" (Stockton, CA: Instituto Fe y Vida/National Association for Lay Ministry, 2008), 13–14. Because of the uneven reporting of this information by dioceses, Johnson-Mondragón depended on the mass-goer social networking website www.masstimes.org to compile these statistics. The information on that site is updated by parishes themselves (automatically requested every six months by the site), and parishes are dropped after three years without an update. Moreover, a "church" on the site may also include a school, university, or chapel that offers public masses. Thus, the information from this site may not coalesce with official church statistics. Nevertheless, it offers us the preliminary look that Johnson-Mondragón intends. For more information about masstimes.org's methods, see http://www.masstimes.org/dotnet/About.aspx#_How_can_a_1.

49. Parishes and missions that have mass on the weekend. A handful of diocesan parishes and missions do devote themselves either in part or wholly to Native American ministry.

50. See "Oregon History: Statehood to the Present," on *Oregon Blue Book,* official state directory and fact book (Salem, OR: Oregon State Archives, 2009), http://bluebook.state.or.us/cultural/history/historypost.htm (accessed 26 June 2009). U.S. Census data on race for Oregon: non-Hispanic whites went from 95.8 percent of the state population in 1970 to 93.3 percent in 1980 to 90.8 percent in 1990 to 83.5 percent in 2000 to 78.5 percent in 2010. Moreover, in 1980, for

example, 94 percent of all African Americans, 79.4 percent of all Asians/Pacific Islanders, and 64 percent of all Latino/as (but only 48.9 percent of all Native Americans) lived in metropolitan areas outside the Diocese of Baker.

51. All figures compiled through assessment of parish mass data on diocesan websites, 25 June 2009.

52. Johnson-Mondragón, "Ministry in Multicultural and National/Ethnic Parishes," 14.

53. Michael W. Foley and Dean R. Hoge, *Religion and the New Immigrants: How Faith Communities Form Our Newest Citizens* (New York: Oxford University Press, 2007), 74–77. The Catholic immigrant groups studied were Salvadorans (along with a small number of other Latino/as), Nigerian Igbos, and Francophone Africans from Senegal and the Gambia. Interestingly, Protestant immigrant communities in the same area occurred in exactly the inverse. Only 27 percent shared the congregation, not all of them worshipping separately (60 percent). Seventy-three percent had stand-alone congregations.

54. Office of Research and Planning of Archdiocese of Chicago, "Data Composite: Facts and Figures for Year Ending 2007" (Chicago: Archdiocese of Chicago, June 2008), 59–60.

55. R. Stephen Warner, "Work in Progress Toward a New Paradigm for the Sociological Study of Religion in the United States," *American Journal of Sociology* 98, no. 5 (March 1993): 1044–1093.

56. Garces-Foley, "From the Melting Pot to the Multicultural Table," 27–53. See also Garces-Foley, "Comparing Catholic and Evangelical Integration Efforts," 17–22.

57. Eric H. F. Law, *Sacred Acts, Holy Change: Faithful Diversity and Practical Transformation* (St. Louis, MO: Chalice Press, 2002), 15–20.

58. Scholars Linda Tuhiwai Smith and Sandra Harding distinguish between methodology and method. I am following Smith's sense of terminology derived from Harding here, where methodology refers to the theoretical-hermeneutical framework that guides the work of research, and methods refer to the specific technical procedures for examining evidence. Linda Tuhiwai Smith, *Decolonizing Methodologies: Research and Indigenous Peoples* (New York: Zed Books, 1999), 143.

59. Gregory A. Smith, "Attitudes toward Immigration: In the Pulpit and Pew," Pew Forum on Religion and Public Life (Washington, DC: Pew Research Center, 2006). http://pewresearch.org/pubs/20/ attitudes-toward-immigration-in-the-pulpit-and-the-pew.

1. ALL SAINTS FROM VILLAGE CHURCH TO SHARED PARISH

1. Rhys H. Williams, "Religion and Place in the Midwest: Urban, Rural, and Suburban Forms of Religious Expression," in *Religion and Public Life in the Midwest: American's Common Denominator?*, ed. Philip Barlow and Mark Silk, Religion by Region Series (Walnut Creek, CA: AltaMira Press, 2004), 187–199.

2. Stephen J. Shaw, "The Cities and the Plains, a Home for God's People," in *The American Catholic Parish: A History from 1850 to the Present*, vol. 2, *Pacific States,*

Intermountain West, Midwest, ed. Jay P. Dolan (New York: Paulist Press, 1987), 284.

3. Black, *History of the Port Jefferson Diocese*, 14–34, 52–53.

4. Timothy L. Smith, "The Ohio Valley: Testing Ground for America's Experiment in Religious Pluralism," *Church History* 60, no. 4 (Dec. 1991): 461–479; Shaw, "The Cities and the Plains," 284–292; and Black, *Port Jefferson Diocese*, 67–73, 93–102.

5. Zolberg, *A Nation by Design*, 128–135; and David Noel Doyle, "Irish as Urban Pioneers in the United States, 1850–1870," *Journal of American Ethnic History* 10, no. 1/2 (Fall 1990/Winter 1991): 36–59.

6. Conzen, *Making Their Own America*, 1–8.

7. Shaw, "The Cities and the Plains," 284–303; and Black, *Port Jefferson Diocese*, 49–54.

8. Jay P. Dolan, *In Search of an American Catholicism: A History of Religion and Culture in Tension* (New York: Oxford, 2002), 93–94.

9. Alba and Nee, *Remaking the American Mainstream*, 59.

10. Dolores Liptak, *Immigrants and Their Church*, The Bicentennial History of the Catholic Church in America, ed. Christopher J. Kauffman (New York: Macmillan, 1989), 100.

11. For example, Fr. Bede O'Connor, "A Missionary's Views on Catholic Religious Behavior, 1854," in *Keeping Faith: European and Asian Catholic Immigrants*, ed. Jeffrey M. Burns, American Catholic Identities: A Documentary History, ed. Christopher J. Kauffman (Maryknoll, NY: Orbis, 2000), 58–59; Shaw, "The Cities and the Plains," 309; and Shaw, *The Catholic Parish as Way-Station*, 43.

12. Shaw, "The Cities and the Plains," 304–315; Gleason, *The Conservative Reformers*, 19–20, 29–40; Shaw, *Way-Station*, 71–87; and Liptak, *Immigrants and Their Church*, 92–113.

13. Zolberg, *Nation by Design*, 202–205.

14. Gleason, *The Conservative Reformers*, 46–51; see also, for example, the English program for the "Golden Jubilee of St. Mary's Church," in Avila, Indiana, 1903.

15. See Alba and Nee, *Remaking the American Mainstream*, 59–63.

16. Herbert J. Gans, "Symbolic Ethnicity: The Future of Ethnic Groups and Cultures in America," *Ethnic and Racial Studies* 2 (1979): 1–20; and Shaw, "The Cities and the Plains," 335–336.

17. Robert A. Orsi, *The Madonna of 115th Street: Faith and Community in Italian Harlem, 1880–1950* (New Haven, CT: Yale University Press, 1985), 14–54; Michael P. Carroll, *American Catholics in the Protestant Imagination: Rethinking the Academic Study of Religion* (Baltimore: Johns Hopkins University Press, 2007), 80–87; Richard M. Linkh, *American Catholicism and European Immigrants, 1900–1924* (Staten Island, NY: Center for Migration Studies, 1991), 35–38; and Shaw, "The Cities and the Plains," 336.

18. Orsi, *The Madonna of 115th Street*, 50–74; Linkh, *European Immigrants*, 38–44, 109–110; Shaw, *Way Station*, 101–123; and Shaw, "The Cities and the Plains, 336–340.

19. Black, *Port Jefferson Diocese,* 171.
20. Alba and Nee, *Remaking the American Mainstream,* 102–123; Linkh, *European Immigrants,* 19–33; and David A. Badillo, *Latinos and the New Immigrant Church* (Baltimore: Johns Hopkins University Press, 2006), 121.
21. Alba and Nee, *Remaking the American Mainstream,* 113–114, 126–131.
22. Parish census records, 1863, All Saints Parish, Havenville.
23. Black, *Port Jefferson Diocese,* 97; and Nowak and the Sesquicentennial Committee, *The History of All Saints Catholic Church,* 8–10.
24. Colonel Charles Sabatte [pseud.], "History of Havenville, Brookton County," 1898, All Saints archives.
25. Stephen Moser [pseud.] et al., "History of Havenville," in *Havenville: The First 150 Years, 1831–1981,* sesquicentennial ed., ed. Robert Johnson [pseud.] (Havenville: Havenville News Printing Co., 1981), 7–11; and Black, *Port Jefferson Diocese,* 15–16, 29–34.
26. Moser et al., "History of Havenville," 7–9; Stephen Moser [pseud.], "Industry Sparks Growth," in *Havenville: The First 150 Years,* 130–132; Carol Buford [pseud.], ed., *Havenville: The Next Ten Years, 1981–1991* (Havenville: News Printing, 1991), 1; and Joanne Sanders [pseud.] et al., "A Walk Through Havenville's Historic District" (Havenville: Havenville Historical Society, 1995).
27. Census of the Population of the United States 1950, vol. 2, Characteristics of the Population.
28. Jo Granfield [pseud.], "Churches Fulfill a Mission," in *Havenville: The First 150 Years,* 193–202; Sabatte, "History of Havenville, Brookton County."
29. "Roman Catholic Lecture," *Havenville Democrat,* 29 February 1844.
30. Yisrael Ellman, "Intermarriage in the United States: A Comparative Study of Jews and Other Ethnic and Religious Groups," *Jewish Social Studies* 49, no. 1 (Winter 1987): 1–26.
31. Shaw, "The Cities and the Plains," 315.
32. Timothy L. Smith, "The Ohio Valley," 461–479.
33. All Saints Parish reports, 1906–1934, Port Jefferson diocesan archives; H. J. Houk [pseud.], *The Port Jefferson Diocese, A Book of Historical Reference, 1669–1907* (Port Jefferson: Archer Printing, 1907), 285–287; Sabatte, "History of Havenville, Brookton County"; and Nowak, *The History of All Saints Catholic Church,* 12.
34. Census of the Population of the United States, 1910, Population. There was an almost complete absence of Italian or Eastern European names in factory and high school group photos from the era.
35. Moser et al., "History of Havenville," 56.
36. Ann Taves, *The Household of Faith: Roman Catholic Devotions in Mid-Nineteenth Century America* (Notre Dame, IN: Notre Dame University Press, 1986), 42–45, 94–111.
37. All Saints Parish records, 1890–1906; Houk, *Port Jefferson Diocese,* 285–287; and Black, *Port Jefferson Diocese,* 162–164, 218–219.

38. *Havenville News-Times,* 26 December 1922; "The Fiery Cross Is Demonstrated," *Havenville Democrat,* 26 December 1922; Black, *Port Jefferson Diocese,* 243–246, 260–264; and Moser et al., "History of Havenville," 63.
39. Ann Grace Rogers [pseud.], "Nostalgia," memoir, typewritten (photocopy), ca. 1995, Rogers family archives, Havenville.
40. All Saints Parish records, 1925–1926; and parish baptismal records, All Saints Parish, Havenville.
41. Lee Shai Weissbach, *Jewish Life in Small-Town America: A History* (New Haven, CT: Yale University Press, 2005), 144–145, 352; "Jewish Historical Resources: Brookton County," Department of Historical Preservation and Archaeology [state website]; and American Jewish Committee, *American Jewish Yearbook* (New York: Jewish Publication Society of America, 1907, 1919).
42. All Saints Parish reports to diocese, 1934–1935.
43. Moser et al., "History of Havenville," 142; Buford, *Havenville: The Next Ten Years,* 13.
44. Parish baptismal records, All Saints Parish, Havenville.
45. Nowak, *The History of All Saints Catholic Church,* 17–18; All Saints Parish reports, 1934–1946.
46. E. Brooks Holifield, "Toward a History of American Congregations," in *New Perspectives in the Study of Congregations,* vol. 2 of *American Congregations,* ed. James P. Wind and James W. Lewis (Chicago: University of Chicago Press, 1994), 43.
47. All Saints Parish reports, 1946–1949.
48. Census of the Population of the United States, 1890, 1910, 1920, 1930, 1950, and 1970.
49. Matt Cheney, "Showing Havenville," website for *Sundown Towns: A Hidden Dimension of American Racism* by James W. Loewen; Granfield, "Churches Fulfill a Mission," 193; and Dialogue Consultants [pseud.], "A Report on the Impact of Changing Demographics and Growing Diversity in the City of Havenville: Issues, Challenges & Opportunities" (Havenville: Community Relations Commission, 2007), 6.
50. Havenville Historical Society, *Havenville: Having a Great Time,* ed. Derrick R. Jones [pseud.] (Havenville: Havenville Historical Society, 1990), 38.
51. Joan Grycz [pseud.], *Port Jefferson Catholic,* 21 November 2004.
52. Nowak, *The History of All Saints Catholic Church,* 23; All Saints church bulletin, January 21, 1962, All Saints Parish archives; and All Saints Parish reports, 1951–1959.
53. Susan Kellogg and Steven Mintz, "Family Structures," in *Encyclopedia of American Social History,* vol. 3, ed. Mary K. Gorn, Elliot J. Williams, and Peter W. Cayton (New York: Charles Scribner's Sons, 1993), 1938.
54. All Saints Parish reports, 1960–1980.
55. Robert N. Bellah et al., *Habits of the Heart: Individualism and Community in American Life* (Berkeley: University of California Press, 1985, 1996); Robert

Putnam, *Bowling Alone: The Collapse and Renewal of American Community* (New York: Simon & Schuster, 2000); and Robert Wuthnow, *Loose Connections: Joining Together in America's Fragmented Communities* (Cambridge, MA: Harvard University Press, 1998, 2002).

56. In an interview, a former city councilwoman claimed that downtown business was declining even before the stores came outside of town.

57. Housing Development Inc. [pseud.], "Housing Assessment for Havenville" (Havenville: City of Havenville, 2004), 22.

58. Housing Development Inc., "Housing Assessment," 3, 13–17.

59. Owen D. Gutfreund, *Twentieth Century Sprawl: Highways and the Reshaping of the American Landscape* (New York: Oxford University Press, 2004), 129–153.

60. Township school district per capita income figures from 1979 to 1999 provided by state board of education; Census of the Population of the United States, 1940–2000.

61. Ned M. Crankshaw, "Plowing or Mowing? Rural Sprawl in Nelson County, Kentucky," *Landscape Journal* 28, no. 2 (September 1, 2009): 218–234.

62. All Saints Parish reports, 1983 and 1993 (includes non-Catholic family members).

63. Black, *Port Jefferson Diocese*, 476–477; Bert Milosz [pseud.], "All Saints Church Represents Second Largest Denomination in Havenville," *The Paper*, 14 December 1993, 8.

64. Stewardship is a shorthand term for church programs to increase commitment on multiple levels. They usually draw on biblical language to ask people to commit their "time, talents, and treasure," often not only to the church but to other charitable endeavors as well.

65. Wuthnow, *Loose Connections*, 9–31, 135–156.

66. State figures on Brookton County.

67. M. J. Broadway, "From City to Countryside: Recent Changes in the Structure and Location of the Meat and Fish Processing Industries," in *Any Way You Cut It: Meat Processing and Small-Town America*, ed. D. Stull, M. Broadway, and D. Griffith (Lawrence: University Press of Kansas, 1995), 17–40.

68. Andrew J. Sofranko and Mohamed M. Samy, "Growth, Diversity, and Aging in the Midwest: An Examination of County Trends, 1990–2000," in *The American Midwest: Managing Change in Rural Transition*, ed. Norman Walzer (Armonk, NY: M. E. Sharpe, 2003), 41–69.

69. Katharine M. Donato and Carl L. Bankston III, "The Origins of Employer Demand in a New Destination: The Salience of Soft Skills in a Volatile Economy," in *New Faces in New Places: The Changing Geography of American Immigration*, ed. Douglass Massey (New York: Russell Sage, 2010), 124–148.

70. Frank D. Bean and Gillian Stevens, *America's Newcomers and the Dynamics of Diversity*, Rose Series in Sociology (New York: Russell Sage, 2003), 30–31.

71. For example, John S. Macdonald and Leatrice D. Macdonald, "Chain Migration: Ethnic Neighborhood Formation and Social Networks," *Milbank Memorial Fund Quarterly* 42 (January 1963), 82–97; and Bin Yu, *Chain Migration Explained: The Power of the Immigration Multiplier*, The New Americans series, ed. Steven J. Gold and Rubén Rumbaut (New York: LFB Publishing, 2008), 1–40.

72. Douglas Massey, Jorge Durand, and Nolan J. Malone, *Beyond Smoke and Mirrors: Mexican Immigration in an Era of Economic Integration* (New York: Russell Sage Foundation, 2002), 19; Carlos Garcia, *"Buscando Trabajo:* Social Networking among Immigrants from Mexico to the United States," *Hispanic Journal of Behavioral Sciences* 27 (2005): 3–22; and Bean and Stevens, *America's Newcomers,* 33–34.

73. Alejandro Portés and Rubén G. Rumbaut, *Legacies: The Story of the Immigrant Second Generation* (Berkeley: University of California Press, 2001), 64–69.

74. Garcia, *"Buscando Trabajo,"* 8–18.

75. The Census Bureau of the U.S. government uses the term "Hispanic" rather than "Latino."

76. State department of education figures.

77. Suro et al., "Changing Faiths: Latinos and the Transformation of American Religion," 15. In the 1990 Census of the Population of the United States, 70 percentof the Hispanic residents of Havenville identified as Mexican. In the 2000 Census, it was 86 percent.

78. While this was noted in interviews, it was also confirmed in a senior history thesis from the local college: Joanna Burrows [pseud.], "The Migration of Latin Americans into the City of Havenville, 1946–2002" (undergraduate thesis, Havenville College, 2002), 22–30.

79. Parish baptismal records, All Saints Parish, Havenville.

80. Mary Jo Glanton [pseud.], "Bountiful Faith at Family Orchard," *Port Jefferson Catholic,* 14 November 2004.

81. Peter Baumgartner [pseud.], "Mexican Americans, Part 3," *Havenville News,* 16 December 1971.

82. Again, I am grateful for confirmation of this information from Burrows, "The Migration of Latin Americans," 7–17.

83. All Saints Parish reports, 1974–1975.

84. Ibid., 1978.

85. Parish baptismal records, All Saints Church, Havenville.

86. Latino ethnicity determined by the first and/or surnames of parents.

87. U.S. Census Bureau, Census of the Population, 1980.

88. Dominic Johns [pseud.], "Havenville May Be at Tipping Point," *Brookton Times* [pseud.], 17 September 2007.

89. Cornell and Hartmann, *Ethnicity and Race,* 41–74.

90. Ibid., 75–106.

91. Kathleen Neils Conzen, "German-Americans and the Invention of Ethnicity," in *Immigration, Language, Ethnicity,* vol. 1 of *America and the Germans: An Assessment of a Three-Hundred-Year History,* ed. Frank Trommler and Joseph McVeigh (Philadelphia: University of Pennsylvania Press, 1985), 131–147.

92. See Cornell and Hartmann, *Ethnicity and Race,* 186–191. For more on the new institutionalism, see Paul J. DiMaggio and Walter W. Powell, introduction to *The New Institutionalism in Organizational Analysis,* ed. Walter W. Powell and Paul DiMaggio (Chicago: University of Chicago Press, 1991),1–38; also Ann Swidler, *Talk of Love: How Culture Matters* (Chicago: University of Chicago Press, 2001).

93. Catálogo de Ministerios 2007 [Catalog of Ministries], All Saints Parish, Havenville.

94. Ibid.

95. John Paul II, *Ecclesia in America* (Rome: Libreria Editrice Vaticana, 1999), 16. The concept is developed in Ken Johnson-Mondragón, "Ministry in Multicultural and National/Ethnic Parishes," 9–12.

96. For example, many Euro-Americans erroneously believed that the Spanish mass collection was smaller than the English masses because the church in Mexico was supported by the government. Some Mexicans believed that Euro-American parishioners were involved in the Ku Klux Klan, even though no evidence existed to suggest this was true; journalistic accounts of the KKK indicated that members came from other areas.

97. Jean Comaroff and John Comaroff, *The Dialectics of Modernity on a South African Frontier,* vol. 2 of *Of Revelation and Revolution* (Chicago: University of Chicago Press, 1998), 406–407.

98. For example, *Havenville News [pseud.],* "My Turn" column for anonymous reader feedback, 2 September 2007 and 23 September 2007; and *Brookton Times [pseud.],* electronic message board responses, 16 September 2007.

99. Leo R. Chavez, *The Latino Threat: Constructing Immigrants, Citizens, and the Nation* (Stanford, CA: Stanford University Press, 2008), 21–43.

100. For example, individualistic "first come, first served" conceptions that respect competitive norms (rather than more collectivist recognition of special needs, vulnerability of groups, or number of persons involved).

101. See Edward Said, *Orientalism* (New York: Vintage, 1979).

102. Jean Comaroff and John Comaroff, *Christianity, Colonialism, and Consciousness in South Africa,* vol. 1 of *Of Revelation and Revolution* (Chicago: University of Chicago Press, 1991), 212–213, 213–230, 243–248, 287–288; vol. 2, 5–7; and Said, *Orientalism.*

103. Kathryn Tanner, *Theories of Culture,* Guides to Theological Inquiry (Minneapolis: Fortress Press, 1997), 56.

104. State department of education figures. The *posadas* at the school had students dressed as the Virgin Mary and Joseph in search of hospitality. The students said the rosary in English and sang a traditional song in Spanish that goes with the search.

105. The equivalent of the Parent-Teacher Association (PTA).

2. MAKING SENSE OF A CHANGED WORLD

1. Jerome Baggett, *Sense of the Faithful: How American Catholics Live Their Faith* (New York: Oxford University Press, 2009), 109–113.
2. See Rhys Williams, "Religion and Place in the Midwest," in *Religion and Public Life in the Midwest: America's Common Denominator?* ed. Philip Barlow and Mark Silk, Religion by Region series (Walnut Creek, CA: Altamira Press, 2004), 202–204; and Robert Wuthnow, *Remaking the Heartland: Middle America Since the 1950s* (Princeton, NJ: Princeton University Press, 2011), 126–170.
3. Swidler, *Talk of Love*, 24–40.
4. Steve Derné, "Cultural Conceptions of Human Motivation and Their Significance for Cultural Theory," in *Sociology of Culture: Emerging Theoretical Perspectives*, ed. Diana Crane (Cambridge, MA: Blackwell, 1994), 267–287.
5. Swidler, *Talk of Love*, 103–107.
6. Ibid., 105.
7. Ibid., 107.
8. Clifford Geertz, *Local Knowledge: Further Essays in Interpretive Anthropology* (New York: Basic Books, 1983), 73–93.
9. Thomas Hobbes, *Leviathan* (Cambridge: Cambridge University Press, 1904), 84.
10. John Locke, *Two Treatises on Government* (London: Butler et al., 1821), 189–199.
11. Bellah et al., *Habits of the Heart*; Jan E. Dizard and Howard Gadlin, *The Minimal Family* (Amherst: University of Massachusetts Press, 1990); Amitai Etzioni, *The New Golden Rule* (New York: Basic Books, 1996); and Putnam, *Bowling Alone*.
12. Clifford Geertz, *The Interpretation of Cultures* (New York: Basic Books, 1977); and Dennis H. Wrong, *The Problem of Order: What Unifies and Divides Society* (New York: Free Press, 1994), 33–34.
13. See Edward L. Cleary, *How Latin America Saved the Soul of the Catholic Church* (New York: Paulist, 2009).
14. Swidler, *Talk of Love*, 89–107.
15. Joseph L. Klesner, "Social Capital and Political Participation in Latin America: Evidence from Argentina, Chile, Mexico, and Peru," *Latin American Research Review* 42, no. 2 (2007): 1–32.
16. For this reason, the historian Mae M. Ngai describes the undocumented as "impossible subjects."
17. Maxine Baca Zinn, "Familism Among Chicanos: A Theoretical Review," *Humboldt Journal of Social Relations* 10, no. 1 (Fall/Winter 1982/1983): 224–38; Richard Griswold del Castillo, *Chicano Families in the Urban Southwest, 1848 to the Present* (Notre Dame, IN: University of Notre Dame Press, 1984); Roberto Alvarez, *Families: Migration and Adaptation in Baja and Alta California from 1800 to 1975* (Berkeley: University of California Press, 1987); Maxine Baca Zinn, "Mexican-Heritage Families in the United States," in *Handbook of Hispanic Cultures in the United States,* ed. Nicólas Kanellos and Claudio Esteva-Fabregat, vol. 2,

Sociology, ed. Félix Padilla (Houston: Arte Público Press and Instituto Cooperación Iberoamericana, 1994), 168–169; Joan Moore, "The Social Fabric of the
Hispanic Community Since 1965," in *Hispanic Catholic Culture in the U.S.: Issues
and Concerns,* ed. Jay Dolan and Allan Figueroa Deck, Notre Dame History of
Hispanic Catholics in the U.S., ed. Jay Dolan (Notre Dame, IN: University of
Notre Dame Press, 1994), 17, 26; and William Vega, "The Study of Latino Families: A Point of Departure," in *Understanding Latino Families: Scholarship, Policy,
and Practice,* ed. Ruth E. Zambrana (Thousand Oaks, CA: Sage, 1995), 3–8.

18. Roberto Goizueta, *Caminemos con Jesus: A Hispanic/Latino Theology of Accompaniment* (Maryknoll, NY: Orbis, 1995), 18–46.

19. James W. Wilkie, *The Mexican Revolution and Social Change Since 1910* (Berkeley:
University of California Press, 1967), xix–xx.

20. David Shirk, *Mexico's New Politics: The PAN and Democratic Change* (Boulder,
CO: Lynne Rienner Publishers, 2005), 15–48.

21. Latinobárometro survey, 2008.

22. Chavez, *Latino Threat Narrative,* 41–42.

23. Mary Douglas, *Purity and Danger: An Analysis of Concepts of Pollution and Taboo*
(Baltimore: Penguin Books, 1966), 48.

24. Chavez, *Latino Threat Narrative,* 41–53, 188–210.

25. Ibid., 154–165.

26. Clifford Geertz, *Local Knowledge: Further Essays in Interpretive Anthropology*
(New York: Basic Books, 1983), 73-93.

27. Swidler, *Talk of Love,* 98.

28. Second Vatican Council, *Sacrosanctum Concilium* 14, in *Vatican Council II:
The Conciliar and Post-Conciliar Documents,* ed. Austin Flannery, new rev. ed.
(Grand Rapids, MI: Eerdmans, 1992).

29. Andrew Greeley, *The American Catholic: A Social Portrait* (New York: Basic
Books, 1977); Andrew Greeley, "Ethnic Variations in Religious Commitment,"
in *The Religious Dimension: New Directions in Quantitative Research,* ed. Robert
Wuthnow (New York: Academic Press, 1979), 113–134; George Gallup Jr. and Jim
Castelli, *The American Catholic People: Their Beliefs, Practices, and Values* (Gar-
den City, NY: Doubleday, 1987); and William D'Antonio, James D. Davidson,
Dean R. Hoge, and Mary L. Gautier, *American Catholics Today: New Realities of
Their Faith and Their Church* (New York: Rowman and Littlefield, 2007), 177.

30. Massa, *Catholics and American Culture,* 148–171.

31. It is customary in dioceses in the United States, if a person for whatever reason
is unable to receive communion, for the priest or lay minister of communion to
make the sign of the cross over the person.

32. Meredith McGuire, *Lived Religion: Faith and Practice in Everyday Life* (New York:
Oxford University Press, 2008), 100.

33. The Mexican custom of kneeling only during the "consecration," the recitation of
Jesus's words instituting the Eucharist, is the norm for most of the Roman Catholic
world and has been since Vatican II. However, the U.S. bishops chose to continue

the American pre–Vatican II posture of kneeling throughout the Eucharistic prayer in 1969. Frank C. Quinn, "Posture and Prayer," *Worship* 72, no. 1 (January 1998): 67–78. The bishops opted to continue this practice and successfully petitioned the Vatican to keep it when the *General Instruction for the Roman Missal* was revised for the third time and published in English in 2003. Joyce Ann Zimmerman, "What Does GIRM Say About Posture During the Eucharistic Prayer?" *Understanding the Mass and the General Instruction for the Roman Missal* (Collegeville, MN: Liturgical Press, 2003), #6. Cf. United States Conference of Catholic Bishops, *General Instruction for the Roman Missal,* liturgy documentary series 2 (Washington, DC: USCCB, 2003), #43; and Conference of Bishops of Colombia, *Instrucción general del misal romano* (Bogotá: Conferencia Episcopal de Colombia, 2007), #43.

34. Actual church law proscribes lay people preaching the homily at mass. See canons (cc.) 766–767 of the 1983 Code of Canon Law in *The Code of Canon Law: Text and Commentary,* ed. James Coriden, Thomas Joseph Green, and Donald E. Heintschel (New York: Paulist Press, 1985).

35. Catherine Bell, *Ritual Theory, Ritual Practice* (New York: Oxford University Press, 1992), viii.

36. Ibid., 90.

37. Ibid., 90–91.

38. John Paul II, *Ecclesia in Eucharistia* 51 (Rome: Liberia Editrice Vaticana, 2003). Emphasis in the original.

39. John Paul II, *Ecclesia in Eucharistia* 10.

40. Congregation for Divine Worship and the Discipline of the Sacrament, Instruction: *Redemptionis Sacramentum* 11 (Rome: Liberia Editrice Vaticana, 2005).

41. Baggett, *Sense of the Faithful,* 51–52, 131–132, 158–161.

42. At the very least, the sacraments and Eucharist of the Eastern Orthodox churches are considered valid in official Roman Catholic teaching. See Congregation for the Doctrine of the Faith, *Dominus Iesus* 17 (Vatican City: Congregation for the Doctrine of the Faith, 2000).

43. McGuire, *Lived Religion,* 39.

44. Ibid., 42.

45. Ibid., 37–38.

46. Baggett, *Sense of the Faithful,* 66–67.

47. James Empereur and Eduardo Fernandez, *La Vida Sacra: Contemporary Hispanic Sacramental Theology* (Lanham, MD: Rowman and Littlefield, 2006), 11; and Adrian Bantjes, "Religion and the Mexican Revolution: Toward a New Historiography," in *Religious Culture in Mexico,* ed. Martín Agustín Nesvig, Jaguar Books on Latin America (Lanham, MD: Rowman and Littlefield, 2007), 227.

48. Translations from the Spanish are by the author unless otherwise indicated. *Doña* is a title historically given to nobility, now more often given to older or respected persons in the community. Because there were so few people over fifty, virtually anyone of that age received that title.

49. In fact, when I encouraged use of more English-rooted terminology in interviews (for example, "devotions" or "practices"), responses indicated that some
Latino interviewees did not know what we were talking about. Some of the
controversy around the term "popular religion" comes from its relationship to
a Marxist division of the world into elites and "the people" (hence, *popular*).
However, as the historian and religious studies scholar Carlos M. N. Eire has
argued persuasively, the distinction between "elite" or "official" religion and
popular religion is persistent in Western Christianity, much older than Marx-
ism. Carlos M. N. Eire, "The Concept of Popular Religion," in *Local Religion in
Colonial Mexico*, ed. Martin Austin Nesvig, Diáologos (Albuquerque: University
of New Mexico Press, 2006), 1–36.

50. Cf. Virgilio P. Elizondo, "Popular Religion as Support of Identity: A Pastoral-Psy-
chological Case Study Based on the Mexican American Experience in the USA,"
Popular Religion 186 (1986): 36–43; Peter W. Williams, *Popular Religion in America:
Symbolic Change and the Modernization Process in Historical Perspective*, reprint ed.
(Urbana, IL: University of Illinois Press, 1989); Diego Irarrazaval, "Religión Popular" (Popular Religion), in *Mysterium Liberationis: Conceptos fundamentales de la
teología de la liberación*, ed. Jon Sobrino and Ignacio Ellacuría (Madrid: Editorial
Trotta, 1990), 345–375; Anthony Stevens-Arroyo and Ana María Díaz-Stevens,
eds., *An Enduring Flame: Studies on Latino Popular Religiosity*, PARAL (Program
for the Analysis of Religion Among Latinos) Studies, vol. 1 (New York: Bildner
Center for Western Hemisphere Studies, 1994); Otto Maduro, "Religious Production of Latino Popular Religiosity," Program for the Analysis of Religion Among
Latinos, Occasional Paper #7, 1996; Carroll, *American Catholics in the Protestant
Imagination*, 113–148; and McGuire, *Lived Religion*, 45–66.

51. McGuire, *Lived Religion*, 60.

52. Daniel Groody, *Border of Death, Valley of Life: An Immigrant Journey of Heart and
Spirit* (Lanham, MD: Rowman and Littlefield, 2002), 29.

53. Broader sociological evidence suggests that religious involvement is associated
with emotional well-being, particularly in the United States. Phillip Connor,
"A Balm for the Soul: Immigrant Religion and Emotional Well-Being," *International Migration* 50, no. 2 (April 2012): 130–157.

54. Richard R. Flores, "Para el Niño Dios: Sociability and Commemorative Senti-
ment in Popular Religious Practice," in Stevens-Arroyo and Díaz-Stevens, *An
Enduring Flame*, 171–189; Roberto Goizueta, *Caminemos con Jesus*, 47–76; and
Orlando Espín, "Juan Soldado, 'Santa Muerte,' and Other Border Crossing
Saints" (session paper, Catholic Theological Society of America conference, San
Jose, California, June 11, 2011).

55. William Christian, Jr., "Catholicisms," in Nesvig, *Local Religion in Colonial
Mexico*, 259–268; and Adrian Bantjes, "Religion and the Mexican Revolution,"
227.

56. McGuire, *Lived Religion*, 46, 60–66.

57. Doña Claudia [pseud.] returned to Mexico in the winter of 2008–2009; her husband had been deported the previous summer.

58. Cf. Rosa María Icaza, ed., *Faith Expressions of the Southwest,* 3rd ed. revised (San Antonio, TX: Mexican American Cultural Center, 2003), 12.

59. The exceptions were *posadas* held in the parish school and by an association for people from the state of Hidalgo, who held the event at a closed nightclub.

60. I also noticed fewer home altars or sacred images in Latino homes in Havenville than I saw in the homes of the same people's relatives in Mexico. This may be due to a common perception that life in Havenville was provisional.

61. "Long live Mexico!"

62. "Long live the United States!"

63. McGuire, *Lived Religion,* 57.

64. Translation by Maria Charria.

65. Julie Martinez [pseud.], "Spanish Services Most Everywhere," *Brookton Times,* 21 October 2007.

66. Lewis R. Rambo and Charles E. Farhadian, "Converting: Stages of Religious Change," in *Religious Conversion: Contemporary Practices and Controversies,* ed. Christopher Lamb and M. Darrol Bryant (New York: Cassell, 1999), 23–24; and Lewis R. Rambo, *Understanding Religious Conversion* (New Haven, CT: Yale University Press, 1993).

67. Rambo, *Understanding Religious Conversion,* 7.

68. Sherry B. Ortner, "Patterns of History: Cultural Schemas in the Foundings of Sherpa Religious Institutions," in *Culture Through Time: Anthropological Approaches,* ed. Emiko Ohnuki-Tierney (Stanford, CA; Stanford University Press, 1990), 63.

69. Conferencia Episcopal Latinoamericana (Latin American Conference of Bishops), "Documento de Puebla, III Conferencia General del Episcopado Latinoamericano, 1979," (Document of Puebla, III General Conference of the Latin American Episcopate), Program of the Evangelization of Culture of the Universidad Católica de Argentina, http://www.uca.edu.ar/esp/sec-pec/esp/docs-celam/pdf/puebla.pdf (accessed 15 May 2009), no. 342. Author's translation.

70. Anna L. Peterson and Manuel A. Vásquez, "The New Evangelization in Latin American Perspective," *Cross Currents* 48, no. 3 (Fall 1998): 311–329.

71. Anthony Gill, "The Struggle to Be Soul Provider: Catholic Responses to Protestant Growth in Latin America," in *Latin American Religion in Motion,* ed. Christian Smith and Joshua Prokopy (New York: Routledge, 1999), 17–40.

72. Samuel Escobar, *Changing Tides: Latin America and World Mission Today,* American Society of Missiology (Maryknoll, NY: Orbis, 2002), 31–32.

73. Jean-Pierre Ruiz, "Naming the Other: U.S. Hispanic Catholics, the So-Called 'Sects,' and the New Evangelization," *Journal of Hispanic/Latino/a Theology* 4, no. 2 (1996): 34–59.

74. Peterson and Vasquez, "New Evangelization," 311–329.

75. Ibid., 316–318, 326–327.

76. Swidler, *Talk of Love,* 93–94.

77. Ibid., 96.

78. Cornell and Hartmann, *Ethnicity and Race,* 28.

3. BEING APART TOGETHER

1. Vatican Congregation for Divine Worship, Circular Letter Concerning the Preparation and Celebration of the Paschal Feasts (February 20, 1988), 94.

2. Paul B. Pedersen, "Cross-Cultural Psychology: Developing Culture-Centered Interventions," in *Handbook of Racial and Ethnic Minority Psychology,* Guillermo Bernal et al., eds. (Thousand Oaks, CA: Sage, 2003), 491.

3. Mayor's Message, "Current Debate Here and Everywhere: Immigration," in *Resident's Guide to Havenville City Services* (Havenville: City Services, January 2007); and Dominic Johns [pseud.], "Havenville May Be at Tipping Point," *Brookton Times* [pseud.], 17 September 2007.

4. William B. Gudykunst, "An Anxiety/Uncertainty Management Theory of Effective Communication," in *Theorizing Intercultural Communication,* ed. William B. Gudykunst (Thousand Oaks, CA: Sage, 2005), 281–322.

5. Stella Ting-Toomey, *Communicating across Cultures* (New York: Guilford Press, 1999), 25–54.

6. Ebaugh and Chafetz, *Religion and the New Immigrants,* 112; and Robert Putnam and David E. Campbell, *American Grace: How Religion Unites and Divides Us* (New York: Simon & Schuster, 2010), 229.

7. Ting-Toomey, *Communicating across Cultures,* 57–58.

8. Austin Flannery, "The Post-Conciliar Documents on the Liturgy," in *Vatican Council II: The Conciliar and Post-Conciliar Documents,* 39. In reality, the Vatican Council specifically encouraged mass in the vernacular of migrants, and the pope himself has offered parts of the mass in Spanish while in the United States. Sacred Congregation for Rites, *Inter Oecumenici* (Instruction on the Proper Implementation of the Constitution on the Sacred Liturgy) 41 in *Vatican Council II: The Conciliar and Post-Conciliar Documents.*

9. Portes and Rumbaut, *Legacies,* 272.

10. See Brett C. Hoover, "Memory and Ministry: Young Adult Nostalgia, Immigrant Amnesia," *New Theology Review,* vol. 23. no. 1 (February 2010): 58–67.

11. Portes and Rimbaut, *Legacies,* 272. Portes and Rumbaut do not argue that the dominant culture of the United States has no impact on migrants or that, even in ethnic enclaves, people retain their "pure" home cultures. Along with many other scholars of immigration they distinguish between forceful assimilation and "segmented assimilation," a process by which at different rates and according to a myriad of factors including personal agency, race, and social-economic status, persons and their families adapt to a segment of U.S. society. For a summary of recent theories on the incorporation of immigrants, see Bean and Stevens, *America's Newcomers and the Dynamics of Diversity,* 94–113.

12. Alejandro Portes and Rubén G. Rumbaut, *Immigrant America: A Portrait*, rev. ed. (Berkeley: University of California Press, 1996), 139.

13. That is, 15.5% = 63 out of 399 Euro-American responses in English (total survey responses = 675). 5.5% = 6 out of 108. 19.2% of those over 40 = 56 out of 291. These answers were not evaluated for statistical significance.

14. Swidler, *Talk of Love*, 1–5.

15. Ibid., 112–114.

16. Ibid., 118.

17. Ibid., 128–132.

18. Peter Guardino, "Postcolonialism as Self-Fulfilled Prophecy? Electoral Politics in Oaxaca, 1814–1828," in *After Spanish Rule: Postcolonial Predicaments of the Americas*, ed. Mark Thurner and Andrés Guerrero (Durham, NC: Duke University Press, 2003), 266.

19. Michael Omi and Howard Winant, *Racial Formation in the United States*, 2nd ed. (New York: Routledge, 1994), 55–69.

20. Michael O. Emerson and Rodney Woo, *People of the Dream: Multiracial Congregations in the United States* (Princeton, NJ: Princeton University Press, 2006), 152.

21. Baggett, *Sense of the Faithful*, 148.

22. Elizabeth Eldredge, *Power in Colonia Africa: Conflict and Discourse in Lesotho, 1870–1960* (Madison: University of Wisconsin Press, 2007), 3–13. See also James C. Scott, *Domination and the Arts of Resistance: The Hidden Transcript of Subordinate Groups* (New Haven, CT: Yale University Press, 1990).

23. Gudykunst, "An Anxiety/Uncertainty Management Theory of Effective Communication," 287.

24. Ibid.

25. See, for example, Stephen S. Dudek, "Drawn in the Circle of God's Love: A Congregational Study of Unity and Diversity" (D.Min. thesis, Catholic Theological Union, 2002); Stephen S. Dudek, "Becoming Inclusive Communities of Faith: Biblical Reflection and Effective Frameworks," *New Theology Review* 21, no. 1 (February 2008): 40–51; and Stephen S. Dudek, "Building a Home for a Multicultural Parish: Lessons Learned," *New Theology Review* 13, no. 1 (February 2000): 37–45.

26. The phrase came from my own interview with Fr. Dudek. See also Dudek, "Building a Home for a Multicultural Parish," 39–40.

27. Arlie Russell Hochschild, *The Commercialization of Intimate Life: Notes from Home and Work* (Berkeley: University of California Press, 2003), 84.

28. Wuthnow, *Remaking the Heartland*, 147.

29. Marian Ronan, *Tracing the Sign of the Cross: Sexuality, Mourning, and the Future of American Catholicism* (New York: Columbia University Press, 2009), 8.

30. Marian Ronan, "The Clergy Sex Abuse Crisis and the Mourning of American Catholic Innocence," *Pastoral Psychology* 56 (2008): 330–331.

31. According to the parish survey, 73 percent of Latino adults in the parish were between the ages of eighteen and forty.

32. Gudykunst, "An Anxiety/Uncertainty Management Theory of Effective Communication," 288.

33. Mark Hugo Lopez and Susan Minishkin, "2008 National Survey of Latinos: Hispanics See Their Situation in U.S. Deteriorating," (Washington, DC: Pew Hispanic Center, 2008), 9–12.

34. Cf. Ebaugh and Chafetz, *Religion and the New Immigrants*, 61–62; Kathleen Sullivan, "St. Catherine's Catholic Church," in *Religion and the New Immigrants: Continuities and Adaptations in Immigrant Congregations*, ed. Helen Rose Fuchs Ebaugh and Janet Saltzman Chafetz (Walnut Creek: Altamira Press, 2000), 210–233; Dudek, "Drawn into the Circle of God's Love," 35–43; Kathleen Garces-Foley, "New Opportunities and New Values: The Emergence of the Multicultural Church," *The Annals of the American Academy of Political and Social Science* 612 (July 2007): 216; Garces-Foley, "Comparing Catholic and Evangelical Integration Efforts," 216; and Baggett, *Sense of the Faithful*, 44.

35. Allan Figueroa Deck, "Multiculturalism as Ideology," in *Perspectivas: Hispanic Ministry*, ed. Allan Figueroa Deck, Yolanda Tarango, and Timothy Matovina (Lanham, MD: Rowman & Littlefield, 1995), 32.

36. John Coleman, "Pastoral Strategies for Multicultural Parishes," *Origins* 31, no. 30 (10 January 2002): 503.

37. See *The Roman Missal: The Sacramentary* (New York: Catholic Book Publishing Company, 1985), 135 and 170 (no. 3); and *Misal Romano* (Mexico City: Obra Nacional de La Buena Prensa, A.C., 1989).

38. On power distance in Mexico, see Gregory K. Stephens and Charles R. Greer, "Doing Business in Mexico: Understanding Cultural Differences," *Organizational Dynamics* 24, no. 1 (Summer 1995): 39–55. On power distance as a concept, see Geert H. Hofstede, *Culture's Consequences* (Thousand Oaks, CA: Sage, 2001), 79–144.

39. Translated by Maria Charria.

40. Ann Neville Miller, "When Face-to-Face Doesn't Work: Use of Informal Intermediaries to Communicate Interpersonally in Sub-Saharan Africa," in *Intercultural Communication: A Reader*, 13th edition, ed. Larry A. Samovar, Richard E. Porter, and Edwin R. McDaniel (Boston: Wadsworth, 2009), 171–180.

41. Margaret Connell Szasz, "Introduction," in *Between Indian and White Worlds: Cultural Brokers*, ed. Margaret Connell Szasz (Norman: University of Oklahoma Press, 1994), 3–23.

42. Yanna Yannakakis, *The Art of Being In-Between: Native Intermediaries, Indian Identity, and Local Rule in Colonial Oaxaca* (Durham, NC: Duke University Press, 2008), 1–14.

43. Eugene Nida and Charles Taber, *The Theory and Practice of Translation* (Leiden, Netherlands: Brill, 2003), vii.

44. David Bellos, *Is That a Fish in Your Ear? Translation and the Meaning of Everything* (New York: Faber and Faber, 2011), 66.

45. Susan Bassnett, "The Meek or the Mighty: Reappraising the Role of the Translator," in *Translation, Power, Subversion,* ed. Román Alvarez and M. Carmen
Africa, Topics in Translation 8 (Bristol, PA: Multilingual Matters, Ltd., 1998),
10–24. See also, Jeremy Munday, *Introducing Translation Studies: Theories and
Applications,* 2nd edition (New York: Routledge, 2008), 142–161.

46. Naomi Seidman, *Faithful Renderings: Jewish-Christian Difference and the Politics
of Translation* (Chicago: University of Chicago Press, 2006).

4. THEORIZING THE SHARED PARISH

1. Ebaugh and Chafetz, following Paul Numrich, use the term "parallel congregations." Ebaugh and Chafetz, *Religion and the New Immigrants.*

2. See, for example, Jay P. Dolan, ed., *The American Catholic Parish: A History from
1850 to the Present* (New York: Paulist Press, 1987).

3. James A. Coriden, *The Parish in Catholic Tradition: History, Theology, and Canon
Law* (New York: Paulist, 1997), 19.

4. Ibid., 22–24, 26–27; Peter George Wallace, *The Long European Reformation:
Religion, Political Conflict, and the Search for Conformity, 1350–1750* (New York:
Palgrave Macmillan, 2004), 8–19; and Bernard P. Prusak, *The Unfinished Church:
Ecclesiology Through the Centuries* (New York: Paulist, 2004), 206.

5. Prusak, *The Unfinished Church,* 206; David Chidestar, *Christianity: A Global History* (New York: HarperCollins, 2000), 192–194.

6. Coriden, *The Parish in Catholic Tradition,* 30–31; Fourth Lateran Council, canons
10–11, 14, 21, 51; Council of Trent, session 24, Decree on Reformation, chapters
II, IV, and XIII.

7. Luis N. Rivera Pagán, *Evangelización y Violencia: La Conquista de América*
[Evangelization and violence: The conquest of America] (San Juan, PR: Edito-
rial CEMI, 1992), 191–204; Gustavo Gutierrez, *Las Casas: In Search of the Poor
of Jesus Christ,* transl. Robert R. Barr (Maryknoll, NY: Orbis, 1993), 279–291;
John Frederick Schwaller, *The Church and Clergy in Sixteenth-Century Mexico*
(Albuquerque: University of New Mexico Press, 1987), 67–71; and "The Laws of
Burgos," transl. L.B. Simpson, in *The Spanish Tradition in America,* ed. Charles
Gibson (New York: Harper & Row, 1968), 61–82.

8. Amos Megged, *Exporting the Catholic Reformation: Local Religion in Early-Colonial
Mexico* (New York: E. J. Brill, 1996), 33–61; Coriden, *The Parish in Catholic Tradition,* 32–34; and Luis N. Rivera-Pagán, "A Prophetic Challenge to the Church: The
Last Word of Barolomé de las Casas," (inaugural lecture of Henry Winters Luce
Professor in Ecumenics and Mission, Princeton Theological Seminary, 9 April
2003). Native peoples were often denied communion and always denied ordina-
tion; many priests refused even to learn their languages. For a view that sees the
clergy's offenses as less systematic, see Schwaller, *The Church and Clergy,* 176–181.

9. Michael Carroll, *American Catholics in the Protestant Imagination: Rethinking
the Academic Study of Religion,* 27–46. Cf. Emmet Larkin, "The Devotional

Revolution in Ireland," *American Historical Review* 77 (1972): 625–652; and Eugene Hynes, "Family and Religious Change in a Peripheral Capitalist Society: Mid-Nineteenth-Century Ireland," in *The Religion and Family Connection: Social Science Perspectives,* ed. Darwin L. Thomas (Provo, UT: Religious Studies Center, Brigham Young University, 1988), 161–174.

10. Baggett, *Sense of the Faithful,* 209.

11. John Huels, "Parish Life and the New Code," *Concilium* 185 (1986): 64–65.

12. Christopher Marsh, "Sacred Space in England, 1560–1640: The View from the Pew," *The Journal of Ecclesiastical History* 53, no. 2 (Apr 2002): 286–311; and Mary J. Oates, *The Catholic Philanthropic Tradition in America* (Bloomington: Indiana University Press, 1995), 2–3.

13. Warner, "Work in Progress," 1066.

14. Stanley R. Maveety, "Doctrine in Tyndale's New Testament: Translation as a Tendentious Art," *Studies in English Literature, 1500–1900* vol. 6, no. 1 (Winter 1966): 151.

15. R. Stephen Warner, "The Place of the Congregation in the Contemporary American Religious Configuration," in *New Perspectives in the Study of Congregations,* vol. 2 of *American Congregations,* ed. James P. Wind and James W. Lewis (Chicago: University of Chicago Press, 1994), 54–99; and R. Stephen Warner, "Religion and New (Post-1965) Immigrants: Some Principles Drawn from Field Research," *American Studies* 41, no. 2/3 (Summer/Fall 2000): 267–286. On institutional isomorphism, see Paul DiMaggio and Walter Powell, "The Iron Cage Revisited: Institutional Isomorphism and Collective Rationality in Organizational Fields," in Powell and DiMaggio, *The New Institutionalism in Organizational Analysis,* 63–82.

16. Warner, "Religion and New (Post-1965) Immigrants," 277–278.

17. Paul Numrich, *Old Wisdom in the New World: Americanization in Two Immigrant Theravada Buddhist Temples* (Knoxville: University of Tennessee Press, 1996); R. Stephen Warner and Judith Wittner, eds., *Gathering in Diaspora*; Ebaugh and Saltzman, *Religion and the New Immigrants*; Carl L. Bankston III and Min Zhou, "De Facto Congregationalism and Socioeconomic Mobility in Laotian and Vietnamese Immigrant Communities: A Study of Religious Institutions and Economic Change," *Review of Religious Research* 41 (2000): 453–470; David R. Maines and Michael J. McCallion, "Evidence and Speculations on Catholic *De Facto* Congregationalism," *Review of Religious Research* 46, no. 1 (2004): 92–101; and Fenggang Yang and Helen Rose Ebaugh, "Transformations in New Immigrant Religions and Their Global Implications," *American Sociological Review* 66 (April 2001): 269–288.

18. Warner, "Work in Progress," 1060.

19. Ibid., 1059–1060.

20. Warner, "Religion and New (Post-1965) Immigrants," 277.

21. Patricia M. Y. Yang, "Analysis of the Study of Religious Organizations," in *Handbook of the Sociology of Religion,* ed. Michelle Dillon (New York: Cambridge University Press, 2003), 124–127.

22. Peter Berger, *The Sacred Canopy: Elements of a Sociological Theory of Religion* (New York: Doubleday, 1969).

23. James P. Wind, "Leading Congregations, Discovering Congregational Cultures," *Christian Century* (February 3–10, 1993): 105–110; see also Nancy Ammerman, *Congregation and Community* (New Brunswick, NJ: Rutgers University Press, 1997).

24. See Rodney Stark and Roger Finke, *Acts of Faith: Explaining the Human Side of Religion* (Berkeley: University of California, 2000).

25. Warner, "The Place of the Congregation in the Contemporary American Religious Configuration," 59–61.

26. For such an evaluation, see Wendy Cadge, "De Facto Congregationalism and the Religious Organizations of Post-1965 Immigrants to the United States: A Revised Approach," *Journal of the American Academy of Religion* 76, no. 2 (June 2008): 344–374.

27. See Warner, "Work in Progress," 1067; see also Jay Dolan, "Patterns of Leadership in the Congregation," in *New Perspectives in the Study of Congregations*, vol. 2 of Wind and Lewis, *American Congregations*, 225–256.

28. Cadge, "De Facto Congregationalism," 349–351.

29. James D. Davidson and Suzanne Fournier, "Recent Research on Catholic Parishes: A Research Note," *Review of Religious Research* 48, no. 1 (2006): 76–77.

30. Manuel A. Vásquez, "Historicizing and Materializing the Study of Religion," in *Immigrant Faiths: Transforming Religious Life in America*, ed. Karen I. Leonard, Alex Stepick, Manuel A. Vasquez, and Jennifer Holdaway (New York: Altamira Press, 2005), 230–235.

31. Wendy Cadge, Peggy Levitt, and David Smilde, "De-Centering and Re-Centering: Rethinking Concepts and Methods in the Sociological Study of Religion," *Journal for the Scientific Study of Religion* 50, no. 3 (September 2011): 438–439.

32. David R. Maines and Michael J. McCallion, "Research Note: Evidence of and Speculations on Catholic *De facto* Congregationalism," *Review of Religious Research* 46, no. 1 (2004): 92–101.

33. Warner, "The Place of the Congregation," 78.

34. Perry Dane, "The Corporation Sole and the Encounter of Law and Church," in *Sacred Companies: Organizational Aspects of Religion and Religious Aspects of Organizations*, ed. N. J. Demerath, Peter Dobkin Hall, Terry Schmitt, and Rhys A. Williams (New York: Oxford University Press, 1998), 55.

35. Dane, "The Corporation Sole," 57. On the persistence of centralized power structures in the Catholic Church, see Richard A. Schoenherr, *Goodbye Father: The Celibate Male Priesthood and the Future of the Catholic Church*, ed. David Yamane, foreword by Dean R. Hoge (New York: Oxford University Press, 2002), 64; and José Comblin, *People of God* (Maryknoll, NY: Orbis, 2004), 115–117.

36. Brett C. Hoover, "When Work Culture and Ministry Collide: Lessons from the INSPIRE Project in Chicago," *Seminary Journal* 16, no. 3 (Winter 2010—published 2012): 43–52.

37. Michael O. Emerson and Karen Chai Kim, "Multiracial Congregations: An Analysis of Their Development and a Typology," *Journal for the Scientific Study of Religion* 42, no. 2 (2003): 218.

38. This point is discussed in Maines and McCallion, "Catholic *De Facto* Congregationalism," 99.

39. See Emerson and Woo, *People of the Dream: Multiracial Congregations in the United States*, 48; Mark Chaves and Shawna L. Anderson, National Congregations Survey 1998 [online database], http://www.soc.duke.edu/natcong/explore. html (accessed on 30 November 2008); Garces-Foley, "New Opportunities and New Values: The Emergence of the Multicultural Church," 210; and John Dart, "Hues in the Pews: Racially Mixed Churches an Elusive Goal," *Christian Century* 118, no. 7 (February 21, 2001): 6–8.

40. See Emerson, *People of the Dream,* 60, on churches made multiracial by mandate.

41. Cf. Garces-Foley, "The Emergence of the Multicultural Church," 218–223; Emerson, *People of the Dream*; and Emerson and Kim, "Multiracial Congregations," 217–227.

42. Baggett, *Sense of the Faithful*, 134.

43. I refer to the county as "self-contained" because (1) according to state figures in 2005, only 6.4 percent of residents commuted out of county to work and (2) the federal highways in and out of Havenville contain extensive shopping facilities. Robert D. Putnam frames the space contemporary Americans inhabit in terms of a work-shopping-home triangle: "Our lives are increasingly traced in large suburban triangles, as we move daily from home to work to shop to home." Putnam, *Bowling Alone*, 211.

44. Parsons' reflections are reported on in Graham Day, *Community and Everyday Life* (New York: Routledge, 2006), 12–13.

45. Bellah et al., *Habits of the Heart: Individualism and Commitment in American Life,* 227.

46. Baggett, *Sense of the Faithful,* 42.

47. Warner, "Immigration and Religious Communities in the United States," 17; and Manuel A. Vásquez, "Historicizing and Materializing the Study of Religion," 231.

48. In a somewhat different manner, Jerome Baggett's book *Sense of the Faithful* makes this point. Baggett describes Bay Area Catholics as engaging the symbols and meanings of Catholic tradition on their own terms as they pursue an ongoing process of identity formation. Baggett, however, working in the sociological tradition, sees this as a particularly important phenomenon of modern people. Yet there is significant historical evidence that Catholics always appropriated the symbols on their own terms, though perhaps more often in communities than in the individualistic manner of today. Outside of modernity we often refer to this process as popular religion.

49. Dolan, *The American Catholic Experience,* 158–194.

50. Vegard Skirbekk, Keric Kaufman, and Anne Goujon, "Secularism, Fundamentalism, or Catholicism? The Religious Composition of the United States to 2043," *Journal for the Scientific Study of Religion* 49, no. 2 (June 2010): 293–310.
51. See Allan Figueroa Deck, "Beyond the Polarized Present: New Perspectives on U.S. Latino Migration and Christianity" (Latino Theology and Ministry lecture, Loyola Marymount University, 4 October 2012).
52. John Tracy Ellis, *American Catholicism,* Chicago History of American Civilization, ed. Daniel J. Boorstin, rev. ed. (Chicago: University of Chicago Press, 1969), 167–168.
53. See, for example, Steinfels, *A People Adrift,* 1–5; Samuel P. Huntington, *Who Are We? The Challenges to America's National Identity* (New York: Simon & Schuster, 2004), 59–106; Kristin Heyer, Mark Rozell, and Michael Genovese, eds., *Catholics and Politics: The Dynamic Tension between Faith and Power* (Washington, DC: Georgetown University Press, 2008); and James Carroll, *Practicing Catholic* (New York: Houghton Mifflin Harcourt, 2009).
54. Skirbekk, Kaufman, and Goujon, "Secularism, Fundamentalism, or Catholicism," 296; and Ken Johnson Mondragón, "Hispanic Ministry Fact Sheet 2006," (Stockton, CA: Instituto Fe y Vida, 2006).
55. For example, Carroll in *Practicing Catholic;* and Huntington in *Who Are We.*
56. See Huntington, *Who Are We,* 221–256.
57. Portés and Rumbaut, *Legacies.*
58. James T. Fisher, *Communion of Immigrants: A History of Catholics in America* (New York: Oxford University Press, 2000), x.
59. I also conducted longer, formal interviews with two family members, with a local worker in a neighborhood store who was active in her parish, and with a parish priest.
60. Bryan T. Froehle, "Religious Competition, Community Building, and Democracy in Latin America: Grassroots Religious Organizations in Venezuela," *Sociology of Religion* 55, no. 2 (Summer 1994): 150.
61. James Empereur and Eduardo Fernández, *La Vida Sacra: Contemporary Hispanic Sacramental Theology* (Lanham, MD: Rowman & Littlefield, 2006), 24–40; Orlando O. Espín, *The Faith of the People: Theological Reflections on Popular Catholicism* (Maryknoll, NY: Orbis, 1997), 32–62, 111–155.
62. Christopher P. Scheitle, "Organizational Niches and Religious Markets: Uniting Two Literatures," *Interdisciplinary Journal of Research on Religion* 3, article 2 (2007): 4.
63. Glenn R. Carroll, "Concentration and Specialization: Dynamics of Niche Width in Populations of Organizations," *American Journal of Sociology* 90, no. 6 (May 1985): 1266–1267.
64. Scheitle, "Organizational Niches and Religious Markets," 3. An notable exception is Nancy Eiesland's analysis of the impact of exurban restructuring on the religious ecology of a Georgia town, *A Particular Place: Urban Restructuring and*

Religious Ecology in a Southern Exurb (New Brunswick, NJ: Rutgers University Press, 2000).

65. See the portraits of Northern California parishes in Baggett, *Sense of the Faithful*, 43–54.

66. Eiesland, *A Particular Place*, 53–61.

67. Ashley Palmer-Boyes, "The Latino Catholic Parish as a Specialist Organization: Distinguishing Characteristics," *Review of Religious Research* 51, no. 3 (March 2010): 302–304.

68. Palmer-Boyes, "The Latino Catholic Parish as a Specialist Organization," 314–318.

69. Eiesland, *A Particular Place*, 14.

70. Ebaugh and Chafetz, *Religion and the New Immigrants*, 49–55.

5. CHALLENGING CULTURAL ENCAPSULATION IN THE SHARED PARISH

1. Laurie D. McCubbin and Sara Bennett, "Cultural Encapsulation," in *Encyclopedia of Counseling*, ed. Frederick T. L. Leong (Thousands Oaks, CA: Sage Publications, 2008), 1091.

2. Some Russian immigrants had arrived after World War II and many more after the fall of the Soviet Union in 1990. I never met any Japanese immigrants in Havenville, and there were none present at this meeting.

3. Mark M. Gray, Mary L. Gautier, and Melissa A. Cidade, "The Changing Face of U.S. Catholic Parishes" (Washington, DC: National Association for Lay Ministry, 2011), 11, 39.

4. Ibid., 31–41.

5. Robert D. Putnam, "E. Pluribus Unum: Diversity and Community in the Twenty-First Century," 2006 Johan Skye Prize Lecture, *Scandinavian Political Studies* 30, no. 2 (2007): 141–142.

6. Milton J. Bennett, "Toward Ethnorelativism: A Developmental Model of Intercultural Sensitivity," in *Education for the Intercultural Experience*, ed. R. Michael Paige (Yarmouth, ME: Intercultural Press, 1993), 21; and Jarrod Owens [pseud.] "Intercultural Resource Networking Project," (Havenville: City of Havenville, 2008), 17.

7. Joseph H. Fichter, *One-Man Research: Reminiscences of a Catholic Sociologist* (New York: John Wiley & Sons, 1973), 44–45. Cf. Fichter, *Dynamics of a City Church*, vol. 1 of *The Southern Parish* (Chicago: University of Chicago Press, 1951), 259–271.

8. Baggett, *Sense of the Faithful*, 180–182. There are other ways of framing this question about Catholics and social issues in the parish. In the 1980s, a group of congregational studies scholars did a mission-oriented interfaith study of congregations and parishes in the Hartford, Connecticut, area. In their findings, they divided the local faith communities by four "mission orientations": civic (this-worldly acceptance of present order), sanctuary (private other-worldly focus), activist (this-worldly focus on change), and evangelistic

(public other-worldly focus). The activist orientation—which characterized just less than half of the Catholic churches in the area—emphasized awareness of social issues and teachings. But most Catholic churches had either a civic orientation—which tended to neglect all social issues—or a sanctuary orientation, which looked only at the small number of social issues acceptable to the dominant culture such as crime, children's rights, and drug abuse. David A. Roozen, William McKinney, and Jackson W. Carroll, *Varieties of Religious Presence Mission in Public Life* (New York: Pilgrim Press, 1984), 35–36, 87–93.

9. See Luis Lugo, Gregory Smith, Dan Cox, and Allison Pond, "A Portrait of American Catholics on the Eve of Pope Benedict XVI's Visit: Social and Political Views of Catholics in the U.S" (Washington, DC: Pew Forum on Religion and Public Life, March 2008), http://pewforum.org/docs/?DocID=295#immigration (accessed on 22 July 2009).

10. Kathleen Garces-Foley, *Crossing the Ethnic Divide: The Multi-Ethnic Church on a Mission* (New York: Oxford University Press, 2007), 146–150.

11. Ibid., 149.

12. Garces-Foley, "Comparing Catholic and Evangelical Integration Efforts," 20.

13. Putnam, "E Pluribus Unum," 137.

14. Foley and Hoge, *Religion and the New Immigrants*, 91–95, 105–113.

15. Baggett, *Sense of the Faithful*, 79.

16. Nancy Fraser and Axel Honneth, *Redistribution or Recognition? A Political-Philosophical Exchange* trans. Joel Golb, James Ingram, and Christiane Wilke (New York: Verso, 2003), 11.

17. For example, Coleman, "Pastoral Strategies for Multicultural Parishes," 498; and Chavez, *The Latino Threat*, 179.

18. See Lugo et al., "A Portrait of American Catholics on the Eve of Pope Benedict XVI's Visit."

19. Hochschild, *The Commercialization of Intimate Life*, 99.

20. Ibid., 97.

21. Ibid., 97–99.

22. Alba and Nee, *Remaking the American Mainstream*, 17–18.

23. Huntington, *Who Are We?*, 221–256.

24. Charles Hirschman, "America's Melting Pot Reconsidered," *Annual Review of Sociology* 9 (1983): 397–399; and Philip Gleason, "The Melting Pot: Symbol of Fusion or Confusion?" *American Quarterly* 16, no. 1 (Spring 1964): 20–46.

25. Portes and Rumbaut, *Immigrant America*, 28–32.

26. Black [pseud.], *History of the Port Jefferson Diocese*, 97.

27. Linkh, *American Catholicism and European Immigrants*, 2–3.

28. Frances A. Kellor, "What Is Americanization?," in *Immigration and Americanization: Selected Readings*, ed. Philip Davis (Boston: Atheneum Press, 1920), 623.

29. Gleason, *The Conservative Reformers*, 159–171.

30. Jeffery E. Mirel, *Patriotic Pluralism: Americanization Education and European Immigrants* (Cambridge, MA: Harvard University Press, 2010), 13–47.
31. This historical debate is recounted in Alba and Nee, *Remaking the American Mainstream*, 23–27.
32. Bean and Stevens, *America's Newcomers and the Dynamics of Diversity*, 94–113.
33. U.S. Conference of Catholic Bishops, "Welcoming the Stranger Among Us," 421n5.
34. United States Conference of Catholic Bishops, *Hispanic Ministry: Three Major Documents* (Washington, DC: USCCB Publishing, 1988), 66.
35. Pontifical Council for Culture, "Towards a Pastoral Approach to Culture" (Vatican City, 1999), no. 2.
36. Ibid.
37. See, for example, Kathleen Neils Conzen, "Mainstream and Side Channels: The Localization of Immigrant Cultures," *Journal of American Ethnic History* 11, no. 1 (Fall 1991): 5–20; and Concha Delgado-Gaitan and Henry Trueba, *Crossing Cultural Borders: Education for Immigrant Families in America* (Bristol, PA: Falmer Press, 1991).
38. Alba and Nee, *Remaking the American Mainstream*, 10–13.
39. Fraser and Honneth, *Redistribution or Recognition*, 75.
40. Garces-Foley, "Comparing Catholic and Evangelical Integration Efforts," 18–20; and Garces-Foley, "From the Melting Pot to the Multicultural Table," 27–29. This, however, is not the only way to interpret the bishops' statements and actions on the issue. At different times, episcopal documents have used both cultural pluralism and multiculturalism. They are both defined in terms of "continuing cooperation in pursuit of the common good and with proper respect for the good of each cultural tradition and community." U.S. Conference of Catholic Bishops, "Welcoming the Stranger Among Us," 421n5. This conflating of two policy approaches that specialists see as different commonly occurs among U.S. educators as well. See Faustino M. Cruz, "Religion, Ethnicity, and Immigration in the United States: Engaging Critically with the U.S. Catholic Church's Pastoral Response," *Journal of Sophia Asian Studies* 26 (2008): 17n2. Moreover, what looks like two discrete stages of policy might instead be seen as different emphases emerging from the bishops as they addressed different concerns over time. Garces-Foley admits, for example, that financial concerns influenced the consolidation of multiple cultural ministries into single offices of cultural diversity at diocesan and national levels, which she interprets as a sign of the move from cultural pluralism to multiculturalism. Garces-Foley, "Comparing Catholic and Evangelical Integration Efforts," 19–20. The bishops' initial document on cultural diversity, "Beyond the Melting Pot: Cultural Pluralism in the United States," (1981) decisively embraces "cultural pluralism" in order to teach U.S. Catholics about the homogenizing effects of the "melting pot" mythos and about the connections between cultural diversity in previous and current waves of immigration.

Their document on the growing Latino population, "The Hispanic Presence: Challenge and Commitment" (1983), sought to advocate within the Church for a poor and underrepresented group; this naturally highlighted cultural pluralism and the right to unique cultural expressions of Catholicism. On the other hand, the later document on migration, "Welcoming the Stranger Among Us" (2000), asked nonimmigrants to welcome newcomers; it focused attention on hospitality and unity, values generally associated with multiculturalism.

41. Charles Taylor, "The Politics of Recognition," in *Multiculturalism: Examining the Politics of Recognition,* ed. Amy Gutmann (Princeton, NJ: Princeton University Press, 1994), 28.

42. Ibid., 37–44, 51–61.

43. Bhikhu C. Parekh, *Rethinking Multiculturalism: Cultural Diversity and Political Theory* (Cambridge, MA: Harvard University Press, 2002), 196–197.

44. Taylor, "The Politics of Recognition," 25–66.

45. Susan Petrilli and Augusto Ponzio, "Migration and Hospitality: Homologies Between Australia and Europe," in *Imagined Australia: Reflections Around the Reciprocal Constructions of Identity Between Australia and Europe,* ed. Renata Summo-O'Connell (Bern, Switzerland: Peter Lang, 2009), 320.

46. Panikos Panayi, "Multicultural Britain: A Very Brief History," *British Politics Review* 6, no. 2 (Spring 2011): 4–5.

47. Peter Casarella, "Recognizing Diversity After Multiculturalism," *New Theology Review* 21. no. 4 (November 2008): 19; and Cruz, "Religion, Ethnicity, and Immigration in the United States," 17n2.

48. Casarella, "Recognizing Diversity After Multiculturalism," 22.

49. Cynthia Willett, introduction to *Theorizing Multiculturalism: A Guide to the Current Debate* (Malden, MA: Blackwell, 1998), 7.

50. Fraser, *Redistribution or Recognition,* 36.

51. Ibid., 16–26.

52. Ibid., 36.

53. Michael Sean Winters, "Neuhaus on the Papal Liturgy," All Things blog, *America* magazine online, 18 April 2008, http://www.americamagazine.org/blog/entry.cfm?id=63011337-5056-8960-321E1BC14366DE29 (accessed 20 January 2012).

54. Joseph A. Varacalli, "Multiculturalism, Catholicism, and American Civilization," *Homiletic and Pastoral Review* 94, no. 6 (March 1994): 47–55. See also Richard John Neuhaus, "The Public Square: Three Who Changed the World," *First Things* 170 (February 2007), http://www.firstthings.com/article/2009/02/three-who-changed-the-world-37 (accessed 13 July 2009). And see Stephen H. Webb, "Christ Against the Multiculturalists," address for entering students of Wabash College, class of 2012, *First Things,* On the Square (6 May 2008), http://www.firstthings.com/onthesquare/2008/05/christ-against-the-multicultur (accessed 13 July 2009).

55. Goizueta, *Caminemos con Jesus,* 164.

56. Ibid., 132–172.

57. Faustino M. Cruz, "Immigrant Faith Communities as Interpreters: Educating for Participatory Action," *New Theology Review* 21, no. 4 (November 2008): 28–29.

58. Bennett, "Toward Ethnorelativism," 30.

59. Milton J. Bennett, "Intercultural Communication: A Current Perspective," in *Basic Concepts of Intercultural Communication*, ed. Milton J. Bennett (Yarmouth, ME: Intercultural Press, 1998), 1–3.

60. Emerson and Kim, "Multiracial Congregations," 218.

61. Francis L. K. Hsu, *Rugged Individualism Reconsidered* (Knoxville: University of Tennessee Press, 1983), 411.

62. The expression comes from the Catholic composer Rufino Zaragoza, who used it at a dialogue I attended with Catholic liturgists and pastoral musicians on multicultural liturgy in July 2009 in Orange, California.

63. Renato Rosaldo writes about anthropologists being unable to conceive of *culture* in Philippine villages where the modern globalized capitalist state entered in and changed things. He also spoke about U.S. policies of assimilation attempting to eradicate immigrants' cultures. While he laments the forceful and often brutal imposition of new cultural forms, he emphasizes that this is not the "loss of culture," as if the modern state was somehow "post-cultural." Cultures change; they become a different kind of culture. Rosaldo, *Culture and Truth: The Remaking of Social Analysis*, with new introduction (Boston: Beacon Press, 1993), 207–214.

64. "Ecclesiology" is the general theological term for theologies of the Church (from the Greek *ekklesia*).

65. Cf. Dennis Doyle, *Communion Ecclesiology: Vision and Versions* (Maryknoll, NY: Orbis, 2000), 13.

66. Ibid., 13.

67. Jean-Marie R. Tillard, *Church of Churches: The Ecclesiology of Communion*, trans. R.C. de Peaux (Collegeville, MN: Liturgical Press, 1992), 19.

68. Doyle, *Communion Ecclesiology*, 152–156. According to the biblical story in Acts, Jesus's disciples spoke in their native tongue and yet were understood by visiting pilgrims speaking a multiplicity of languages. According to the Genesis story, God confused the language of the earliest human beings in order to keep them from collaborating on hubristic projects like the great tower at Babel. Scripture scholars do not necessarily regard either as historical events but rather stories with powerful symbolic import.

69. Tillard, *Church of Churches*, 31.

70. John D. Zizioulas, *Communion and Otherness: Further Studies in Personhood and the Church*, ed. Paul McPartlan, foreword by Rowan Williams (New York: T & T Clark, 2006), 5. Italics in the original.

71. Zizioulas, *Communion and Otherness*, 294–306.

72. Doyle, *Communion Ecclesiology*, 160.

73. Zizioulas, *Communion and Otherness,* 2–3.

74. Tillard, *Church of Churches,* 31–33.

75. Jamie T. Phelps, "Communion Ecclesiology and Black Liberation Theology," *Theological Studies* 61 (2000): 693–694.

76. Phelps, "Communion Ecclesiology," 694–695.

77. Tillard, *Church of Churches,* 37–38.

78. Data from Parish Survey, 17–18 May 2008.

79. Jackson Carroll, *God's Potters: Pastoral Leadership and the Shaping of Congregations* (Grand Rapids, MI: Eerdmans, 2006), 25.

80. Ibid., 128.

81. Wendy Griswold, *Cultures and Societies in a Changing World,* 3rd edition, Sociology for a New Century (Thousand Oaks, CA: Pine Forge Press, 2008), 4–11.

82. Ibid., 11.

83. Ibid., 1–20.

84. Carroll, *God's Potters,* 130.

85. Katherine DiSalvo, "Understanding an Outlier: How Parish Culture Matters in a Highly Participatory Catholic Church," *Review of Religious Research* 49, no. 1 (2008): 438–455.

86. Hochschild, *Commercialization of Intimate Life,* 99.

87. Nicholas Healy, *Church, World, and the Christian Life: Practical-Prophetic Ecclesiology* (Cambridge: Cambridge University Press, 2000), 25–51.

88. Christian Batalden Scharen, "'Judicious Narratives,' or Ethnography as Ecclesiology," *Scottish Journal of Theology* 58, no. 2 (2005): 125–142.

89. Swidler, *Talk of Love,* 111–134.

90. Healy, *Church, World, and the Christian Life,* 5.

91. Kathleen Odell Korgen, *Crossing the Racial Divide: Close Friendships Between Black and White Americans* (Westport, CT: Praeger, 2002), 7.

92. Weber's definition discussed in Peter Imbusch, "The Concept of Violence," in *International Handbook of Violence Research,* vol. 1, ed. Wilhelm Heitmeyer and John Hagan (Dordrecht, Netherlands: Kluwer Academic Publishers, 2003), 30–31.

93. For example, Michel Foucault, *Power/Knowledge: Selected Interviews and Other Writings, 1972–1977* (New York: Vintage, 1980); Lisa Wedeen, *Ambiguities of Domination: Politics, Rhetoric, and Symbols in Contemporary Syria* (Chicago: University of Chicago Press, 1999); and Jean Comaroff and John Comaroff, *Of Revelation and Revolution,* vols. 1–2 (Chicago: University of Chicago Press, 1991–1997).

94. Scott, *Domination and the Arts of Resistance,* 11–16.

95. Mark B. Borg, "Engaging Diversity's Underbelly: A Story from an Immigrant Parish," *American Journal of Community Psychology* 37, no.3/4 (June 2006): 191–201.

96. Ibid., 197.

97. Scott, "General Commentary," in *Power: Critical Concepts,* vol. 1, ed. John Scott (New York: Routledge, 1994), n1.

98. Emerson and Woo, *People of the Dream*, 47–73. See also Garces-Foley, "New Opportunities and New Values: The Emergence of the Multicultural Church," 221–222.

99. Garces-Foley, "New Opportunities and New Values," 222.

100. Ibid., 223.

101. Such was the case of a Houston parish identified by Emerson and Woo (*People of the Dream*, 57) that came together out of its conscious mission to welcome all who came through the doors. I have seen this in a Chicago area parish that embraced its multicultural mission as part of a larger commitment to progressive theology and politics. Another parish in Southern California embraced this mission out of a shared commitment to a strong devotional Catholicism.

CONCLUSION

1. For example, Richard Rodriguez, *Brown: The Last Discovery of America* (New York: Viking, 2002); Warner, "Immigration and Religious Communities in the United States," 4; and Peter C. Phan, *Christianity with an Asian Face: Asian American Theology in the Making* (Maryknoll, NY: Orbis, 2003), 4.

2. Alejandro Díaz-Domínguez, "Nota metodológica: Midiendo religión en encuestas de Latinoamérica" [Methodological note: Measuring religión in Latin American surveys], *Perspectivas desde el Barómetro de las Américas* [Perspectives from the Americas Barometer], no. 29 (Vanderbilt University, 2009), 11. *Perspectivas* available at http://www.vanderbilt.edu/lapop-espanol/serie-perspectivas.php.

3. Nathan P. Walters and Edward N. Trevelyan, "The Newly Arrived Foreign-Born Population of the United States: 2010," American Community Survey Briefs (Washington, DC: U.S. Census Bureau, 2011), 3.

4. Timothy Tseng, Antony Alumkal, Peter Cha, Faustino Cruz, Young Lee Hertig, Russell Jeung, Jung Ha Kim, Sharon Kim, Ruth Narita Doyle, Fenggang Yang, and David Yoo, *Asian American Religious Leadership Today: A Preliminary Inquiry* (Durham, NC: Pulpit and Pew Research Reports, 2005), 19. Chinese and Indians in the United States are estimated to be 12 percent and 17 percent Catholic respectively. As a result of Roman Catholic concentration in wartime South Vietnam, Vietnamese in the United States are about 30 percent Roman Catholic.

5. Dolan, *The American Catholic Experience*, 159.

6. For example, Peter R. D'Agostino, "Catholic Planning for a Multicultural Metropolis, 1982–1996," in *Public Religion and Urban Transformation: Faith in the City*, ed. Lowell Livezey (New York: New York University Press, 2000), 268–291; and Foley and Hoge, *Religion and the New Immigrants*. On the other hand, see Virgilio Elizondo and Timothy Matovina, *San Fernando Cathedral: Soul of the City* (Maryknoll, NY: Orbis, 1998).

7. For example, Baggett, *Sense of the Faithful*, 59–88.

8. For example, Geraldine Mossiere, "Emotional Dimensions of Conversion: An African Evangelical Congregation in Montreal," *Anthropologica* 49, no. 1 (2007): 113–124

9. For example, Ileana Gómez, Carmen Meyers, Manuel A. Vásquez, and Philip Williams, "Religious and Social Participation in War-Torn Areas of El Salvador," *Journal of Interamerican Studies and World Affairs* 41, no. 4 (December 1999): 53–71.

10. Orsi, *The Madonna of 115th Street*, 1–74.

11. Linden, *Global Catholicism*, 2.

12. See James Murphy, *A Pilgrim's Guide to Sacramento's Cathedral* (Strasbourg, France: Editions du Signe, 2006), 6–7.

13. David Judson and Ronald E. Steen, *Art for the Cathedral: John Nava: Tapestries from Proposal to Installation* (Los Angeles: Judson Studies, 2003).

14. Stephen J. Dudek, "Building a Home for a Multicultural Parish: Lessons Learned," *New Theology Review* 13, no. 1 (2000): 37.

15. Marilynne Robinson, "Imagination and Community: What Holds Us Together," *Commonweal Magazine* (March 9, 2012).

APPENDIX

1. Kathleen Cahalan, "Pastoral Theology or Practical Theology? Limits and Possibilities," in *Keeping Faith in Practice: Aspects of Catholic Pastoral Theology*, ed. James Sweeney, Gemma Simmonds, and David Lonsdale (London: SCM Press, 2010), 108.

2. See M. León-Portilla, *Bernardino de Sahagún: The First Anthropologist* (Norman, OK: University of Oklahoma Press, 2002); and Susan Castillo, *Colonial Encounters in New World Writing, 1500–1786: Performing America* (New York: Routledge, 2006), 187.

3. Jean Michaud, *Incidental Ethnographers: French Catholic Missions on the Tonkin-Yunnan Frontier, 1880–1930* (Boston: Brill, 2007).

4. Stephen L. Schensul, Jean J. Schensul, and Margaret Diane LeCompte, *Initiating Ethnographic Research: A Mixed Methods Approach* (Lanham, MD: AltaMira Press, 2013), 36.

5. Jean M. Bartunek and Meryl Reis Louis, *Insider/Outsider Team Research*, Qualitative Research Series 40 (Thousand Oaks, CA: Sage Publications, 1996), 12.

6. Ibid., 11–13.

7. Kirin Narayan, "How Native Is a 'Native' Ethnographer?" *American Anthropologist*, New Series 95, no. 3 (September 1993): 671–672, 676–677.

8. Ibid., 675–679.

9. Robert Emerson, Rachel Fretz, and Linda Shaw, *Writing Ethnographic Fieldnotes* (Chicago: University of Chicago Press, 1995), 3.

10. Ann Taves, "Negotiating the Boundaries in Theological and Religious Studies" (paper from Open Convocation, Graduate Theological Union, 22 September

2005), Catholic Studies website at UCSB, http://www.religion.ucsb.edu/faculty/
GTU-FinalLecture.pdf (accessed 17 April 2006).

11. Donald Cozzens, *Freeing Celibacy* (Collegeville, MN: Liturgical Press, 2006),
7–18.

12. Donald Cozzens, *Sacred Silence: Denial and the Crisis in the Church* (Collegeville,
MN: Liturgical Press, 2002); and Paul Lakeland, *Liberation of the Laity: In Search
of an Accountable Church* (New York: Continuum, 2004), 7–13.

13. Bartunek and Louis, *Insider/Outsider Team Research*, 13–15.

14. Clifford Geertz, *Local Knowledge*, 57.

15. Bartunek and Louis, *Insider/Outsider Team Research*, 18, 62.

16. Paul Ricoeur, "The Hermeneutics of Testimony," in *Essays on Biblical Interpretation*, ed. with an introduction by Lewis S. Mudge (Philadelphia: Fortress, 1980),
119–146.

17. Mary Field Belenky, Blythe McVicker Clinchy, Nancy Rule Goldberger, and Jill
Mattuck Tarule, *Women's Ways of Knowing: The Development of Self, Voice, and
Mind*, 10th anniversary edition (New York: Basic Books, 1997), 103–112. For
more on the development of observation in modern scientific thinking, see Ian
G. Barbour, *Science and Religion: Historical and Contemporary Issues*, rev. ed.
(New York: HarperCollins, 1990), 9–23.

18. Peter Donovan, "Neutrality in Religious Studies," in *The Insider/Outsider Problem in the Study of Religion: A Reader*, ed. Russell T. McCutcheon (New York:
Cassell, 1999), 236.

19. Belenky et al., *Women's Ways of Knowing*, 112–118. See also Nancy Goldberger,
Mary Belenky., Blythe Clinchy, and Jill Tarule, eds., *Knowledge, Difference, and
Power: Essays Inspired by Women's Ways of Knowing* (New York: Basic Books,
1996).

20. Stephen A. Tyler, "Post-Modern Ethnography: From Document of the Occult
to Occult Document," in *Writing Culture: The Poetics and Politics of Ethnography*,
ed. James Clifford and George E. Marcus, School of American Research Seminar (Berkeley: University of California Press, 1986), 126.

21. Bartunek and Louis, *Insider/Outsider Team Research*, 62.

22. Ibid., 18.

23. Ernest T. Stringer, *Action Research: A Handbook for Practitioners* (Thousand
Oaks, CA: Sage Publications, 1996), 1–8; Orlando Fals-Borda, "Some Basic
Ingredients," in *Action and Knowledge: Breaking the Monopoly with Participatory
Action Research*, ed. Orlando Fals-Borda and Mohammad Anisur Rahman (New
York: Apex Press, 1991), 4–5.

24. Bartunek and Louis, *Insider/Outsider Team Research*, 24–27.

25. Scott L. Thumma, "'Methods for Congregational Study," in *Studying Congregations: A New Handbook*, 196–239.

26. The short survey asked parishioners who were at least fifteen years of age to
identify whether they were born and raised locally, their cultural background,
state or country of origin, age group, years at the parish, and whether or not

they were involved in ministries; they could select among eight options in terms of how they understood parish unity in a culturally diverse parish. They filled out the surveys during the service, and ushers collected them. Participation was high—675 persons answered the survey out of an approximate Sunday attendance of 1,100–1,200. Choices among the eight options were not evaluated for statistical significance.

27. Thumma, "Methods for Congregational Study," 207–208. See also Michael Agar, *The Professional Stranger: An Informal Introduction to Ethnography* (San Diego: Academic Press, 1996), 139–141.

28. Thumma, "Methods for Congregational Study," 204.

29. Stringer, *Action Research*, 62.

30. George E. Marcus, "Contemporary Problems of Ethnography in the Modern World System," in *Writing Culture*, 166, 172.

31. Michael Burawoy, "Introduction: Reaching for the Global," in *Global Ethnography*, ed. Michael Burawoy et al. (Berkeley: University of California Press, 2000), 21–35.

Alba, Richard, and Victor Nee. *Remaking the American Mainstream: Assimilation and Contemporary Immigration.* Cambridge, MA: Harvard University Press, 2003.

Alvarez, Roberto. *Families: Migration and Adaptation in Baja and Alta California from 1800 to 1975.* Berkeley: University of California Press, 1987.

Ammerman, Nancy T. *Congregations and Community.* New Brunswick, NJ: Rutgers University Press, 1997.

———. "Postmodern Trends in Religious Organization." Paper presented to the annual meeting of the American Sociological Association, 7 August 1999.

Ammerman, Nancy T., Jackson Carroll, Carl S. Dudley, and William McKinney, eds. *Studying Congregations: A New Handbook.* Nashville, TN: Abingdon, 1998.

Baca Zinn, Maxine. "Familism Among Chicanos: A Theoretical Review." *Humboldt Journal of Social Relations* 10, no. 1 (Fall/Winter 1982/1983): 224–238.

———. "Mexican-Heritage Families in the United States." In *Handbook of Hispanic Cultures in the United States,* edited by Nicólas Kanellos and Claudio Esteva-Fabregat. Vol. 2, *Sociology,* edited by Félix Padilla, 161–173. Houston: Arte Público Press and Instituto Cooperación Iberoamericana, 1994.

Badillo, David A. "The Catholic Church and the Making of Mexican-American Parish Communities in the Midwest." In *Mexican Americans and the Catholic Church, 1900-1965,* edited by Jay P. Dolan and Gilberto Hinojosa, 236–308. Notre Dame History of Hispanic Catholics in the U.S., edited by Jay Dolan. Notre Dame, IN: University of Notre Dame Press, 1994.

———. *Latinos and the New Immigrant Church.* Baltimore, MD: Johns Hopkins University Press, 2006.

Baggett, Jerome P. *Sense of the Faithful: How American Catholics Live Their Faith.* New York: Oxford University Press, 2009.

Bankston, Carl L. III, and Min Zhou. "De Facto Congregationalism and Socioeconomic Mobility in Laotian and Vietnamese Immigrant Communities: A Study of Religious Institutions and Economic Change." *Review of Religious Research* 41 (2000): 453–470.

Bantjes, Adrian. "Religion and the Mexican Revolution: Toward a New Historiography." In *Religious Culture in Mexico,* edited by Martín Agustín Nesvig, 223–254. Jaguar Books on Latin America. Lanham, MD: Rowman & Littlefield, 2007.

Barlow, Philip, and Mark Silk. *Religion and Public Life in the Midwest: American's Common Denominator?* Religion by Region. Walnut Creek, CA: AltaMira Press, 2004.

Bartunek, Jean M., and Meryl Reis Louis. *Insider/Outsider Research.* Qualitative
Research series 40. Thousand Oaks, CA: Sage Publications, 1996.

Bassnett, Susan. "The Meek or the Mighty: Reappraising the Role of the Translator." In
Translation, Power, Subversion, edited by Román Alvarez and M. Carmen Africa,
10–24. Topics in Translation 8. Bristol, PA: Multilingual Matters, Ltd., 1998.

Bean, Frank D., and Gillian Stevens. *America's Newcomers and the Dynamics of Diversity.* Rose Series in Sociology of American Sociological Association. New York:
Russell Sage Foundation, 2003.

Becker, Penny Edgell. "Making Inclusive Communities: Congregations and the 'Problem' of Race." *Social Problems* 45, no. 4 (1998): 451–472.

Belenky, Mary Field, Blythe McVicker Clinchy, Nancy Rule Goldberger, and Jill
Mattuck Tarule. *Women's Ways of Knowing: The Development of Self, Voice, and
Mind.* 10th anniv. ed. New York: Basic Books, 1997.

Bell, Catherine. *Ritual Theory, Ritual Practice.* New York: Oxford University Press, 1992.

Bellah, Robert N., Richard Madsen, William M. Sullivan, and Ann Swidler. *Habits of
the Heart: Individualism and Commitment in American Life.* Updated edition with
new introduction. Berkeley: University of California Press, 1996.

Bellos, David. *Is That a Fish in Your Ear? Translation and the Meaning of Everything.*
New York: Faber and Faber, 2011.

Bennett, Milton J. "Intercultural Communication: A Current Perspective." In *Basic
Concepts of Intercultural Communication,* edited By Milton J. Bennett, 1–34. Yarmouth, ME: Intercultural Press, 1998.

———. "Toward Ethnorelativism: A Developmental Model of Intercultural Sensitivity." In *Education for the Intercultural Experience,* edited by R. Michael Paige, 21–72.
Yarmouth, ME: Intercultural Press, 1993.

Bhaba, Homi K. *The Location of Culture.* New York: Routledge, 1994.

Black, Gino [pseud.]. *History of the Port Jefferson Diocese.* Port Jefferson: PJ Catholic
Press [pseud.], 2006.

Bleichner, Howard P. *View from the Altar: Reflections on the Rapidly Changing Catholic
Priesthood.* New York: Crossroad, 2004.

Bourdieu, Pierre. *Outline of a Theory of Practice.* Translated by Richard Nice. Cambridge: Cambridge University Press, 1977.

Brandes, Stanley. "The Cremated Catholic: The Ends of a Deceased Guatemalan." *Body
and Society* 7 (2001): 111–120.

———. *Skulls to the Living, Bread to the Dead: The Day of the Dead in Mexico and
Beyond.* Malden, MA: Blackwell, 2006.

Broadway, M. J. "From City to Countryside: Recent Changes in the Structure and
Location of the Meat and Fish Processing Industries." In *Any Way You Cut It: Meat
Processing and Small-Town America,* edited by Donald Stull, Michael J. Broadway,
and David Griffith, 17–40. Lawrence: University Press of Kansas, 1995.

Bunson, Matthew, ed. *Catholic Almanac 2008.* Huntington, IN: Our Sunday Visitor, 2007.

Burawoy, Michael, ed. *Global Ethnography: Forces, Connections, and Imaginations in a
Postmodern World.* Berkeley: University of California Press, 2000.

Burns, Jeffrey M. "St. Elizabeth's Parish of Oakland and the Resiliency of Parish Life: From German to Latino, From Pre- to Post-Vatican II." *U.S. Catholic Historian* 14, no. 3 (Summer 1996): 57–74.

Burns, Jeffrey M., Ellen Skerrett, and Joseph M. White. *Keeping Faith: European and Asian Catholic Immigrants*. American Catholic Identities: A Documentary History, edited by Christopher Kauffmann. Maryknoll, NY: Orbis, 2000.

Cadge, Wendy. "De Facto Congregationalism and the Religious Organizations of Post-1965 Immigrants to the United States: A Revised Approach." *Journal of the American Academy of Religion* 76, no. 2 (June 2008): 344–374.

Cadge, Wendy, Peggy Levitt, and David Smilde. "De-Centering and Re-Centering: Rethinking Concepts and Methods in the Sociological Study of Religion." *Journal for the Scientific Study of Religion* 50, no. 3 (2011): 437–449.

Cahalan, Kathleen. "Pastoral Theology or Practical Theology? Limits and Possibilities." In *Keeping Faith in Practice: Aspects of Catholic Pastoral Theology*, ed. James Sweeney, Gemma Simmonds, and David Lonsdale, 99–116. London: SCM Press, 2010.

Calavita, Kitty. *Inside the State: The Bracero Program, Immigration, and the I.N.S.* New York: Routledge, 1992.

Carey, Patrick W. *Catholics in America*. Westport, CT: Praeger, 2004.

Carroll, Glenn R. "Concentration and Specialization: Dynamics of Niche Width in Populations of Organizations." *American Journal of Sociology* 90, no. 6 (May 1985): 1262–1283.

Carroll, Michael P. *American Catholics in the Protestant Imagination: Rethinking the Academic Study of Religion*. Baltimore: Johns Hopkins University Press, 2007.

Casarella, Peter. "Recognizing Diversity After Multiculturalism." *New Theology Review* 21, no. 4 (November 2008): 17–26.

Castelli, Jim, and Joseph Gremillion. *The Emerging Parish: The Notre Dame Study of Catholic Life Since Vatican II*. Notre Dame, IN: Notre Dame University Press, 1987.

Cenkner, William, ed. *The Multicultural Church: A New Landscape in U.S. Theologies*. New York: Paulist, 1996.

Center for Applied Research in the Apostolate [CARA]. "Young Adult Catholics." *Special Report*. Washington, DC: CARA, 2002.

Cerulo, Karen A. "Individualism . . . *Pro Tem*: Reconsidering U.S. Social Relations." In *Culture in Mind*, edited Karen A. Cerulo, 135–171. New York: Routledge, 2002.

Chafetz, Janet Saltzman, and Helen Rose Ebaugh, eds. *Religion Across Borders: Transnational Immigrant Networks*. Walnut Creek, CA: Altamira Press, 2002.

Chaves, Mark. *Congregations in America*. Cambridge, MA: Harvard University Press, 2004.

Chaves, Mark, and Shawna L. Anderson. National Congregations Study, 1998. Durham, NC: Duke University, 2008. http://www.soc.duke.edu/natcong/explore.html.

———. National Congregations Study, 2006. Durham, NC: Duke University, 2008. http://www.soc.duke.edu/natcong/cgi-bin/natcong2.cgi.

Chavez, Leo R. *The Latino Threat: Constructing Immigrants, Citizens, and the Nation*. Stanford, CA: Stanford University Press, 2008.

Chidestar, David. *Christianity: A Global History*. New York: HarperCollins, 2000.

Clark, William A. *A Voice of Their Own: The Authority of the Local Parish.* Collegeville, MN: Liturgical Press, 2005.

Cleary, Edward L. *How Latin America Saved the Soul of the Catholic Church.* New York: Paulist, 2009.

Clifford, James, and George Marcus, eds. *Writing Culture: The Poetics and Politics of Ethnography.* Berkeley: University of California Press, 1986.

Coleman, John. "Pastoral Strategies for Multicultural Parishes." *Origins* 31, no. 30 (10 January 2002): 497–505.

Comaroff, Jean, and John Comaroff. *Christianity, Colonialism, and Consciousness in South Africa.* Vol. 1 of *Of Revelation and Revolution.* Chicago: University of Chicago Press, 1991.

Comaroff, Jean, and John Comaroff. *The Dialectics of Modernity on a South African Frontier.* Vol. 2 of *Of Revelation and Revolution.* Chicago: University of Chicago Press, 1997.

Conde-Frazier, Elizabeth. "Participatory Action Research: Practical Theology for Social Justice." *Religious Education* 101, no. 3 (Summer 2006): 321–329.

Conferencia del Episcopado Mexicano [Conference of Mexican Bishops] and United States Conference of Catholic Bishops [USCCB]. "Strangers No Longer: A Pastoral Letter on Migration." Washington, DC: USCCB, 2002.

Conferencia Episcopal Latinoamericana [Latin American Conference of Bishops]. "Documento de Puebla, III Conferencia General del Episcopado Latinoamericano, 1979" [Document of Puebla, III General Conference of the Latin American Episcopate]. Program of the Evangelization of Culture of the Universidad Católica de Argentina.

Congregation for Divine Worship and the Discipline of the Sacraments. Instruction: *Redemptionis Sacramentum.* Rome: Liberia Editrice Vaticana, 2005.

Congregation for the Doctrine of the Faith. *Dominus Iesus.* Vatican City: Congregation for the Doctrine of the Faith, 2000.

Connor, Phillip. "A Balm for the Soul: Immigrant Religion and Emotional Well-Being." *International Migration* 50, no. 2 (April 2012): 130–157.

Conzen, Kathleen Neils. "Foundation of a Rural German-Catholic Culture: Farm and Family in St. Martin, Minn., 1857–1915." Working Paper Series, American Catholic Studies Seminar, no. 2 (Spring 1977).

———. "German-Americans and the Invention of Ethnicity." In *Immigration, Language, Ethnicity,* volume one of *America and the Germans: An Assessment of a Three-Hundred-Year* History, edited by Frank Trommler and Joseph McVeigh, 131–147. Philadelphia: University of Pennsylvania Press, 1985.

———. *Making Their Own America: Assimilation Theory and the German Peasant Pioneer.* New York: Berg Publishers, 1990.

Coriden, James A. *The Parish in Catholic Tradition: History, Theology, and Canon Law.* New York: Paulist, 1996.

Coriden, James A., Thomas Joseph Green, and Donald E. Heintschel, eds. *The Code of Canon Law: Text and Commentary.* New York: Paulist Press, 1985.

Cornell, Stephen, and Douglas Hartmann. *Ethnicity and Race: Making Identities in a Changing World*. 2nd ed. Thousand Oaks, CA: Pine Forge Press, 2007.

Cozzens, Donald B. *Freeing Celibacy*. Collegeville, MN: Liturgical Press, 2006.

——— *Sacred Silence: Denial and the Crisis in the Church*. Collegeville, MN: Liturgical Press, 2002.

Crane, Ken. *Latino Churches: Faith, Family, and Ethnicity in the Second Generation*. New Americans: Recent Immigration and American Society. New York: LFB Scholarly Publishing, 2003.

Crankshaw, Ned M. "Plowing or Mowing? Rural Sprawl in Nelson County, Kentucky." *Landscape Journal* 28, no. 2 (1 September 2009): 218–234.

Cruz, Faustino M. "Immigrant Faith Communities as Interpreters: Educating for Participatory Action." *New Theology Review* 21, no. 4 (November 2008): 27–37.

———. "Ministry for a Multicultural Church and Society." *Reflective Practice: Formation and Supervision in Ministry* 27 (2007): 43–60.

———. "Religion, Ethnicity, and Immigration in the United States: Engaging Critically with the U.S. Catholic Church's Pastoral Response." *Journal of Sophia Asian Studies* 26 (2008): 1–23.

Demerath, N.J., Peter Dobkin Hall, Terry Schmitt, and Rhys A. Williams, eds. *Sacred Companies: Organizational Aspects of Religion and Religious Aspects of Organizations*. New York: Oxford University Press, 1998.

D'Agostino, Peter R. "Catholic Planning for a Multicultural Metropolis, 1982–1996." In *Public Religion, Faith in the City, and Urban Transformation*, edited by Lowell W. Livezey, 268–291. New York: New York University Press, 2000.

———. *Rome in America: Transnational Catholic Ideology from the Risorgimento to Fascism*. Chapel Hill: University of North Carolina Press, 2004.

D'Antonio, William V., James D. Davidson, Dean R. Hoge, and Mary L. Gautier. *American Catholics Today: New Realities of Their Faith and Their Church*. Lanham, MD: Rowman & Littlefield, 2007.

Davidson, James D., and Suzanne Fournier. "Recent Research on Catholic Parishes: A Research Note." *Review of Religious Research* 48, no. 1 (2006): 72–81.

Davis, Cyprian. *The History of Black Catholics in the United States*. New York: Crossroad, 1990.

Day, Graham. *Community and Everyday Life*. New York: Routledge, 2006.

Deck, Allan Figueroa. "Beyond the Polarized Present: New Perspectives on U.S. Latino Migration and Christianity." Latino Theology and Ministry lecture, Loyola Marymount University, 4 October 2012.

———. "Multiculturalism as Ideology." In *Perspectivas: Hispanic Ministry*, edited by Allan Figueroa Deck, Yolanda Tarango, and Timothy Matovina, 28–34. Lanham, MD: Rowman & Littlefield, 1995.

Derné, Steve. "Cultural Conceptions of Human Motivation and Their Significance for Culture Theory." In *The Sociology of Culture*, edited by Diana Crane, 267–287. Cambridge, MA: Blackwell, 1994.

Derné, Steve. "Structural Realities, Persistent Dilemmas, and the Construction of Emotional Paradigms: Love in Three Cultures." *Social Perspectives on Emotion* 2 (1994): 281–308.

de Young, Curtiss Paul, Michael O. Emerson, George Yancey, and Karen Chai Kim. *United by Faith: The Multiracial Congregation as an Answer to the Problem of Race.* New York: Oxford University Press, 2003.

Díaz-Stevens, Ana María. *Oxcart Catholicism on Fifth Avenue: The Impact of the Puerto Rican Migration upon the Archdiocese of New York.* Notre Dame, IN: University of Notre Dame Press, 1993.

Dillon, Michelle. *Catholic Identity: Balancing Reason, Faith, and Power.* New York: Cambridge University Press, 1999.

DiMaggio, Paul J., and Walter W. Powell, eds. *The New Institutionalism in Organizational Analysis.* Chicago: University of Chicago Press, 1991.

DiSalvo, Katherine. "Understanding an Outlier: How Parish Culture Matters in a Highly Participatory Catholic Church." *Review of Religious Research* 49, no. 1 (2008): 438–455.

Dizard Jan E., and Howard Gadlin. *The Minimal Family.* Amherst: University of Massachusetts Press, 1990.

Driskill, Joseph D. "Exploring White Identity Formation in Pastoral Care and Counseling Training." *American Journal of Pastoral Counseling* 7, no. 1 (2003): 3–22.

Dolan, Jay P. *The American Catholic Experience: A History from Colonial Times to the Present.* Notre Dame, IN: University of Notre Dame Press, 1992.

———. *In Search of an American Catholicism: A History of Religion and Culture in Tension.* New York: Oxford, 2002.

Dolan Jay P., and Allan Figueroa Deck, eds. *Hispanic Culture in the United States: Issues and Concerns.* Notre Dame History of Hispanic Catholics in the U.S., vol. 3. Notre Dame, IN: University of Notre Dame Press, 1994.

Donato, Katharine M., and Carl L. Bankston III. "The Origins of Employer Demand in a New Destination: The Salience of Soft Skills in a Volatile Economy." In *New Faces in New Places: The Changing Geography of American Immigration*, edited by Douglass Massey, 124–148. New York: Russell Sage, 2010.

Doyle, David Noel. "Irish as Urban Pioneers in the United States, 1850–1870." *Journal of American Ethnic History* 10, no. 1/2 (Fall 1990/Winter 1991): 36–59.

———. "The Remaking of Irish America, 1845–1880." In *Making the Irish American: History and Heritage of the Irish in the United States*, ed. J.J. Lee and Marion R. Casey, 213–252. New York: New York University Press, 2006.

Doyle, Dennis. *Communion Ecclesiology: Vision and Versions.* Maryknoll, NY: Orbis, 2000.

Dudek, Stephen S. "Becoming Inclusive Communities of Faith: Biblical Reflection and Effective Frameworks." *New Theology Review* 21, no. 1 (Feb. 2008): 40–51.

———. "Building a Home for a Multicultural Parish: Lessons Learned." *New Theology Review* 13, no. 1 (February 2000): 37–45.

———. "Drawn in the Circle of God's Love: A Congregational Study of Unity and Diversity." D.Min. thesis, Catholic Theological Union, 2002.

Ebaugh, Helen Rose, and Janet Salztman Chafetz. *Religion and the New Immigrants: Continuities and Adaptations in Immigrant Congregations*. Abridged student edition. Lanham, MD: Altamira Press, 2000.

Eiesland, Nancy. *A Particular Place: Urban Restructuring and Religious Ecology in a Southern Exurb*. New Brunswick, NJ: Rutgers University Press, 2000.

Eldredge, Elizabeth. *Power in Colonial Africa: Conflict and Discourse in Lesotho, 1870–1960*. Madison: University of Wisconsin Press, 2007.

Eliasoph, Nina. "'Close to Home': The Work of Avoiding Politics." *Theory and Society* 26 (1997): 605–647.

Elizondo, Virgilio, and Timothy Matovina. *San Fernando Cathedral: Soul of the City*. Maryknoll, NY: Orbis, 1998.

Ellis, John Tracy. *American Catholicism*. Rev. ed. The Chicago History of American Civilization, edited by Daniel J. Boorstin. Chicago: University of Chicago Press, 1969.

Ellman, Yisrael. "Intermarriage in the United States: A Comparative Study of Jews and Other Ethnic and Religious Groups." *Jewish Social Studies* 49, no. 1 (Winter 1987): 1–26.

Emerson, Michael O., and Karen Chai Kim. "Multiracial Congregations: An Analysis of Their Development and a Typology." *Journal for the Scientific Study of Religion* 42, no. 2 (2003): 217–227.

Emerson, Michael O., and Rodney Woo. *People of the Dream: Multiracial Congregations in the United States*. Princeton, NJ: Princeton University Press, 2006.

Emerson, Robert M., Rachel I. Fretz, and Linda L. Shaw. *Writing Ethnographic Fieldnotes*. Chicago: University of Chicago Press, 1995.

Empereur, James, and Eduardo Fernández. *La Vida Sacra: Contemporary Hispanic Sacramental Theology*. Celebrating Faith: Explorations in Latino Spirituality and Theology, ed. Virgilio Elizondo. New York: Rowman & Littlefield, 2006.

Escobar, Samuel. *Changing Tides: Latin America and World Mission Today*. American Society of Missiology. Maryknoll, NY: Orbis, 2002.

Espín, Orlando O. *The Faith of the People: Theological Reflections on Popular Catholicism*. Maryknoll, NY: Orbis, 1997.

———. "Juan Soldado, 'Santa Muerte,' and Other Border Crossing Saints." Session paper, Catholic Theological Society of America conference, San Jose, CA, June 11, 2011.

Etzioni, Amitai. *The New Golden Rule*. New York: Basic Books, 1996.

Fals-Borda, Orlando, and Mohammed Anisur Rahman, eds. *Action and Knowledge: Breaking the Monopoly with Participatory Action-Research*. New York: Apex Press, 1991.

Fichter, Joseph H. *Dynamics of a City Church*. Vol. 1 of *The Southern Parish*. Chicago: University of Chicago Press, 1951.

Fichter, Joseph H. *One-Man Research: Reminiscences of a Catholic Sociologist.* New York: Wiley, 1973.

Finke, Roger, and Rodney Starke. *The Churching of America, 1776–1950: Winners and Losers in Our Religious Economy.* 2nd ed. New Brunswick, NJ: Rutgers University Press, 2005.

Fisher, James T. *Communion of Immigrants: A History of Catholics in America.* New York: Oxford University Press, 2000.

Flannery, Austin, ed. *Vatican Council II: The Conciliar and Post Conciliar Documents.* Vatican Collection, vol. 1. Grand Rapids, MI: Eerdmans, 1992.

Foley, Michael W., and Dean R. Hoge. *Religion and the New Immigrants: How Faith Communities Form Our Newest Citizens.* New York: Oxford University Press, 2007.

Fornet-Betancourt, Raúl. *Hacia una filosofía intercultural latinoamericana* [Toward an intercultural Latin American philosophy]. 1st ed. Colección universitaria. San José, Costa Rica: Editorial DEI, 1994.

Fornet-Betancourt, Raúl, ed. *Interaction and Asymmetry between Cultures in the Context of Globalization.* Frankfurt, Germany: IKO, 2002.

Foster, Charles R. *Embracing Diversity: Leadership in Multicultural Congregations.* Herndon, VA: Alban Institute, 1997.

Foucault, Michel. *Power/Knowledge: Selected Interviews and Other Writings, 1972–1977.* Edited by Colin Gordon. Translated by Colin Gordon, Leo Marshall, John Mepham, and Kate Soper. New York: Pantheon Books, 1980.

Fraser, Nancy, and Axel Honneth. *Redistribution or Recognition? A Political-Philosophical Exchange.* Translated by Joel Golb, James Ingram, and Christiane Wilke. New York: Verso, 2003.

Freire, Paulo. *La educación como práctica de la libertad* [Education as liberatory practice]. Translated by Lilién Ronzoni. Mexico, DF: Siglo Veintiuno Editores, 1969.

———. *Pedagogy of the Oppressed.* 30th anniv. ed. Translated by Myra Bergman Ramos. Introduction by Donaldo Macedo. New York: Continuum, 2000.

Froehle, Bryan T. "Religious Competition, Community Building, and Democracy in Latin America: Grassroots Religious Organizations in Venezuela." *Sociology of Religion* 55, no. 2 (Summer 1994): 145–162.

Gallup, George Jr., and Jim Castelli. *The American Catholic People: Their Beliefs, Practices, and Values.* Garden City, NY: Doubleday, 1987.

Gans, Herbert J. "Symbolic Ethnicity: The Future of Ethnic Groups and Cultures in America." *Ethnic and Racial Studies* 2 (1979): 1–20.

Garcia, Carlos. "*Buscando Trabajo:* Social Networking among Immigrants from Mexico to the United States." *Hispanic Journal of Behavioral Sciences* 27 (2005): 3–22.

Garces-Foley, Kathleen. "Comparing Catholic and Evangelical Integration Efforts." *Journal for the Scientific Study of Religion* 47, no. 1 (2008): 17–22.

———. *Crossing the Ethnic Divide: The Multiethnic Church on a Mission.* New York: Oxford University Press, 2007.

———. "From the Melting Pot to the Multicultural Table: Filipino Catholics in Los Angeles." *American Catholic Studies* 120, no. 1 (2009): 27–53.

———. "New Opportunities and New Values: The Emergence of the Multicultural Church." *Annals of the American Academy of Political and Social Science* 612, no. 1 (2007): 209–224.

Geertz, Clifford. *The Interpretation of Cultures.* New York: Basic Books, 1973.

———. *Local Knowledge: Further Essays in Interpretive Anthropology.* New York: Basic Books, 1983.

Gill, Anthony. "The Struggle to Be Soul Provider: Catholic Responses to Protestant Growth in Latin America." In *Latin American Religion in Motion,* edited by Christian Smith and Joshua Prokopy, 17–40. New York: Routledge, 1999.

Gleason, Philip. *The Conservative Reformers: German-American Catholics and the Social Order.* Notre Dame, IN: University of Notre Dame Press, 1968.

———. "In Search of Unity: American Catholic Thought 1920–1960." *Catholic Historical Review* 65, no. 2 (April 1979): 185–205.

———. "The Melting Pot: Symbol of Fusion or Confusion?" *American Quarterly* 16, no. 1 (Spring 1964): 20–46.

Goizueta, Roberto. *Caminemos con Jesus: Toward a Hispanic/Latino Theology of Accompaniment.* Maryknoll, NY: Orbis, 1995.

Goldberger, Nancy Rule, Mary Belenky, Blythe Clinchy, and Jill Tarule, eds. *Knowledge, Difference, and Power: Essays Inspired by Women's Ways of Knowing.* New York: Basic Books, 1996,

Gray, Mark M., Mary L. Gautier, and Melissa A. Cidade. "The Changing Face of U.S. Catholic Parishes." Washington, DC: National Association for Lay Ministry, 2011.

Greeley, Andrew. *The American Catholic: A Social Portrait.* New York: Basic Books, 1977.

———. *The Catholic Imagination.* Berkeley: University of California Press, 2000.

———. "Ethnic Variations in Religious Commitment." In *The Religious Dimension: New Directions in Quantitative Research,* edited by Robert Wuthnow, 113–134. New York: Academic Press, 1979.

Griswold, Wendy. *Cultures and Societies in a Changing World.* Thousand Oaks, CA: Pine Forge Press, 1994.

Griswold del Castillo, Richard. *Chicano Families in the Urban Southwest, 1848 to the Present.* Notre Dame, IN: University of Notre Dame Press, 1984.

Groody, Daniel. *Border of Death, Valley of Life: An Immigrant Journey of Heart and Spirit.* Lanham, MD: Rowman & Littlefield, 2002.

Guardino, Peter. "Postcolonialism as Self-Fulfilled Prophecy? Electoral Politics in Oaxaca, 1814–1828." In *After Spanish Rule: Postcolonial Predicaments of the Americas,* ed. Mark Thurner and Andrés Guerrero, 248–271. Durham, NC: Duke University Press, 2003.

Gudykunst, William B. "An Anxiety/Uncertainty Management Theory of Effective Communication." In *Theorizing Intercultural Communication,* edited William B. Gudykunst, 281–322. Thousand Oaks, CA: Sage, 2005.

Gutierrez, Gustavo. *Las Casas: In Search of the Poor of Jesus Christ.* Translated by Robert R. Barr. Maryknoll, NY: Orbis, 1993.

Healy, Nicholas M. *Church, World, and the Christian Life: Practical-Prophetic Ecclesiology*. Cambridge: Cambridge University Press, 2000.

Healy, Nicholas M. "Practices and the New Ecclesiology: Misplaced Concreteness?" *International Journal of Systematic Theology* 5, no. 3 (November 2003): 287–308.

Hennesey, James. *American Catholics: A History of the Roman Catholic Community in the United States*. New York: Oxford University Press, 1981.

Hess, Mary E. "Collaborating with People to Study 'The Popular': Implementing Participatory Action Research Strategies in Religious Education." *Religious Education* 96, no. 3 (November 2001): 271–293.

Hinsdale, Mary Ann, Helen M. Lewis, and S. Maxine Waller. *It Comes from the People: Community Development and Local Theology*. Philadelphia: Temple University Press, 1995.

Hirschman, Charles. "America's Melting Pot Reconsidered." *Annual Review of Sociology* 9 (1983): 397–423.

Hochschild, Arlie Russell. *The Commercialization of Intimate Life: Notes from Home and Work*. Berkeley: University of California Press, 2003.

Hofstede, Geert H. *Culture's Consequences*. Thousand Oaks, CA: Sage, 2001.

Hoover, Brett C. "Memory and Ministry: Young Adult Nostalgia, Immigrant Amnesia." *New Theology Review* 23. No. 1 (February 2010): 58–67.

———. "When Work Culture and Ministry Collide: Lessons from the INSPIRE Project in Chicago," *Seminary Journal* 16, no. 3 (Winter 2010, published 2012): 43–52.

Hopewell, James F. *Congregation: Stories and Structures*. Edited by Barbara G. Wheeler. Philadelphia: Fortress, 1987.

Hsu, Francis L. K. *Rugged Individualism Reconsidered*. Knoxville: University of Tennessee Press, 1983.

Huels, John. "Parish Life and the New Code." *Concilium* 185 (1986): 64–65.

Huntington, Samuel. *Who Are We? The Challenges to America's National Identity*. New York: Simon & Schuster, 2004.

Hynes, Eugene. "Family and Religious Change in a Peripheral Capitalist Society: Mid-Nineteenth-Century Ireland." In *The Religion and Family Connection: Social Science Perspectives*, edited by Darwin L. Thomas, 161–174. Provo, UT: Religious Studies Center, Brigham Young University, 1988.

Icaza, Rosa María, ed. *Faith Expressions of the Southwest*. 3rd ed. revised. San Antonio, TX: Mexican American Cultural Center, 2003.

International Committee on English in the Liturgy. *General Instruction for the Roman Missal*. Liturgy Documentary series 2. Washington, DC: USCCB, 2003.

Irarrazaval, Diego. "Religion Popular" [Popular religion]. In *Mysterium Liberationis: Conceptos fundamentals de la teología de la liberación* (The mystery of liberation: Fundamental concepts of the theology of liberation), edited by Ignacio Ellacuría and Jon Sobrino, vol. 2, 345–375. Madrid: Editorial Trotta, 1990.

Isasi-Díaz, Ada María. *En la Lucha/In the Struggle: Elaborating a Mujerista Theology*. 10th anniv. ed. Minneapolis: Fortress Press, 2004.

Isasi-Diaz, Ada Maria, and Yolanda Tarango. *Hispanic Women: Prophetic Voices in the Church*. Minneapolis: Fortress Press, 1992.

John Paul II. *Ecclesia in America*. Rome: Libreria Editrice Vaticana, 1999.

John Paul II. *Eucharistia in Ecclesia*. Rome: Libreria Editrice Vaticana, 2003.

Johnson-Mondragón, Ken. "Ministry in Multicultural and National/Ethnic Parishes: Evaluating the Findings of the Emerging Models of Pastoral Leadership Project." Stockton, CA: Instituto Fe y Vida/National Association for Lay Ministry, 2008.

Judson, David, and Ronald E. Steen. *Art for the Cathedral: John Nava: Tapestries from Proposal to Installation*. Los Angeles: Judson Studies, 2003.

Kantowicz, Edward R. "Cardinal Mundelein of Chicago and the Shaping of Twentieth-Century American Catholicism." *Journal of American History* 68, no. 1 (Jun. 1981): 63–68.

Kellogg, Susan, and Steven Mintz. "Family Structures." In *Encyclopedia of American Social History*, vol. 3, edited by Mary K. Gorn, Elliot J. Williams, and Peter W. Cayton, 1925–1941. New York: Charles Scribner's Sons, 1993.

Kellor, Frances A. "What Is Americanization?" In *Immigration and Americanization: Selected Readings*, edited by Philip Davis, 625–626. Boston: Atheneum, 1920.

Klesner, Joseph L. "Social Capital and Political Participation in Latin America Evidence from Argentina, Chile, Mexico, and Peru." *Latin American Research Review* 42, no. 2 (2007): 1–32.

Kosmin, Barry A.. "Research Report: The National Survey of Religious Identification, 1989–90." New York: Graduate Center of the City University of New York, 1991.

Kosmin, Barry A., Egon Mayer, and Ariela Keysar, "American Religious Identification Survey, 2001." New York: Graduate Center of the City University of New York, 2001.

Korgen, Kathleen Odell. *Crossing the Racial Divide: Close Friendships Between Black and White Americans*. Westport, CT: Praeger, 2002.

Lakeland, Paul. *The Liberation of the Laity: In Search of an Accountable Church*. New York: Continuum, 2004.

———. *Postmodernity: Christian Identity in a Fragmented Age*. Guides to Theological Inquiry. Minneapolis: Fortress Press, 1997.

Larkin, Emmet. "The Devotional Revolution in Ireland." *American Historical Review* 77 (1972): 625–652.

Law, Eric H. F. *Sacred Acts, Holy Change: Faithful Diversity and Practical Transformation*. St. Louis, MO: Chalice Press, 2002.

LeBeau, Bryan. *Religion in America to 1865*. New York: New York University Press, 2000.

Levitt, Peggy. *God Needs No Passport: Immigrants and the Changing American Religious Landscape*. New York: New Press, 2007.

Linden, Ian. *Global Catholicism: Diversity and Change Since Vatican II*. New York: Columbia University Press, 2009.

Linkh, Richard M. *American Catholicism and European Immigrants, 1900–1924*. New York: Center for Migration Studies, 1991.

Liptak, Dolores. *Immigrants and Their Church*. Bicentennial History of the Catholic Church in America, edited by Christopher J. Kauffman. New York: Macmillan, 1989.

Loewen, Jacob A. "Roles: Relating to an Alien Social Structure." *Missiology* 4, no. 2 (April 1976): 217–242.

Lopez, Mark Hugo, and Susan Minishkin. "2008 National Survey of Latinos: Hispanics See Their Situation in U.S. Deteriorating." Washington, DC: Pew Hispanic Center, 2008.

Lugo, Luis, Gabriel Escobar, Sandra Stencel, Gretchen Livingston, John C. Green, Shirin Hakimzadeh, Gregory A. Smith, Dan Cox, and Sahar Chaudhry. "Changing Faiths: Latinos and the Transformation of American Religion. Washington, DC: Pew Research Center, 2007.

Lugo, Luis, Gregory Smith, Dan Cox, and Allison Pond. "A Portrait of American Catholics on the Eve of Pope Benedict XVI's Visit: Social and Political Views of Catholics in the U.S." Washington, DC: Pew Forum on Religion and Public Life, March 2008.

Luis Lugo, Sandra Stencel, John Green, Gregory Smith, Dan Cox, Allison Pond, Tracy Miller, Elizabeth Podrebarac, Michelle Ralston, Hilary Ramp, Andrew Kohut, Paul Taylor, and Scott Keeter. "U.S. Religious Landscape Survey 2008." Washington, DC: Pew Forum on Religion and Public Life, 2008.

Maines, David R., and Michael J. McCallion. "Evidence and Speculations on Catholic on *De Facto* Congregationalism." *Review of Religious Research* 46, no. 1 (2004): 92–101.

Marsh, Christopher. "Sacred Space in England, 1560–1640: The View from the Pew." *Journal of Ecclesiastical History* 53, no. 2 (Apr 2002): 286–311.

Massa, Mark S. *Catholics and American Culture: Fulton Sheen, Dorothy Day, and the Notre Dame Football Team*. New York: Crossroad, 1999.

Massey, Douglas, Jorge Durand, and Nolan J. Malone. *Beyond Smoke and Mirrors: Mexican Immigration in an Era of Economic Integration*. New York: Russell Sage Foundation, 2002.

Matovina, Timothy, and Gerald E. Poyo, eds. *¡Presente! U.S. Latino Catholics from Colonial Origins to the Present*. American Catholic Identities: A Documentary History, edited by Christopher Kauffmann. Maryknoll, NY: Orbis, 2000.

Maveety, Stanley R. "Doctrine in Tyndale's New Testament: Translation as a Tendentious Art." *Studies in English Literature, 1500–1900* 6, no. 1 (Winter 1966): 151–158.

McCubbin, Laurie D., and Sara Bennett, "Cultural Encapsulation." In *Encyclopedia of Counseling*, edited by Frederick T. L. Leong, 1091–1092. Thousand Oaks, CA: Sage, 2008.

McCutcheon, Russell T. *The Insider/Outsider Problem in the Study of Religion: A Reader*. New York: Cassell, 1999.

McGreevy, John T. *Parish Boundaries: The Catholic Encounter with Race in the Twentieth-Century Urban North*. Historical Studies of Urban America. Chicago: University of Chicago Press, 1998.

McGuire, Meredith B. *Lived Religion: Faith and Practice in Everyday Life*. New York: Oxford University Press, 2008.

Megged, Amos. *Exporting the Catholic Reformation: Local Religion in Early-Colonial Mexico*. New York: E. J. Brill, 1996.

Meier, Matt S., and Feliciano Ribera. *Mexican Americans—American Mexicans: From Conquistadors to Chicanos*. Rev. ed. New York: Hill and Wang, 1993.

Michaud, Jean. *Incidental Ethnographers: French Catholic Missions on the Tonkin-Yunnan Frontier, 1880–1930*. Boston: Brill, 2007.

Miller, Ann Neville. "When Face-to-Face Doesn't Work: Use of Informal Intermediaries to Communicate Interpersonally in Sub-Saharan Africa." In *Intercultural Communication: A Reader*, 13th ed., edited by Larry A. Samovar, Richard E. Porter, and Edwin R. McDaniel, 171–180. Boston: Wadsworth, 2009.

Mirel, Jeffery E. *Patriotic Pluralism: Americanization Education and European Immigrants*. Cambridge, MA: Harvard University Press, 2010.

Murphy, James. *A Pilgrim's Guide to Sacramento's Cathedral*. Strasbourg, France: Editions du Signe, 2006.

Narayan, Kirin. "How Native Is a 'Native' Ethnographer?" *American Anthropologist*, New Series, 95, no. 3 (September 1993): 671–686.

Nesvig, Martin Austin, ed. *Local Religion in Colonial Mexico*. Diáologos series. Albuquerque, NM: University of New Mexico Press, 2006.

Neuhaus, Richard John. "The Public Square: Three Who Changed the World." *First Things* 170 (February 2007). http://www.firstthings.com/article/2009/02/three-who-changed-the-world-37. Accessed 13 July 2009.

Ngai, Mae M. *Impossible Subjects: Illegal Aliens and the Making of Modern America*. Politics and Society in Twentieth Century America. Princeton, NJ: Princeton University Press, 2005.

Nida, Eugene, and Charles Taber. *The Theory and Practice of Translation*. Leiden, Netherlands: Brill, 2003.

Numrich, Paul. *Old Wisdom in the New World: Americanization in Two Immigrant Theravada Buddhist Temples*. Knoxville: University of Tennessee Press, 1996.

Oates, Mary J. *The Catholic Philanthropic Tradition in America*. Bloomington: Indiana University Press, 1995.

Office of Research and Planning of Archdiocese of Chicago. "Data Composite: Facts and Figures for Year Ending 2007." Chicago: Archdiocese of Chicago, June 2008.

Omi, Michael, and Howard Winant. *Racial Formation in the United States from the 1960s to the 1990s*. 2nd ed. New York: Routledge, 1994.

Ong, Walter. *Orality and Literacy: The Technologizing of the Word*. New York: Methuen, 1982.

Orsi, Robert A. *Between Heaven and Earth: The Religious Worlds People Make and the Scholars Who Study Them*. Princeton, NJ: Princeton University Press, 2004.

———. *The Madonna of 115th Street: Faith and Community in Italian Harlem, 1880–1950*. New Haven, CT: Yale University Press, 1985.

Ortner, Sherry. "Patterns of History: Cultural Schemas in the Founding of Sherpa Religious Institutions." In *Culture Through Time: Anthropological Approaches,* edited by
Emiko Ohnuki-Tierney, 57–93. Stanford, CA: Stanford University Press, 1990.

———. "Theory in Anthropology Since the Sixties." *Comparative Studies in Society and
History* 26 (1984): 126–166.

Palmer-Boyes, Ashley. "The Latino Catholic Parish as a Specialist Organization: Distinguishing Characteristics." *Review of Religious Research* 51, no. 3 (March 2010): 302–323.

Panayi, Panikos. "Multicultural Britain: A Very Brief History." *British Politics Review* 6,
no. 2 (Spring 2011): 4–5.

Parekh, Bhikhu C. *Rethinking Multiculturalism: Cultural Diversity and Political Theory.*
Cambridge, MA: Harvard University Press, 2002.

Perl, Paul, Jennifer Z. Greely, and Mark M. Gray. "How Many Hispanics Are Catholic?" Center for Applied Research in the Apostolate. Washington, DC: Georgetown
University/CARA, 2005.

Pedersen, Paul B. "Cross-Cultural Psychology: Developing Culture-Centered Interven-
tions." In *Handbook of Racial and Ethnic Minority Psychology,* edited by Guillermo
Bernal, Joseph E. (Everett) Trimble, Ann Kathleen Burlew, and Frederick T. L.
Leong. Thousand Oaks, CA: Sage, 2003.

Peterson Anna L., and Manuel A. Vásquez. "The New Evangelization in Latin American Perspective." *Cross Currents* 48, no. 3 (Fall 1998): 311–329.

Phan, Peter. *Christianity with an Asian Face: Asian-American Theology in the Making.*
Maryknoll, NY: Orbis, 2004.

Phelps, Jamie T. "Communion Ecclesiology and Black Liberation Theology." *Theological Studies* 61, no. 4 (2000): 672–699.

Pitti, Gina Marie. "'A Ghastly International Racket': The Catholic Church and the Bracero Program in California, 1942–1964." Working Paper Series, Cushwa Center for
the Study of American Catholicism, series 33, no. 2 (Fall 2001): 1–21.

———. "To 'Hear About God in Spanish': Ethnicity, Church, and Community Activism
in the San Francisco Archdiocese Mexican-American Colonias, 1943–1965." Ph.D.,
diss., Stanford University, 2003.

Portes, Alejandro, and Rubén Rumbaut. *Immigrant America: A Portrait.* 2nd ed. Berkeley: University of California Press, 1996.

Portes, Alejandro, and Rubén Rumbaut. *Legacies: The Story of the Immigrant Second
Generation.* Berkeley: University of California Press, 2001.

Prusak, Bernard P. *The Church Unfinished: Ecclesiology Through the Centuries.* New
York: Paulist, 2004.

Putnam, Robert D. *Bowling Alone: The Collapse and Revival of American Community.*
New York: Simon & Schuster, 2000.

———. "E. Pluribus Unum: Diversity and Community in the Twenty-First Century."
2006 Johan Skye Prize Lecture. *Scandinavian Political Studies* 30, no. 2 (2007):
137–174.

Putnam, Robert D., and David E. Campbell. *American Grace: How Religion Unites and
Divides Us.* New York: Simon & Schuster, 2010.

Quinn, Frank C. "Posture and Prayer." *Worship* 72, no. 1 (January 1998): 67–78.

Rambo, Lewis R. *Understanding Religious Conversion*. New Haven, CT: Yale University Press, 1993.

Rambo, Lewis R., and Charles E. Farhadian. "Converting: Stages of Religious Change." In *Religious Conversion: Contemporary Practices and Controversies*, edited by Christopher Lamb and M. Darrol Bryant. New York: Cassell, 1999.

Ray, Melissa L. "Partial Alienation as Organizational Parent-Member Accommodation: An Urban, Midwestern Catholic Parish." *Sociology of Religion* 55, no. 1 (Spring 1994): 53–64.

Richey, Russell E., Kenneth E. Rowe, and Jeanne Miller Schmidt. *American Methodism: A Compact History*. Nashville,TN: Abingdon Press, 2010.

Ricoeur, Paul. *Essays on Biblical Interpretation*, edited by Lewis Mudge. Philadelphia: Fortress Press, 1980.

Rivera Pagán, Luis N. *Evangelización y Violencia: La Conquista de América* [Evangelization and violence: The conquest of America]. San Juan, PR: Editorial CEMI, 1992.

———. "A Prophetic Challenge to the Church: The Last Word of Barolomé de las Casas." Inaugural lecture of Henry Winters Luce Professor in Ecumenics and Mission, Princeton Theological Seminary, 9 April 2003.

Robinson, Marilynne. "Imagination and Community: What Holds Us Together." *Commonweal*, March 9, 2012.

Rodriguez, Richard. *Brown: The Last Discovery of America*. New York: Viking, 2002.

Ronan, Marian. "The Clergy Sex Abuse Crisis and the Mourning of American Catholic Innocence." *Pastoral Psychology* 56 (2008): 321–339.

———. *Tracing the Sign of the Cross: Sexuality, Mourning, and the Future of American Catholicism*. New York: Columbia University Press, 2009.

Roozen, David A., William. McKinney, and Jackson W. Carroll. *Varieties of Religious Presence: Mission in Public Life*. New York: Pilgrim Press, 1984.

Rosaldo, Renato. *Culture and Truth: The Remaking of Social Analysis*. Boston: Beacon Press, 1993.

Ruiz, Jean-Pierre. "Naming the Other: U.S. Hispanic Catholics, the So-Called 'Sects,' and the New Evangelization." *Journal of Hispanic/Latino/a Theology* 4, no. 2 (1996): 34–59.

Said, Edward. *Orientalism*. New York: Vintage Books, 1978.

Sandoval, Moises. *On the Move: A History of the Hispanic Church in the United States*. Maryknoll, NY: Orbis, 1990.

Scharen, Christian Batalden. "'Judicious Narratives,' or Ethnography as Ecclesiology." *Scottish Journal of Theology* 58, no. 2 (2005): 125–142.

Scheitle, Christopher P. "Organizational Niches and Religious Markets: Uniting Two Literatures." *Interdisciplinary Journal of Research on Religion* 3, article 2 (2007).

Schensul, Stephen L., Jean J. Schensul, and Margaret Diane LeCompte. *Initiating Ethnographic Research: A Mixed Methods Approach*. Lanham, MD: AltaMira Press, 2013.

Scheper-Hughes, Nancy. *Death Without Weeping: The Violence of Everyday Life in Brazil.* Berkeley: University of California Press, 1992.
———. "The Primacy of the Ethical: Propositions for a Militant Anthropology." *Current Anthropology* 36, no. 3 (June 1995): 409–440.
Schneiders, Sandra M. *The Revelatory Text: Interpreting the New Testament As Sacred Scripture.* Collegeville, MN: Liturgical Press, 1999.
Schoenherr, Richard A. *Goodbye Father: The Celibate Male Priesthood and the Future of the Catholic Church.* Edited by David Yamane. Foreword by Dean Hoge. New York: Oxford University Press, 2002.
Schwaller, John Frederick. *The Church and Clergy in Sixteenth-Century Mexico.* Albuquerque: University of New Mexico Press, 1987.
Scott, James C. *Domination and the Arts of Resistance: Hidden Transcripts.* New Haven, CT: Yale University Press, 1990.
Seidman, Naomi. *Faithful Renderings: Jewish-Christian Difference and the Politics of Translation.* Chicago: University of Chicago Press, 2006.
Sewell, William H., Jr. "The Concept(s) of Culture." In *Beyond the Cultural Turn: New Directions in the Study of Society and Culture,* edited by Victoria E. Bonnell and Lynn Hunt, 35–61. Berkeley: University of California Press, 1999.
Shaw, Stephen J. *The Catholic Parish as Way-Station of Ethnicity and Americanization: Chicago's Germans and Italians, 1903-1939.* Chicago Studies in the History of American Religion. Editor's preface by Martin E. Marty. Brooklyn, NY: Carlson Publishing, 1991.
Shaw, Stephen J. "The Cities and the Plains, a Home for God's People: A History of the Catholic Parish in the Midwest." In *Pacific States, Intermountain West, Midwest.* Vol. 2 of *The American Catholic Parish: A History from 1850 to the Present,* edited by Jay P. Dolan, 277–380. New York: Paulist Press, 1987.
Shirk, David. *Mexico's New Politics: The PAN and Democratic Change.* Boulder, CO: Lynne Rienner, 2005.
Skirbekk, Vegard, Keric Kaufman, and Anne Goujon. "Secularism, Fundamentalism, or Catholicism? The Religious Composition of the United States to 2043." *Journal for the Scientific Study of Religion* 49, no. 2 (June 2010): 293–310.
Smith, Gregory A. "Attitudes toward Immigration: In the Pulpit and Pew." Pew Forum on Religion and Public Life. Washington, DC: Pew Research Center, 2006.
Smith, Linda Tuhiwai. *Decolonizing Methodologies: Research and Indigenous Peoples.* New York: Zed Books, 1999.
Smith, Timothy L. "New Approaches to the History of Immigration in Twentieth-Century America." *American Historical Review* 71, no. 4 (July 1966), 1267–1269.
———. "The Ohio Valley: Testing Ground for America's Experiment in Religious Pluralism." *Church History* 60, no. 4 (December 1991): 461–479.
Sofranko, Andrew J., and Mohamed M. Samy. "Growth, Diversity, and Aging in the Midwest: An Examination of County Trends, 1990-2000." In *The American Midwest: Managing Change in Rural Transition,* edited by Norman Walzer, 41–69. Armonk, NY: M. E. Sharpe, 2003.

Steinfels, Peter. *A People Adrift: The Crisis of the Roman Catholic Church in America.* New York: Simon & Schuster, 2004.

Stephens, Gregory K., and Charles R. Greer. "Doing Business in Mexico: Understanding Cultural Differences." *Organizational Dynamics* 24, no. 1 (Summer 1995): 39–55.

Stepick, Alex, Terry Rey, and Sarah J. Mahler, eds. *Churches and Charity in the Immigrant City: Religion, Immigration, and Civic Engagement in Miami.* New Brunswick, NJ: Rutgers University Press, 2009.

Stevens-Arroyo, Anthony M. "The PARAL Study: The National Survey of Leadership for Latino Parishes and Congregations." Part 1. Brooklyn, NY: Religion in Society and Culture, 2002.

Stevens-Arroyo, Anthony M., and Ana María Díaz-Stevens. *An Enduring Flame: Studies on Latino Popular Religiosity.* PARAL [Program for the Analysis of Religion Among Latinos] Studies series. Vol. 1. New York: Bildner Center for Western Hemisphere Studies, 1994.

Stringer, Ernest T. *Action Research: A Handbook for Practitioners.* Thousand Oaks: Sage Publications, 1996.

Swidler, Ann. "Culture in Action: Symbols and Strategies." *American Sociological Review* 51 (April 1986): 273–286.

———. *Talk of Love: How Culture Matters.* Chicago: University of Chicago Press, 2001.

Szasz, Margaret Connell, ed. *Between Indian and White Worlds: Cultural Brokers.* Norman: University of Oklahoma Press, 1994.

Tanner, Kathryn. *Theories of Culture.* Guides to Theological Inquiry. Minneapolis: Fortress Press, 1997.

Taves, Ann. *The Household of Faith: Roman Catholic Devotions in Mid-Nineteenth Century America.* Notre Dame, IN: Notre Dame University Press, 1986.

———. "Negotiating the Boundaries in Theological and Religious Studies." Paper from Open Convocation, Graduate Theological Union, 22 September 2005. Catholic Studies website at UCSB. http://www.religion.ucsb.edu/faculty/GTU-FinalLecture.pdf. Accessed 17 April 2006.

Taylor, Charles. "The Politics of Recognition." In *Multiculturalism: Examining the Politics of Recognition,* edited Amy Gutmann, 25–73. Princeton, NJ: Princeton University Press, 1994.

Tillard, Jean-Marie Roger. *Church of Churches: The Ecclesiology of Communion.* Translated by R. C. De Peaux. Collegeville, MN: Liturgical Press, 1992.

Ting-Toomey, Stella. *Communicating across Cultures.* New York: Guilford Press, 1999.

Tseng, Timothy, et al. *Asian American Religious Leadership Today: A Preliminary Inquiry.* Durham, NC: Pulpit and Pew Research Reports, 2005.

U.S. Census Bureau. American Community Survey (Annual).

U.S. Census Bureau. Census of the Population of the United States (Decennial).

U.S. Census Bureau. "Profile of the Foreign-Born Population in the United States: 2000," by Dianne Schmidley. Current Population Reports: Special Studies. Washington, DC: U.S. Census Bureau, 2001.

United States Catholic Bishops' Committee for Social Development and World Peace. "Beyond the Melting Pot: Cultural Pluralism in the United States." *Origins* 10, no. 31 (15 January 1981): 481–489.

United States Conference of Catholic Bishops. *Hispanic Ministry: Three Major Documents.* Washington, DC: USCCB Publishing, 1988.

———. "The Hispanic Presence: Challenge and Commitment." *Origins* 13, no. 32 (19 January 1984): 529–541.

———. "Welcoming the Stranger Among Us." *Origins* 30, no 26 (7 December 2000): 407–421.

United States Conference of Catholic Bishops' Office of Media Relations. "Catholic Information Project." Washington, DC: USCCB, 2006.

Varacalli, Joseph A. "Multiculturalism, Catholicism, and American Civilization." *Homiletic and Pastoral Review* 94, no. 6 (March 1994): 47–55.

Vásquez, Manuel A. "Historicizing and Materializing the Study of Religion." In *Immigrant Faiths: Transforming Religious Life in America,* edited by Karen I. Leonard et al., 219–242. New York: Altamira Press, 2005.

Vega, William. "The Study of Latino Families: A Point of Departure." *Understanding Latino Families: Scholarship, Policy, and Practice,* edited by Ruth E. Zambrana, 3–17. Thousand Oaks, CA: Sage, 1995.

Wallace, Peter George. *The Long European Reformation: Religion, Political Conflict, and the Search for Conformity, 1350–1750.* New York: Palgrave Macmillan, 2004.

Warner, R. Stephen. "Religion and New (Post-1965) Immigrants: Some Principles Drawn from Field Research." *American Studies* 41, no. 2/3 (Summer/Fall 2000): 267–286.

———. "Work in Progress Toward a New Paradigm for the Sociological Study of Religion in the United States." *American Journal of Sociology* 98, no. 5 (1993): 1044–1093.

Warner, R. Stephen, and Judith G. Wittner, eds. *Gatherings in Diaspora: Congregations and the New Immigration.* Philadelphia: Temple University, 1998.

Webb, Stephen H. "Christ Against the Multiculturalists." Address for entering students of Wabash College, class of 2012. *First Things,* On the Square (6 May 2008). http://www.firstthings.com/onthesquare/2008/05/christ-against-the-multicultur. Accessed 13 July 2009.

Weissbach, Lee Shai. *Jewish Life in Small-Town America: A History.* New Haven, CT: Yale University Press, 2005.

Werner, Oswald, and G. Mark Schoepfle. *Foundations of Ethnography and Interviewing.* Vol. 1 of *Systematic Fieldwork.* Newbury Park, CA: Sage Publications, 1987.

Wilkie, James W. *The Mexican Revolution and Social Change Since 1910.* Berkeley: University of California Press, 1967.

Willett, Cynthia, ed. *Theorizing Multiculturalism: A Guide to the Current Debate.* Malden, MA: Blackwell, 1998.

Wind, James P. "Leading Congregations, Discovering Congregational Cultures." *Christian Century* 110, no. 4 (3–10 February 1993): 105.

Wind, James P., and James W. Lewis, eds. *Portraits of Twelve Religious Communities.* Vol. 1 of *American Congregations.* Chicago: University of Chicago Press, 1994.

———. *New Perspectives in the Study of Congregations.* Vol. 2 of *American Congregations.* Chicago: University of Chicago Press, 1994.

Woolever, Cynthia, et al. "Characteristics of U.S. Congregations, by Faith Group - Part 1." US Congregational Life Survey (2001). Louisville, KY: US Congregations, 2005. Online report. http://www.uscongregations.org/charact-cong.htm. Accessed 3 September 2008.

Wrong, Dennis H. *The Problem of Order: What Unifies and Divides Society.* New York: Free Press, 1994.

Wuthnow, Robert. *Loose Connections: Joining Together in America's Fragmented Communities.* Cambridge, MA: Harvard University Press, 2002.

———. *Remaking the Heartland: Middle America since the 1950s.* Princeton, NJ: Princeton University Press, 2011.

Yang, Fenggang, and Helen Rose Ebaugh. "Transformations in New Immigrant Religions and Their Global Implications." *American Sociological Review* 66 (April 2001): 269–288

Yannakakis, Yanna. *The Art of Being In-Between: Native Intermediaries, Indian Identity, and Local Rule in Colonial Oaxaca.* Durham, NC: Duke University Press, 2008.

Yoo, David, and Ruth H. Chung, eds. *Religion and Spirituality in Korean America,* Champaign: University of Illinois Press, 2008.

Zimmerman, Joyce Ann. "What Does GIRM Say About Posture During the Eucharistic Prayer?" *Understanding the Mass and the General Instruction for the Roman Missal* 6. Collegeville, MN: Liturgical Press, 2003.

Zizioulas, John D. *Communion and Otherness: Further Studies in Personhood and the Church.* Edited by Paul McPartlan. New York: T & T Clark, 2006.

Zolberg, Aristide R. *A Nation by Design: Immigration Policy in the Fashioning of America.* Cambridge, MA: Harvard University Press, 2006.

Brett C. Hoover is Assistant Professor of Theological Studies at Loyola Marymount University in Los Angeles. He earned his Ph.D. in the interdisciplinary study of religion at the Graduate Theological Union in Berkeley, California. He is the author of several books and articles.